# Arthur

*Phillip*

## Also by Derek Parker:

The Fall of Phaethon (1954)

Company of Two (with Paul Casimir, 1955)

Beyond Wisdom (verse play, 1957)

Byron and his World (1968)

The Twelfth Rose (ballet libretto, 1969)

The Question of Astrology (1970)

The Westcountry (1973)

John Donne and his World (1975)

Familiar to All: William Lilly and 17th century astrology (1975)

Radio: the great years (1977)

The Westcountry and the Sea (1980)

The Memoirs of Cora Pearl (fiction, as William Blatchford, 1983)

God of the Dance: Vaslav Nijinsky (1988)

The Trade of Angels (fiction, 1988)

The Royal Academy of Dancing: the first 75 years (1995)

Writing Erotic Fiction (1995)

Nell Gwyn (2000)

Roman Murder Mystery: the true story of Pompilia (2001)

Casanova (2002)

Benvenuto Cellini (2004)

Voltaire (2005)

Outback (2008, paperback published 2009 by Woodslane Press)

Banjo Paterson (2009, Woodslane Press)

# ARTHUR

## AUSTRALIA'S FIRST GOVERNOR

# DEREK PARKER

WOODSLANE

**Woodslane Press Pty Ltd**
7/5 Vuko Place, Warriewood, NSW 2102
**Email:** info@woodslane.com.au
**Website:** www.woodslane.com.au

© 2009 Woodslane Press, text © 2009 Derek Parker

National Library of Australia Cataloguing-in-Publication entry

| | |
|---|---|
| Author: | Parker, Derek. |
| Title: | Arthur Phillip : Australia's first governor / Derek Parker. |
| Edition: | 1st ed. |
| ISBN: | 9781921203992 (hbk.) |
| Notes: | Includes index. |
| Subjects: | Phillip, Arthur, 1738-1814. |
| | Governors--New South Wales--Biography. |
| | First Fleet, 1787-1788. |
| Dewey Number: | 994.401 |

Design and layout by Robyn Latimer
Printed in China

*Dedicated with admiration to*

H.E. Professor Marie Bashir, A.C., C.V.O.
THIRTY-SEVENTH GOVERNOR OF NEW SOUTH WALES

# FOREWORD

At first it seems perfectly possible to visualise Arthur Phillip, first Governor of New South Wales – a tall, lean figure striding down towards the water's edge at Port Jackson in his naval uniform, moving with a certain care (a continual tenderness in his side made movement painful), his features somewhat aquiline, his nose straight, lips full, eyes cool and unwavering, seeming to see everything.

But the more one tries to focus on him, to see something of the man behind the icon, the more blurred the image becomes. The outline may still be clear, but the detail is missing.

The problem faced by anyone attempting a biography of Phillip is the lack of personal records. Apart from one, the only letters of his to have survived were written 'on business'; they betray nothing of the man except that part of him – substantial, indeed – concerned with his career either as a naval officer or as Governor. If he wrote letters to either of his wives, they have not survived, and his second wife appears to have destroyed any and every document she could find which had anything to do with him. He had no close personal friends. Those who wrote *of* him did so as a colleague or a senior officer, and all too often as a man of whom to complain.

As he prepared to leave Sydney at the end of his term – an end upon which he had himself insisted, though his masters in England did all they could to dissuade him from retiring – a convict, Richard Atkins, who had become a magistrate at Parramatta and almost a friend, remarked that people might exclaim against the Governor, but he doubted whether any other man could do as well. In retrospect, one must agree that certainly no other man who travelled to Port Jackson with the First Fleet could have done as well; the idea of the Lieutenant-Governor, the splenetic and vastly unpopular Major Ross, at Government House is the stuff of nightmare.

Over the two centuries since his appointment, commentators have been as surprised at the choice of Arthur Phillip as some were at the time (the First Lord of the Admiralty, to mention only the most distinguished critic). But was it really so surprising? What did the Home Office and the Admiralty expect of a man who was to navigate a fleet to the antipodes, and when he got it there unload its cargo of unregenerate criminals and forge them into some sort of a working colony? Apart from the necessary seamanship, they needed a man with a cool head who understood men and how to control them, a man capable of governing himself, possessed of calm and understanding and a thorough grasp of reality, with complete loyalty to the Crown and Government and a determination to plan and carry through an enterprise unlike any other within living memory. Fortunately, there were one or two men at the Admiralty who understood that Arthur Phillip possessed all these credentials.

It has been complained that he was an undistinguished, run-of-the-mill naval officer of whom the best that could be said was that he had not made any serious mistakes during his career. There was, however, more to him than that. We may not have succeeded in discovering just what services he did for his government during the mysterious months when he disappeared from the naval record books, but we can safely assume that they were of value. So too was the experience he gained as an officer in the Portuguese navy of whom Marquis of Lavradio, the Viceroy of Brazil, wrote that he was 'one of the officers of the most distinct merit that the Queen has in her service in the Navy', a brave and truthful man who took no-one at face value, always said what he thought, was calm and unflappable, zealous and honourable. This does not sound like a run-of-the-mill officer.

It would have been perfectly possible to appoint Phillip merely as the commander of the First Fleet, with a civil servant to take up the position of Governor when it arrived in New South Wales. Such a step never seems to have been considered, and we may guess that the reason for this is that Phillip was seen as a man who was capable of exercising perfect control over the seamen and marines of the fleet, and therefore of the convicts also in his care. He had, after all, come up through the ranks. He knew about life on the lower decks, he knew about crime and punishment on His Majesty's ships, and this experience was of enormous value to him. He knew the value of a captain who stood no nonsense, upheld strict discipline, could order severe punishment when it was needed but was seen above all to be fair. He was himself a stern but not severe disciplinarian – on one occasion chastising an officer for striking a member of his crew without due cause. He was not a compulsive hanger and flogger, and while he was driven by circumstances to extremes of punishment (circumstances which he did not contemplate on leaving England), this was not by choice; he did not become the sort of monster who stood by taking snuff while the skin and flesh was stripped from a man's back.

If those who appointed him believed him to be a career naval officer who would get quietly on with his work without troubling them about details, accepting their yea as yea and their nay as nay, they swiftly found they had backed the wrong man. Phillip did not simply accept his commission and disappear from view while the preliminary work was put in train. He spent a considerable amount of time thinking about the whole task – the voyage, but also what was to come when it ended. He was exercised, for instance, about the Indigenous people of New South Wales. He knew nothing about them but that he was expected to confiscate their country, and wanted to do so if possible without violence and without giving them too much offence. Like any man of his time, he was not unduly concerned about the confiscation of territory; it was what powerful countries did, and had always done. Nor did he understand that the sudden arrival of the white men and women would necessarily begin utterly to change the way of life of the Aborigines. This was in no way regrettable, for it was the duty of the educated white races to educate and civilise the 'natives' – the value of making the black men and women as nearly as possible into facsimiles of their white counterparts was a given; it was a main point of the age of enlightenment. If his superiors had thought about this at all, it was as an intellectual exercise rather than a practical plan of action. Phillip spent time actually considering how a relationship between his crews and convicts and the Aborigines might be nurtured, and the difficulties which would undoubtedly arise.

He expected hostility from the natives as a matter of course; why should they go out of their way to be friendly to those who were stealing their land? It is clear from his attitude and actions during his time with the Portuguese navy that he did not lack personal bravery, and this showed in his dealings with the Aborigines. He took the view that there was no reason for them to attack the white men unless the latter showed antagonism towards them, but there is surely a gap between taking this view and putting it into practice by walking calmly, unarmed, up to a group of natives carrying dangerous-looking spears and appearing ready to use them. On one occasion indeed this almost led to his death; but the incident did not change his attitude, and notably he took no revenge on the man who attacked him. He was determined from the start to treat the Aborigines as fairly as possible: from the moment he raised the flag on shore, he was the Governor of the Indigenous people as well as of the whites. He kept this pledge largely to himself, which was probably wise – few of his officers and none of the marines, sailors or convicts would have understood it. He also kept it to an astonishing extent, and through a great deal of criticism; he even allowed himself to be argued out of the initially extreme reaction to the murder of one of his close servants. In a strange way he had a fellow-feeling for the Aborigines, which made him almost their friend – not only in his relationship with those he took to live at Government House, but in casual encounters, when we can see him smiling and even laughing with them in a way completely different to his relationship with any white man, free or convicted. His treatment of the two Aborigines he brought back with him to London may seem to us in some ways ludicrous, but was without doubt astonishingly generous.

The time and care he spent considering the care and nurture of the convicts showed a humanity foreign to almost anyone else concerned with the prison service. The well-being of prisoners was something with which his superiors were not at all seriously concerned. They did not care that the prisons and prison hulks were delivering to Phillip convicts who at best were weak and ill-nurtured, and at worst diseased and almost at the point of death. They were uninterested in the fact that the prisoners had barely enough clothes with which to cover themselves, and sometimes not even that. Phillip did, and he nagged and nagged and nagged at the Home Office on the subject – and nagged and nagged and nagged the Admiralty about the unpreparedness of the marines and of the seamen. The fact that it got him nowhere – the stone was simply too large for him to roll uphill – was not his fault.

His care for the convicts and Aborigines was severely pragmatic. He was not interested in saving the souls of either.

As poor Mr Johnson, the First Fleet's unfortunate pastor, was to discover, Arthur Phillip was just so much of a Christian as was required by his commission: there is absolutely no sign that he was interested in religion *per se*. He had been commanded to see that the colony was a Christian colony, and did so with a minimum of interest and action, regularly disregarding Johnson's plea for a proper place of worship and, as far as we know, attending services only when absolutely required to by protocol. He gave little thought to the principles of original sin or redemption; he certainly believed that some human beings were naturally evil, but did not trouble himself with saving the souls of sinners; it was trouble enough to ensure that they were fed. He despised their crimes (showing no sign of undue sympathy with the often dreadful circumstances which too often prompted them) but believed in treating them in a civilised manner, provided they showed they were worthy of it. His fury at the conditions under which they were imprisoned on the ships of the Second Fleet almost prompted him to burst through the conventional prose of his dispatches to his lords and masters in England – you can feel it bubbling between the lines. On at least one occasion his complaints about the Government's blindness to the misbehaviour of the masters of the transports vessels border on insolence.

He was by no means an intellectual: we do not hear of him ever reading or even possessing a book. The style of his dispatches shows no talent for writing; his prose can best be described as utilitarian. Nor did he have any pretentions as an artist: while he had had sufficient training to be able to draw a chart, unlike many of his officers he kept no sketch-book. In that sense he was a typical career naval officer of his time – with the exception that he said what he thought, with no consideration of the effect that might have on his advancement.

Though we know nothing definite about the illness from

which he suffered from the age of 20, we do know that while there may have been periods when it only slightly affected his life, there were other periods when it became seriously troublesome, and during the whole of his time in New South Wales it was more or less seriously so. He did not allow this to prevent him from doing his daily duty. He worked until he dropped, or at least until he was forced to sit down; he even went on a number of explorative expeditions – though these became sufficiently arduous for him to have to cut them short – and he was seen to be obviously in pain on some public occasions. Continual pain has its effect upon the personality, and may well have contributed to the impression he gave of being distant and unfriendly. It would be unrealistic to expect him to have made friends among his fellow officers: a Governor in his position could no more be familiar with his fellows than the captain of a ship. People like his irritable Lieutenant-Governor would always be ready to accuse him of favouritism – the last thing of which he was capable. On the other hand, from time to time the occasional remark betrays the fact that he could unbend – send a lady a small present of some kind, or entertain at Government House with a show of pleasant hospitality, with music played in the next room while the guests dined.

The emotional circumstances of his two marriages are a closed book. Did he marry for money? If so, it shows a talent for charm which he does not betray elsewhere; perhaps he could indeed lay himself out as the gallant, handsome naval officer. If so he did so with success, for fortunes came with both his wives. So, however, did marital failure – at least in the case of his first marriage, and there are strong hints that his second was not altogether successful. How far this was his fault, again, one can only surmise. After a brief period during which he seems to have played the attentive husband, escorting his wives into society, he retired; in the first case to the New

Forest, when farming seemed to occupy all his time, and in the second case away from home on various duties until this retirement forced him to share a house with his wife.

Though he showed no signs of wanting to return to New South Wales, he would probably have liked to have been given the opportunity to decline to do so; if he hoped for or expected honours – or any kind of official appreciation of his service – he was equally disappointed. Nor did honours come with his death: no obituaries were published; as far as we know there was no official attendance at his funeral. He was hurried into a relatively obscure grave.

Did he merit St Paul's or Westminster Abbey? In retrospect, surely so. As a personality he had none of the obvious marks of greatness, though his capacity for taking pains was notable enough. No historian would set him down as one of the pillars of late eighteenth century British history. Australia should see him differently, however, remembering Edmund Burke's definition of great men as 'the guide-posts and landmarks in the state.' One tiny corner of the continent between 1787 and 1792 hardly constituted a state, but Arthur Phillip guided it with sureness and acumen, and his period as Governor must certainly be recognised as a major landmark in the history of not only the state but of the country. Under his hand the muddy or parched sparse settlements of Sydney and Rose Hill began to take on the shape and character of real towns, and within a preposterously short period New South Wales itself was to begin to look less like a wasteland temporarily disturbed by the aberration of civilisation and more like the embryo of a sophisticated colony.

Had he remained at Government House, or returned to it for another five or even 10 years (had his health permitted it) would he have been able to restrict the growing power of the New South Wales Corps and the greed of its officers which led eventually to the Rum Rebellion of 1808 and the removal of Governor Bligh? He had certainly shown himself capable of standing up to Major Ross and his successor, though his mistaken permission to the officers to trade with Cape Town might be regarded as starting the rot which in the end led to the Rum riots. In any event, the difficulties to come were, in respect of the disreputable New South Wales Corps, considerably greater than those he already faced, and while in his prime he may have dealt with them, his growing ill-health and age might well have led to his defeat.

Above all, however, we can remember that the development of Sydney and Parramatta, and the beginning of the free settlements around them, though still vestigial when he left, owed everything to Arthur Phillip.

# ONE

At last, after months of prevarication, obfuscation and argument, an outbreak of typhus and a seamen's strike, the little fleet finally set to sea, sailing out of Portsmouth harbour at three in the morning of Sunday, 13 May 1787.

The sprightly, if barely seaworthy, little *Sirius* was the flagship, followed by three store-ships – the *Borrowdale, Golden Grove* and *Fishburn* – and six convict transports – the *Alexander, Supply, Charlotte, Scarborough, Friendship, Prince of Wales* and *Lady Penhryn*. On the deck of the *Sirius* stood the man in charge of the enterprise – the commander of what would be known as the First Fleet, Captain Arthur Phillip, Governor Designate of the colony of New South Wales.[1] Though he had had his problems with the Government and the Admiralty here he was, finally, setting out on the great enterprise. As the deck of the *Sirius* lifted to the waves of the Channel, then to the more robust breakers of the Atlantic, so rough that he could scarcely keep his seat at his desk as he began the first entries in his log, he braced himself for the task which faced him. Astern of the flagship, crowded below decks, 736 convicts began to feel the initial queasiness which was soon to introduce them to the full horror of sea-sickness in the dark crowded conditions below decks.

Nothing, even given Phillip's well-conceived mistrust of his masters in London, could have prepared him for the rigours which were to test him - a semi-retired naval officer, summoned from a comfortable life as a gentleman farmer in Hampshire to run a colony on the other side of the world. He must, even at the very start of the project, and certainly many times during it, have wondered whether he had been wise to accept the offer.

Arthur Phillip was born on 11 October 1738, in Bread Street in the parish of All Hallows in London. He was the second child of Jacob Phillip, a German who had come to London from Frankfurt who is described in one of the early memoirs of Phillip's as a teacher of 'the languages'. What this means is obscure – perhaps simply that he supported himself as a teacher of German. Jacob appears for the first time as the second husband of Elizabeth Herbert, the widow of a captain in the Royal navy; their names attached to the baptismal record of their daughter Rebecca, born in June, 1737.

Mrs Elizabeth Phillip had been a Miss Breach, of a moderately prominent family from the parish of St Botolph without Aldgate. She married her first husband, John Herbert, on 30 November, 1728. He sailed on a number of ships before joining the frigate *Tartar* in 1730 as an ordinary seaman. The *Tartar* sailed for the Caribbean in October, cruised for a year, then needed re-fitting before returning to England. The ship put in to Port Royal in the summer of 1731, and while she was refitting Herbert died in the naval hospital, presumably of fever.

Elizabeth, though childless, was probably left in poor circumstances, like the widows of so many ordinary seamen. How she survived for the next five years we can only guess; we next hear of her in 1737, living in Bread Street as the wife of Jacob Phillip. Their daughter Rebecca was born in the early summer of that year, and a son, Arthur, followed 16 months later. However Jacob managed to support his family at that time, they were clearly not the poorest of the poor. A diligent researcher[2] has found that he contributed a rather more substantial sum

2

than most to the Poor Rate of his parish. However, it is clear that, perhaps as a result of Jacob's death (the circumstances of which are obscure), the family later fell on hard times, for in 1751 Arthur was admitted to the Charity School of the Royal Hospital for Seamen at Greenwich – his father was listed in the entry book as a 'steward' (which suggests, as does Arthur's acceptance at the school, that Jacob must at some time have gone to sea).

The Charity School was for the sons of former seamen who had been disabled by their service, or had been killed in action, whose families could not afford to give them an education. Arthur was 14 when he entered the school, which raises the question of what had happened to him during the previous several years. Mrs Phillip could not have afforded to have a boy of working age lounging around at home. It has been suggested that he went, or was sent, to sea when he was nine. This would not have been uncommon; but we can only guess at the circumstances – it may be that some influence was exerted by Michael Everitt, a relative by marriage of Arthur's mother, of whom more will shortly be told. Four years at sea would certainly have prepared the boy for any rigours he was likely to experience in the British navy, for which he was now clearly headed.

The Greenwich Hospital School offered excellent training for a young seaman in circumstances which, if not luxurious, were at the very least a considerable improvement on the life he had led at sea as some sort of lowly cabin boy (if that indeed is what had happened to him in the previous few years). He now found himself provided with good clothes, text books and instruments (such as a sextant) and with regular meals – good bread and cheese for breakfast and supper and hearty dinners (even with meat on Sundays); meals would have been accompanied by half a pint of beer at breakfast and supper, with a pint at dinner.

The school's position, at Greenwich, on the bank of the

Thames, set its pupils at the very heart of British naval history. From here many heroic ships had set sail, and most had returned with treasure in gold and knowledge of the world. The Royal Hospital itself was populated by seamen who had been injured in their country's service, and whose tales of life at sea delighted the boys of the school.

After two and a half years at school Arthur Phillip was considered ready for service. He had learned to read and write (a Bible and Book of Common Prayer had been provided for the purpose), and, to some extent, to calculate. For some reason he had spent more than the average time at the school - normally, boys stayed for a year only. Did he show particular promise? There is no evidence of it. When the Governors met to consider his future, there was no question of his being sent straight to a naval vessel – instead, he was apprenticed for seven years to the master of a whaling ship.

This must surely have been a disappointment to the boy as he staggered out of the school, carrying his books and coping as best he could with a sea-chest containing a selection of hard-wearing clothes for use at sea. His master was to be one William Readhead, who had guaranteed to instruct him 'in the best way and manner for making him an able seaman and as good an artist as he can', and promised not to 'immoderately beat or misuse him.'[3]

Readhead's ship was the *Fortune*, built to sail to and from the coastal waters of Greenland to hunt whales and bring back their blubber. The job was both unpleasant and highly dangerous. The hunting was done in small boats, from which the whales were harpooned. It could take up to twelve hours to kill a large animal. The blubber was then stripped, either on shore or on shipboard, cut into manageable pieces and boiled down. All this took place in bitterly cold weather, and on a far from generous allowance of food.

The *Fortune* sailed on 1 April 1754 with 30 other whalers and returned towards the end of July. It sounds a brief enough period but it would have been quite long enough for Arthur Phillip, who at 15 and the most junior and least important body on board, would have had the worst jobs, carried out in devastating cold and in a landscape which must have seemed like a frozen hell.

His second voyage was considerably more comfortable – to the Mediterranean, on a jobbing voyage transporting various cargos to various ports. The *Fortune*, with a crew of twelve including Arthur Phillip, left London in August 1754 for Barcelona, then on to Leghorn and home via Sète and Rotterdam. There is no record of the cargo, but the voyage introduced Arthur to the sights, sounds and smells of Europe, to Mediterranean warmth and the lion sun, infinitely preferable to the freezing cold of the arctic wastes. (Much later, he was to find the sun as cruel as the most freezing of winds.) Eight months of sailing in warmer waters to countries more hospitable than the coast of Greenland must have been extremely welcome.

Too soon, however, back in the pool of London, Readhead signed on a new crew, and the *Fortune* sailed again for Greenland. The voyage happily lasted only three months, and when Readhead paid off his crew in July 1755, Arthur Phillip was very probably glad to see the last of him. Somehow, he managed to wriggle free of his indentures, and joined the Royal Navy.

His first naval ship was the *Buckingham*, a proud 68-gun battleship under the command of Captain Michael Everitt. Here, in all likelihood, lies the key to Arthur's sudden and easy transfer from one seagoing discipline to another, for we know he was a distant relative of the Captain's on his mother's side. The Captain looks steadily out of his portrait, the very picture of an open-faced, agreeable naval commander, rather negligently holding a telescope and regarding the world with perfect, calm assurance.

In October, 17-year-old Arthur climbed up onto the top of a coach, wrapped himself up as best he could against the cold wind (the cold, again!) and bucketed down the rough uneven road from London to Plymouth to join the *Buckingham*, lying in the Sound, where he found himself one of a quintet of 'young gentlemen' in training, including Everitt's own two sons, Robert and George, and the two sons of Vice-Admiral Temple West, who also sailed on the *Buckingham*. Everitt had gone so far as to persuade the Admiralty to provide a schoolmaster to assist in their further education and the Admiralty had agreed, for the training of young men for the service was considered invaluable as Britain prepared for war against the French.

Whether a schoolmaster was actually on board when the *Buckingham* sailed out of Plymouth on 7 November, as part of a squadron commanded by Admiral John Byng, we cannot know. In any case, the boys were no doubt excited to be almost immediately seeing action, for the *Buckingham* soon captured a 74-gun French warship, set her on fire and sunk her. While there is no reason to suppose that Phillip particularly distinguished himself, or indeed had the opportunity to do so, he certainly held his own, for in November he was listed as Able Bodied, and a month later as Corporal - no special promotion, but an indication of disciplined good behaviour.

In the new year the ship put in to Spithead for a refit, then sailed to Gibraltar under Admiral Byng's command as part of a squadron carrying troops and munitions. On the voyage out Phillip may have had the opportunity to observe the problem of keeping a crew healthy during a relatively lengthy voyage, for the food provided was bad and insufficient, clothes were poor and there was an almost total lack of bedding. In fact, provision for the voyage seems to have been appalling, and it is unsurprising that there was a great deal of sickness on all the vessels.

Byng had learned, when he had briefly put in at Gibraltar, that his small force was massively out-gunned in the Mediterranean by a French squadron of twelve battleships and a number of frigates, all heavily manned. These were set to defend Minorca, occupied by the French except for Fort St Philip, a British-held garrison now under siege. Not only out-gunned but with many men of his ships' crews sick, Byng's squadron met with the French on 20 May, and the *Buckingham* and two other British ships were confronted by nine French vessels.

Battle was joined, and the British ships under the command of Vice-Admiral Temple West immediately did some damage to the French, and *vice versa*. The *Buckingham* and two other vessels faced off against the French ships, with casualties on both sides, but inexplicably the vessels under Byng's command advanced at such a lethargic pace that they took over an hour to get within range of their opponents, and some did not fire a single shot; Byng's flagship, the *Ramilles*, was barely engaged before withdrawing. It seemed as though he realized that the French were in command of the situation – as indeed they were – so it is surprising that in this very odd battle they suddenly decided to withdraw. Seeing the French sail off, Byng considered his next step, and decided to withdraw to Gibraltar, leaving Minorca to the French, and the garrison at Fort St Philip with no option other than ignominious surrender.

Byng was relieved of his command, and on his return to England was court-martialled on his own quarter-deck, convicted of neglect of duty, and shot (the incident was famously commemorated by Voltaire in *Candide* by the statement that the English found it advisable to shoot an admiral from time to time *pour enourager les autres*).

The Admiralty was clearly hesitant to convict, let along execute, Byng, whose main defect was, like Hamlet's, the inability to make up his mind. Colleagues of his own rank were, on the whole, sympathetic to the unfortunate Admiral, believing with some justice that political machinations alone demanded such severe punishment. Otherwise, all England seems to have been convinced of Byng's cowardice, and Arthur Philip was among those who condemned him unequivocally. Describing his own adventures in a letter to his sister – one of the very few personal documents of his own to have survived – he emphasized the damage done to the French ships, but commented that while the *Buckingham* was engaging the enemy, 'Admiral Byng lay with his Top Sails aback, and only fired now & then, & that at too great a distance to doe, or Receive any damage.'

As hot-headed and patriotic as one might expect a teenager to be, Phillip proudly boasted that 'every man in our Fleet burned with the greatest ardour imaginable, and theirs by their behaviour i.e. the French with a great dastardness, for their not coming to a close engagement when they had Such Odds as their Whole Fleet against our Division Plainly Shewed that most of them had rather Run than Fight . . . I need not mention the great Courage & conduct of our Admiral and Captains shewed that Day in our Division, nor the Cowardice of the Only person Admiral Byng, that kept the French fleet from being Distroyed, and the Island from being relieved. For no doubt all England will Soon be convinced of the merit of Admiral West, and the downright Cowardice of Admiral Byng.'[4]

With his patron, Captain Everitt, temporarily removed from his command in order to give evidence at Byng's court-martial, and with war now officially declared against France, Phillip transferred to another warship, the *Princess Louise*, as captain's clerk, and sailed on board her as part of a squadron sent to cruise the Mediterranean. There, no doubt, the young man's ardour was somewhat dampened by the fact that for four months none of his new ship's 60 guns fired a single shot in anger. Phillip transferred again, this time to the *Ramilles*, and he found himself back at Spithead in January 1757.

He may have been more than a little dismayed to find himself listed, on the *Ramilles*, as a mere 'able bodied seaman'. If so, immediate relief was at hand, for on 3 February he joined the 98-gun battleship *Neptune* at Portsmouth as a midshipman, his elevation no doubt owing something to the fact that his commanding officer was once more none other than Captain Everitt. He also had the pleasure of a reunion with his four young contemporaries, the West's and Everitt's sons.

His promotion was a not inconsiderable step on the rigging.[5] He was for the first time in command of other men, and the ambition to become an officer was now feasible. Moreover, he was paid £2 5s a month, some of which he may well have remitted to his mother and sister (though apart from the single letter to Rebecca we have no evidence of his relationship with them, and can only suppose that they were still both alive and that he was a dutiful brother and son). Apart from all that, he now had the right to beat members of the crew, or order them to be beaten, with some of them men twice his own age.[6]

The *Neptune* sailed from Portsmouth, but only to Spithead, where she lay idly at anchor for five months. Presumably, despite the relative inactivity of life in port, Arthur had the opportunity to learn something about his duties on the lowest rank of the ladder of command and his part in the smooth running of the ship.

However, at the end of five months or so, he left *Neptune*, and vanishes from our sight for almost two years. The gap is complete, and there is no discovering what happened to him during that time. Alan Frost[7] suggests that he was perhaps ill, or at least that this was the reason for his discharge; and it is certainly possible. He also supposes that Phillip may have spent some time serving with Everitt on a ship called the *Union*, which also seems possible, though unproven.

He was now, after over five years at sea – more if we assume an earlier experience – well versed in maritime discipline, and it was a discipline which was to serve him particularly well when he came to govern a colony. The training he had had was excellent: by 16 he and his contemporaries were competent seamen, able to work aloft, reef sails and steer the ship. As a midshipman he had revived what he had been taught of mathematics and drawing and had begun to understand more thoroughly how to calculate an accurate position, lay down a course, map a coastline. He had learned the value of teamwork while living in a mess with men with the same skills, sharing the chores, observing how others worked, whether officers, rigging ship, or as gun crew.

There is a general impression, fostered by popular novels and by television and film, that the navy in the eighteenth century was unbearably brutal and cruel, with sadistic officers administering frequent lashings, and with life below decks barely better than that of animals in a zoo. Punishment was certainly harsh, but it should be remembered that the lash was not peculiar to naval life; on land physical punishment was common for all manner of delinquency, and whereas prison was a possible alternative on shore, on board ship there was very limited room to imprison a man; it was much more convenient to punish him and return him to duty. Moreover, a public flogging was almost a theatrical event, with the whole crew mustered to watch the punishment, marines with loaded muskets standing between the crew and officers in case of trouble. Once seen by a young seaman, it was never forgotten.

There is no suggestion that Arthur Phillip ever suffered the lash, but he must more than once have witnessed such punishment, and observed to what extent it was, or was not, a deterrent. In later life, often reluctantly, he was to order or approve similar punishment on almost innumerable occasions.

He also saw, if he did not himself experience, the effects of drink, and observed very keenly the tendency of some men to use alcohol to render themselves insensible whenever reality became too much for them. An average daily consumption of eight pints of beer, accompanied by liberal tots of rum-and-water when available, was one thing; the opportunity to drink much more heavily, especially at leisure when the alcohol could not be burned off by hard work, was quite another. If for the rest of his life Phillip was to be a very moderate drinker, and to mistrust others who misused alcohol, he had learned the lesson early, and learned it well.

In general, if the cruelty of life on board a ship has been somewhat exaggerated, the poor living conditions have not. The latter were certainly often damaging both to morale and to health (as during Byng's unfortunate voyage to the Mediterranean). The officers and commanders, who were frequently almost as subject to such conditions as the crew, knew that shortages of food were almost always due to the fact that the Admiralty failed to provide sufficient funds to supply it, and that the reason for this was usually due to the niggardly provision politicians made for the support of the Navy. Phillip and his contemporaries will, in low voices, have discussed all this, spoken of their superiors and criticized them; they will have begun, too, to discuss the international politics of the time, the activities of the French and Spanish navies and how they might be hindered, the strategies of blockading foreign ports and how the war in Europe could affect Britain's trade with India and the far east.

The next definite sighting of Phillip is as midshipman on the 36-gun frigate *Aurora,* sailing to and from Gibraltar in July/September 1759 as escort to a convoy of merchantmen, then cruising the English, French and Dutch coasts between October and January 1760, when Phillip left her to join the *Stirling Castle,* again under Captain Everitt. The *Stirling Castle* was fitted out first at Woolwich, then at Spithead for a voyage to the West Indies. She sailed to Antigua, and thence during December 1760 began patrolling among the Windward Islands.

The uneventful cruising went on until November of the next year, when the ship joined the squadron of Admiral George Rodney, who had been sent from England to capture Martinique and any other French island whose 'liberation' from the French seemed practicable. Phillip had by now been promoted to fourth lieutenant on the *Stirling Castle* and served with her as she accompanied a force of 12,000 men that landed on Martinique and secured the island within a fortnight. It was a brief and uneventful excitement, after which Captain Everitt gave up command and returned to England. Phillip remained with the ship, which was promptly sent with 10 others to blockade the French fleet sheltering at Haiti, then to support the attack on a French fort guarding the harbour of Havana.

The business of attacking and securing the town was lengthy and tedious in stiflingly hot and humid weather. An attempt to bombard El Morro, the fort guarding the town, was bungled, and one of the British ships, the *Cambridge*, was badly damaged and its captain and several crewmen killed. To Phillip's chagrin his new commanding officer, James Campbell, played a major part in the slipshod attempt at an attack, appearing to disobey orders and withdraw from the action for no other reason than securing his ship's safety. His view of Campbell is unlikely to have been more charitable than his opinion of Byng. The captain was court-martialled and dismissed from the service.

In July the tedious and mismanaged campaign ended when additional troops were landed and took Havana. The cost had been great, with many men killed – over 5,000 soldiers and 3,000 sailors. Moreover 800 sailors and 500 marines died from sickness contracted as a result of outbreaks of fever exacerbated by the climate – old hands had complained that they smelt fever and dysentery in the air, and they had been right. What with the length of time away from port and the damage done in battle, the fleet was in a state of disrepair – the *Stirling Castle* herself was said to be so decrepit that 'it was quite impracticable to repair her without a dock so as to be safe to proceed to sea.'[8] She was eventually scuttled and sunk in harbour, while Philip and the rest of her company were transferred to the *Infanta*, a captured French ship. He remained on the *Infanta* while she sailed to England, reaching Portsmouth in mid-March 1763. There, Phillip's promotion to lieutenant was confirmed, and he was paid off.

While only occasionally exciting, the long voyage added to his experience of how a ship's company should be kept in order – sometimes by the harsh discipline of flogging (up to 600 lashes were not unusual, for desertion, and pro rata punishment for such offences as drunkenness or failure to obey orders). Phillip would have by now been capable of making up his own mind as to how far severe punishment resulted in better behaviour and less crime, and how far it made a crew resentful and discontented. Coming up through the ranks could have two effects: it could result in an officer exercising tyrannous command, or it could convince him that a careful balance between strictness and a certain amount of give and take had more positive results where the general atmosphere on board was concerned. Phillip took the latter view, though he did not hesitate to punish strictly when he thought such action justified for the good of the ship or – later – the colony.

In England, and presumably living in London, Phillip was paid off and living on half-pay of 14 shillings a week – about £60 in the currency of 2010. This was bare subsistence, but he had also received a share of the prize money awarded to the squadron as the result of the capture of the *Havana*, and this amounted to £130, or today about £10,600. Scarcely riches – indeed one would have thought he would hesitate to marry on such an income – but the records of St Augustine's Church, Watling Street confirm that, on 19 July 1763, he wed (like his father before him) a widow – 41-year-old Mrs Margaret Charlotte Denison, *née* Tybott.

Presumably he had first met Miss Tybott sometime during 1757-8, the only period when he may have had free time in London. She would have been single then; she married John Denison, her first husband – a cloth and wine merchant in a good way of business – in August 1759, while Phillip was in the Mediterranean. That marriage lasted barely six months before Denison died, leaving his wife a very rich woman indeed, not only in possession of his estate but of a fortune in trust of £120,000 – not far short of 10 million pounds in today's currency.[9] She must have found the young lieutenant Phillip uncommonly attractive, for she certainly did not marry him for his money. Did he marry her for hers? It seems unlikely that he married for love, and there is nothing in his character that we know of to suggest that he had a strong sex-drive; it seems quite possible that he was a man to whom work, and the company of his fellow men, was more interesting and attractive than women. Not that he seems to have been particularly familiar even with those men with whom he worked most closely. All the evidence suggests that he was a man to whom his work was all-important, and that he needed very little else.

He and his wife lived in London for two years, then moved to Lyndhurst, in the New Forest, to a farm called 'Vernals', with a house and outbuildings standing in 22 acres, and he bought a little additional land adjoining. The records of this period are sparse. Professor Alan Frost[10] suggests that Phillip may have taken an interest in the trade of his wife's first husband, and dealt in cloth and wine from Portugal and Spain, but whether this, or indeed farming, seriously engaged his interest seems on the whole unlikely. With his wife's fortune he certainly did not need to work.

Soon enough, however, the necessity to earn an income of his own began to press, for within five years the marriage began to break down. Who can know the reason? Mrs Phillip may have been disappointed in her husband's lack of ardour – if at first he had made a pretence at domestic bliss, the 16 years age difference and perhaps a longing for greater activity than was provided by a little light farming may have weakened his resolve. At all events in April 1769 they parted, the agreement allowing Mrs Phillip the household furniture and all her personal effects; presumably Phillip was able to keep the house, but he lost the large income from his wife's fortune and certainly could not touch the capital which her father had placed in trust for her. After the strain of the divorce he went off to France for several months, to reappear in November 1770 once more as an active naval officer – fourth lieutenant on board the 74-gun battle ship *Egmont*.

No doubt he was relieved to be back on shipboard with the prospect of forwarding his career. Unfortunately, while there initially seemed hope of action in the Falklands, where there was trouble with Spain over its expulsion of British settlers, that controversy was settled before the Egmont could complete her refit and set sail. Instead, Lieutenant Phillip found himself told off to lead a press gang. Only a totally insensitive man could have found this a pleasant experience, but it was a very necessary operation, used since 1664 to crew warships with 'eligible men of seafaring habits between the ages of 18 and 45 years.'

In the 1770s the navy was looking for at least 40,000 men. Conventional recruiting was not easy: no man with seagoing experience would choose to serve on a navy ship unless he was really intent on getting ahead in the service. Naval pay was around half that paid by merchantmen, and lower than that paid to a farm labourer. Astonishingly, it had been set in 1653 and was not to be increased until April 1797 (after the mutiny at Spithead). About half of all navy crews were impressed – and impressed men not only received lower wages than volunteers but were not allowed to go ashore when their ships were in port, and were sometimes even put in irons to prevent their escape. No wonder men scampered and dispersed when there was the slightest hint of a press gang in the streets – and not only those with seagoing experience were targeted, for though landsmen were legally exempt from impressments this was often ignored; two men without seagoing experience were considered by captains to be the equivalent of one Able Seamen. The technique for persuading such a man to join was simple: he would first be asked to volunteer, and if he refused he would be asked at least to drink the health of the navy, and taken when he was drunk. If that failed, he was simply knocked out.

How successful Arthur Phillip was as the leader of a press gang we cannot know; what we know of his character suggests that he will not have been an enthusiast for the practice, which might well have sickened him, and which he may well privately have considered counter-productive. An impressed man was unlikely to make the kind of seaman really committed to his work. The fourth lieutenant would, however, have been pleased when the *Egmont* sailed. Sadly this was only down the coast to Spithead, where she moored with no prospect of going anywhere. Phillip left her, once more on half pay, on the excuse that his health was again sufficiently poor to make it necessary for him to take sick leave; he went off to France 'for the sake of his health'. Whether his health was really bad enough for us to accept this statement at face value is perhaps questionable; certainly his health never seems to have been robust, but he remained abroad for almost four years, and it is surely unlikely that he spent those years as an invalid. He returned to England with a considerable amount of money, which he certainly did not save from his half-pay. There is little point in speculating about his activities – the wine or cloth trade, again? A study of engineering? An early account of him suggests that he studied fortification and military engineering, perhaps in Paris with a German Professor of Artillery and Fortification at the École Militaire. Certainly he returned with a good command of the French language, which was to be of service to him later.

While facts are sparse as far as those years go, the next firm news we have of Arthur Phillip is, on the face of it, surprising: in December 1774 he travelled to Lisbon to join the Portuguese navy.

# TWO

'At a loose end' would be a reasonable description of Arthur Phillip's situation in 1774. He could, of course, re-join the navy; on the other hand, what would his prospects be? After 13 years he was still only a lieutenant, and though certainly he had made no great effort to better his condition, there was not a great deal he could do in peace time, when promotion was dependent to a great extent on the caprice of senior officers, rather than on excellent service.

Happily, out of the blue there came a surprising offer, brokered by Captain Augustus Hervey, who had commanded the *Sterling Castle* during the attacks on Havana, and was now at the Admiralty. Hervey had been approached by the Portuguese Ambassador in London to arrange for some of Britain's half-pay officers to join the Portuguese navy at a time of excited dispute between Portugal and Spain. Spain had supported France during the Seven Years War, while Portugal had taken the part of Britain. At the end of the war the French navy was crippled, and the British Admiralty was quite aware that only an ambitious rebuilding program and collaboration with the Spanish fleet would see it again able to challenge the Royal Navy's command of the sea. Any support given to the Portuguese was seen as energy well spent. So Hervey recommended Phillip as an officer who, though only a lieutenant, was a man who could be trusted.

Phillip presented himself to the Portuguese Ambassador, Pinto de Souza, and declared himself ready to serve, on certain conditions: that he was paid at the same rate as a British naval officer on active service, that he should be allowed half pay when placed on the retired list, and that he should hold the rank of captain. This was all considered eminently reasonable, indeed more than reasonable; he was awarded twice the pay of an equivalent Portuguese officer, with an extra sum if commanding a frigate and even more if he was in command of a ship of the line. The Portuguese did not recognize 'half pay', but he would be adequately rewarded at the end of his commission.

Phillip arrived in Lisbon early in 1775, was commissioned captain in the Portuguese navy, and appointed second captain on the *Nossa Senhora de Belém*; his co-captain was one António de Sales e Noronha. Phillip found the idea of two captains serving on the same vessel a peculiar one; but it was the Portuguese custom, and he had to accept it. On 9 February, Phillip and Sales e Noronha, having travelled to the court to take a formal farewell of the King, sailed for Rio de Janeiro, where they reported to Luis de Almeida Portugal, Marquis of Lavradio and Viceroy of Brazil. It was here that Phillip came under the command of one Robert M'Douall, another British naval officer on loan to the Portuguese navy. Lavradio and M'Douall were completely different characters, and had little time for each other. M'Douall, indeed, had little time for anyone except himself, and was disliked not only by the Viceroy but by the officers under his command.

Lavradio had not only received warm recommendations of Phillip's soundness from Portugal, but liked him on sight, and during the four months after his arrival made a point of getting to know Phillip, while he in turn began to learn Portuguese, study charts of the harbour and naval yard (of possible future use to the Admiralty) and familiarise himself with the political complexities of the situation in which he now found himself.

This involved the conflict between Spain and Portugal over rights to certain areas of South America, particularly around Colonia do Sacramento, a colony founded in 1680 by Portugal but disputed by the Spanish from their own settlements on the opposite bank of the river at Buenos Aries. In 1680 Colonia was captured by José de Garro and returned to Portugal the following year, only to be conquered again by the Spanish in 1705 after a five month siege. The Treaty of Utrecht, however, signed by the representatives of Louis XIV of France and Philip V of Spain on the one hand, and representatives of Queen Anne of Great Britain, the Duke of Savoy, and the United Provinces on the other, restored the colony to Portugal. Portugal held it still when Phillip arrived in Buenos Aries and, to the fury of Spain, continued to use it – as they had for many years – as a dispersal point for illicit trade.

In mid-August, Phillip was given command of the *Pilar*, a 26-gun frigate, and was ordered to sail to Santa Catarina with another ship, transporting three companies of infantry and artillery to Colonia, where a crumbling fort was defended by troops weakened by fever; it was said that the sentries were so debilitated that they had to sit while on duty. Dismayed by the weakness and prevarication of Francisco José da Rocha, the Governor of Colonia, Phillip took matters into his own hands and, when two Spanish ships came in his view rather too close to the land, fired on them, damaging one. A little while later, he fired on two more. Da Rocha panicked, and sent an officer to apologise to the Spanish commander of San Carlos, claiming that he had personally instructed Phillip to refrain from violence (which indeed was the truth). The Spanish were careful, however, to keep their ships out of range in future.

The firmness of Portugal's latest British captain was impressive, especially in contrast to the indecision of M'Douall. We can presume that the latter was not best pleased at Lavradio's applause for Phillip's actions – for when M'Douall was ordered to attack the Spanish, and Phillip and the *Pilar* were sent forward in support, M'Douall ordered the junior officer to go off on a fruitless hunt for Spanish ships in the Plate estuary, then himself abandoned the attack after an initial failure and took his squadron back to Santa Catarina, where Phillip rejoined it. Lavradio was enraged, and sent off a broadside to M'Douall, complaining at his dismissal of the *Pilar* from the action: 'The vessels you sent were manned by the worst sailors of the Fleet. You used inexperienced officers while those who had been in battle, and under fire, such as Arthur Phillip . . . and other officers of great value on account of their honour and energy, were left out, and sent to do that which the others could have done equally well.'[11]

Almost immediately, however, a truce was declared from Lisbon, although both sides in the dispute kept their troops and ships in readiness, and Lavradio sent the *Pilar* with two other ships under Phillip's command back to Colonia, where they protected Portuguese vessels against Spanish depredations and captured two ships. Spain protested, and the Viceroy withdrew two ships, leaving only the *Pilar*, with Phillip in charge. The latter spent the four months from September 1775 protecting local fishing boats from pirates, who had the habit of capturing them and selling the crews into slavery. He also took the opportunity of thoroughly exploring the waters through which he sailed, drawing or updating charts, taking note of the strengths and weaknesses of Spanish ports such as Maldonade, Montevideo and Buenos Aries, and acquiring and passing on to the British Admiralty some extremely sensitive and important observations.

His work at Colonia also occupied him, and he emphasised to Lavradio the necessity of seeing that the colony was properly supplied. In the winter there were shortages of food, coal and wood: the *Pilar* also needed repair, but the necessary material was not available. Moreover, a single frigate was in his opinion insufficient to guard the place properly. Lavradio, though he was able to do little enough to remedy the situation, was all the more impressed by Phillip, whom he now considered to be a much more efficient, decisive and authoritative officer than M'Douall.

Doubtless the news in November that a huge Spanish fleet – 20 warships escorting 96 transports carrying 10,000 troops - had sailed from Cádiz made Lavradio wish that he could have sent for Phillip to advise him rather than M'Douall. When the waiting Portuguese squadron sighted the Spanish fleet, it was so huge that it was impossible to count the number of ships. Phillip tried desperately to persuade M'Douall to attack, but as usual he prevaricated – the most he would do is send a ship to dart in now and again and try to pick off a single Spanish ship. When this did not work, he turned the squadron away from the oncoming fleet. Phillip sent him a private letter, imploring him, for the sake of his own honour and that of the English nation, not to refrain from attacking. It did no good.

Eventually, M'Douall's prevarication was such that any chance of a successful attack against the massed Spanish ships would be virtual suicide. At that point, he called all his captains to a meeting, at which he managed to persuade them that inaction was the best possible course; at all costs the squadron must be preserved. Five of the eight captains signed a statement approving of his view, and agreed that they should sail back to Rio for further instructions. One wavered, only one argued for an immediate attack. Phillip reluctantly concluded that in the situation as it now was, with no chance of additional ships or troops being available, he must also assent to a return to Rio. So the squadron ran for port – 'fleeing like a Chinaman', as one Portuguese official later put it.

At Rio, under the furious eye of Lavradio, the squadron

refitted before sailing again on 1 April, and at last Phillip saw some action. With another similarly minded captain, he led the assault on a 70-gun Spanish battleship, the *San Agustin*. He sneaked in under the guard of the Spanish, who could not think that such a small and inoffensive vessel could be an armed adversary. The *Pilar* fired, but quick nightfall and a failing wind deprived Phillip of success until the following morning, when dawn showed the Spanish captain that he was almost in the middle of a Portuguese squadron. He surrendered, and Phillip escorted the captured vessel back to Rio as a prize, where she became the most effective ship in the Portuguese squadron – with Arthur Phillip as her commander.

In August, Lavradio heard that peace discussions were underway in Europe, and ordered the cessation of hostilities – not a moment too soon, for Colonia had been forced to surrender. In October 1777 the Treaty of San Ildefonso awarded Colonia to Spain, while it returned Santa Catarina to Portugal. Lavradio bundled M'Douall on a ship to Lisbon to be court-martialled for contributing to the loss of Santa Catarina, and though Phillip remained highly valued and praised by the Viceroy, the *San Agustin* had to be returned to Spain, and so he lost his command.

No doubt at Phillip's request, Lavradio gave him command of the *Santo Antonio* (which had been M'Douall's flagship) and engaged him to escort a convoy carrying diamonds to Lisbon. He sailed into port on 20 August, and four days later relinquished his commission. Lavradio's report to his superiors in Lisbon was glowing: Phillip was

> one of the officers of the most distinct merit that the Queen has in her service in the Navy, and I think that it will be a most important acquisition to retain him in the Royal Service . . . As regards his disposition,

he is somewhat distrustful; but, as he is an Officer of education and principle, he gives way to reason, and does not, before doing so, fall into those exaggerated and unbearable excesses of temper which the majority of his fellow-countrymen do, more especially those who have been brought up at sea. He is very clean-handed; is an Officer of great truth and very brave; and is no flatterer, saying what he thinks, but without temper or want of respect. The length of my Report upon this Officer implies that I regret his departure very much, and I confess that I do. It is the consequence of my having noted the great difference in the way he served, as compared with the greater part of the others.[12]

The British Ambassador wrote to the Lord Commissioners of the Admiralty to support this view: the Portuguese Court was 'extremely satisfied with the conduct of this Gentleman, & . . . he has served in the Brasils with great Zeal & Honour.'

Returning to London, Phillip's intention was to re-join the Royal Navy; soon after arrival, he learned that he would do so as master and commander, and immediately did himself some good by reporting to the Secretary of the Admiralty that on the voyage from Lisbon he had observed a French fleet of more than 30 ships, sailing south. Four days later, he reported to the 74-gun battleship *Alexander* as first lieutenant under Captain Richard Kempenfelt, with a crew of 600 men.

# THREE

Phillip cannot have been entirely pleased when, rather than being given command of his own ship, he found himself a first lieutenant – not an insignificant rank, but somewhat of a comedown after having been in command of his own battleship. However, there was nothing he could do but wait and hope that the Lords of the Admiralty would not forget the praise given him for the service he had done in Portugal.

Understandably nervous of the combined forces of Spain and France, massed only a short sail from the English coast, their Lordships had decided on a show of strength, and the *Alexander* joined the Channel fleet off Spithead in June, 1778. For six weeks the two fleets did a stately dance around each other, coming within sight of each other's sails but never close enough to provoke violence. Then, back at Spithead, Phillip heard that his position as master and commander was to be recognised: he was appointed to captain the fireship *Basilisk*.

How much of a compliment was this? A fireship was not a battleship, but an old hulk unfit for further service. Packed with readily combustible material it would be set on fire, then sailed among an enemy fleet to set as many ships as possible alight. Though there was good danger money to be made by captain and crew, and though clearly a man placed in command must have shown himself to be cool and brave in dangerous situations, it was not a position to be sought. Moreover, even among wrecks the *Basilisk* was notably frail, incapable even for the time of leaving harbour.

Phillip therefore requested a transfer to the *Victory*, the flagship of the Channel fleet (a quarter of a century later to earn herself, at Trafalgar, a place as the most famous of all English battleships). There is no evidence that his request was granted, but neither is there reason to believe that it was not. In fact it seems likely that it was at this time he made the acquaintance of the purser of the *Victory*, Evan Nepean, who was to become Secretary of the Admiralty[13], and of whom we shall learn more later.

If Phillip did sail on the *Victory* it would have been as a volunteer, which would explain the absence of his name from her records. In any case, he did not see any action, and when she returned to port he learned – perhaps with relief – that it had been decided that the *Basilisk* was beyond repair, and that he was summoned to London for consultation with the First Lord of the Admiralty, Lord Sandwich, presumably about his knowledge of affairs in South America.

It was now the summer of 1780 and, uncertain about his future and eager to see some action, Phillip took the liberty of writing a personal letter to the First Lord, reminding him that he had done the state some service and asking for what was due to him – that is, active service in any part of the world. 'Nothing could hurt me so much as remaining unemploy'd in times like the present,' he wrote.[14]

His plea had little effect – at least until January 1781, when a sudden complete blanket of silence descends, and we hear no more of him for nine months. Those who subscribe to the belief that from time to time Phillip, with his excellent command of French, was in some way employed as a spy, might well claim that this explains the complete absence of evidence about his life between January and October, when his name appears in records as acting captain of the frigate *Ariadne*, which he was directed to sail to the Elbe to escort a transport ship back to England.

While the voyage did not run up against the enemy, it was by no means easy – it was bitterly cold when he reached Cuxhaven at the mouth of the Elbe, and the transport had been run ashore to avoid being iced in and perhaps crushed. Phillip himself had for the same reason decided to run the *Ariadne* onto the mud, first unloading her guns and equipment to lighten her. Rather defensively, he explained later to the Secretary of the Admiralty that he had 'consulted with the Pilots and acted for the best, the running of the Ship into the mud [being] the only means of saving her, and that was not done until many hours after the Pilots who were on board declared it to be absolutely necessary, and refused either to carry her to Sea or to take any further charge of her if she remained at Anchor.'[15] The transport finally sailed early in March, and the *Ariadne* was refloated and reached England almost three weeks later. There, her captain saw to it that her refit was completed to his satisfaction before she sailed again at the end of June to patrol the Channel. It was on the *Ariadne* that he first met a man who was to become a colleague and friend in his New South Wales adventure, Lieutenant Philip Gidley King. Finally, in December 1781, he received the news for which he had waited: he was to captain the 64-gun *Europe* – at last, he was to command a real warship.

Sadly, the following twelve months failed to provide any excitement, but he cannot have been dissatisfied with his progress. He had started his naval career with no advantages in the way of money or great influence, though one should not underestimate the importance of his distant relationship with Captain Everitt. He had advanced steadily through his own efforts and talents – not least his talent for languages and his command of French, German and Portuguese. Some of his activities remain slightly obscure: what, for instance, was the real nature of his usefulness to Sandwich? We can assume his knowledge of what he had seen during his time in the Portuguese navy will have been valuable, but more valuable may have been what he really did during his travels in France – just as he had made the most of his forced stay in Cuxhaven. It is unlikely that his activities abroad could be safely described as 'spying', but his keen observation and nose for valuable information had made him of use, and his superiors had affirmed that he had a safe pair of hands, and was to be trusted.

Whatever Phillip might have expected during his next months of duty, it would certainly not have been a voyage to India.

The voyage arose as the result of the hope of the British that the Mexicans, Peruvians and Chileans might successfully revolt against Spanish rule in South America, and the desire to help them to do so. A successful revolt and the defeat of Spain would open out enormous markets for British traders in the area, and with any luck the gratitude of the prevailing native people would encourage them to be open and generous. A number of more or less wild suggestions for British intervention had been put forward over the past few years, including the sending of military forces – either formal forces or privateers unofficially supported by the Government – to support the rebels whether covertly or openly.

In the end, the idea which gained favour was that of sending a military expedition – say 1,500 troops – first to India, where they would be joined by another 2,000 Sepoys, then on to New Zealand, whence it would sail to South America to support a British offer of independence. Spain's instant defeat was envisaged, after which there would be untold gold to be gained from the opening out of trade.

Robert M'Douall had advised 'distressing' Spain by sending a small squadron to the mouth of the River Plate to disrupt the passage of Spanish ships between Spain and Buenos Aries and capture Spanish treasure ships. In the end it was decided to dispatch a naval force of three 50-gun warships, two frigates, a sloop and two fireships, with the usual supporting supply vessels, to the Plate, there either to take Buenos Aries and encourage the rebels in the area or, if Spanish forces seemed too great, to cruise around disrupting trade as M'Douall had suggested. However, no sooner had this plan been accepted than the British declared war on the United Provinces because of Holland's determination to continue to send ammunition and stores to France, Spain and the American colonies. This made it highly probable that a number of ports *en route* to India would fall under the control of Britain's enemies, so the River Plate plans were set aside, and it was decided that the proposed forces should proceed to Cape Town (one of the ports in question) and take it.

Phillip was called to the Admiralty to supply some of his charts of the South American coast. He was able to make several practical suggestions about the possibility of British ships finding safe landing places along the east coast where they could pick up water and wood. There was also talk of loading munitions for the rebels in Peru. The naval force sailed in mid-March, M'Douall meandering up and down the coast seeing what he could see while another force under Richard Johnstone sailed for the Cape, his ships damaged by a fight, on the way, with a Spanish force. The damage strongly suggested that Johnstone should not engage at the Cape, and so he ordered the troop carriers and supply ships on to India while he laid up briefly at St Helena before cruising off the Plate.

Phillip may or may not have sailed with Johnstone; he certainly made careful provision for his charts to be available, should they be needed while he was 'called for', which suggests that he left Britain, or at least London, for a while – though there is no concrete evidence that the call ever came. Professor Frost, in his *Arthur Phillip, his Voyaging*, records several suggestions, some the result of anecdote – among them that he sailed more or less privately to South America on a reconnoitring voyage and that it was at this time that he was recruited into the British espionage service, and perhaps was engaged in secret service work. Neither speculation can be proved, and it is perhaps best simply to acknowledge ignorance of his movements until late 1782, when Phillip was commissioned captain of the *Europe*, which was to sail to India via South America in company with three other warships.

An expedition was planned, once again, with the idea of supporting insurrection, now popularly believed to be so violent that Spain could not resist it. It was suggested that five warships, two frigates, two sloops and 10 transports carrying 2,000 troops should sail for the Plate. A successful operation there would release a proportion of the force to go on to India.

The squadron sailed on 16 January 1783 – three days before Spain sued for peace. The warships *Elizabeth, Grafton* and *Iphigenia* sailed with the *Europe*, under Phillip's command. In the Bay of Biscay the small flotilla was so buffeted by strong storms – violent gales and towering waves – that only Phillip, in the *Europe*, battled on; the other warships, damaged, returned to port. Madeira was the destination named in Phillip's orders but, still plagued by stormy weather – so stormy that the hatches were continually battened down, with the result that the air below decks was musty and thick – he discovered that his compasses were faulty, so that the ship was at least 300 kilometres from its supposed position. Moreover, scurvy had broken out among the crew. No longer capable of reaching Madeira, he took the *Europe* on to Port Praia in the Portuguese Cape Verde islands, off the western coast of Africa. There he was able to do some repairs to the ship and take on supplies.

With no news or sight of the rest of the squadron, he decided to sail on to India. Bad weather once again intervened, and he was forced to make for Rio, then sail on for São Sebastião. Unexpectedly, a shot was fired across his bow by the fort at

Santa Cruz. There was no reason for this, for the Viceroy knew his ship was in the area. Furious, Phillip stormed ashore and demanded the Viceroy order the fort commander to offer a personal apology – for 'the insult offered to His Majesty's Colours' – or he would be forced to fire on the fort. The commandant apologised, Phillip gave the fort a salute of 15 guns, the fort replied with a salute of 19 guns, and everyone's honour was satisfied.

In port the *Europe* was more thoroughly repaired while Phillip kept his ears open for information about the settlements in the country around – there was no doubt, in his opinion, that an assault on Monte Video would succeed, and the defeat of the Spanish would be a matter of course. By the time he reported this, if at all, the opportunity was lost.

He sailed from Rio on 5 May, with 50 bulls on board, apart from other supplies, and when he reached the Comoro Island was presented by the ruling family with half a dozen bullocks. He also gathered there a considerable amount of fruit, useful against the scurvy, before sailing on through now placid weather past the Maldives and Ceylon to Madras, where the India squadron waited under the command of Sir Edward Hughes, to whom he presented a bullock or two. Hughes was appalled at the poor state of the *Europe*, and ordered extensive repairs before sending her home under the command of Sir Richard King.

The homeward bound flotilla met extremely stormy weather *en route* to Cape Town, and there were many deaths from scurvy and almost 2,000 men sick by the time the ships anchored in Table Bay. At first the Dutch Governor was reluctant to allow the sick to be landed – he had not heard that a truce had by now been struck between the British and Dutch. He eventually agreed that the most seriously sick men be landed on Robben Island, while once more necessary repairs were done to the storm-damaged ships, one of which was so seriously smashed that she had to be abandoned and burnt at her moorings.

The heavy weather continued through December and January, and Philip and Hughes moved into more comfortable lodgings on shore while they oversaw repairs and re-provisioned the ships with goods reluctantly provided by the Dutch, who by now had been convinced that peace had broken out but were no doubt still less than confidently friendly. Phillip's 'astonishment', expressed in a letter to the Governor, that there seemed to be a reluctance to supply his ships at a time of peace and 'in friendship with great Britain' was perhaps a little feigned.

The re-fit and provisioning of the little fleet was taking so long and the weather continued to be so bad that Hughes decided to send Phillip on ahead with his dispatches, together with a complaint about how long it was taking the Dutch to reach an accommodation with visiting naval ships at Cape Town The *Europe* reached England by the end of April, and the crew was paid off. Having made his report at the Admiralty, the next we hear of Phillip is of an application for leave so that he could travel to Grenoble 'on Account of my Private Affairs.' The fact that he was given prompt permission is not particularly surprising, but eyebrows might have been slightly raised at the fact that he was also given £150 in respect of salary and expenses. This would amount, today, to something over £13,000. We do not know what proportion was allotted to 'expenses', but need not wonder how they were incurred, for it is obvious that he was being paid to spy on French naval activities in and around the arsenals on the coast between Toulon and Nice, reaching Toulon in January 1785 and receiving another £170 in expenses from the Admiralty's secret service fund towards the end of the year.

Whether or not he had previously being employed in spying, or at least covert observation, it is no wonder that he was seen as a useful man to have in France. He spoke French like a Frenchman and, as a practical naval officer knew precisely what to look out for at a naval base. He observed and reported that the French navy had 14 battleships and eleven frigates refitting at Toulon, and contrived to discover that orders had been given to fit seven battleships for immediate service, five to be ready in the near future. Such details could only have come from the French, very possibly as a result of the careful expenditure of his 'expenses'. Along the coast to Nice, he was unable to gain access to any of the arsenals but may have gone about obtaining additional information from elsewhere – his movements for the rest of the year are obscure. He was back in England, briefly, in late October, presumably to make a personal report, then returned to the Toulon area with a further supply of money for 'expenses' – this time £160.

Centred on Hyères, between Toulon and Bormes-les-Mimosas, he rattled along the coast over appalling roads in unsprung carriages, and by the end of 1786 must have been hoping that on his return to England he would be ordered off to sea again. He was.

# FOUR

The size of the English prison population had been a problem for some years before anyone thought of expelling prisoners from their homeland to some more or less remote place – sufficiently far away to make them invisible to ordinary law-abiding people and the politicians who longed to be free of them.

The invisibility of prisoners was an important aspect of the Georgian prison system. Sinners (and the sin was generally seen by Christian law-makers to be as despicable as the actual crime) were not put in prison in order that they might repent or reform; they were put there largely to be forgotten – to be out of sight and out of mind. Transportation was a bright idea which put the prisoner even further out of sight and mind than imprisoning him or her in a cell in some insalubrious part of town. In the case of the latter the people to whom prisoners were not invisible, of course, were those who made a profit by imprisoning them – those who owned and ran the gaols – people like the Bishops of Ely and Durham and the Dukes of Portland and Leeds, whose employees could load prisoners down with chains until and unless they paid heavily for them to be removed. Then there was money to be made from providing bedding and food and drink (even water), for sharing a straw bed with another prisoner and even for simply inhabiting a cell.

The idea of transportation had been around for centuries – in 1597 Queen Elizabeth's government passed a law 'for the Punyshment of Rogues, Vagabonds and Sturdy Beggars' which would banish them from England 'to such parts beyond the seas as shall be assigned by the Privy Council', while in 1611 convicts were sent to America to work in the plantations in Virginia and a century later Britain began officially transporting criminals to the North American colonies. There was a tariff – minor theft might result in transportation for seven years (as opposed to being branded or flogged), while a prisoner condemned to death might have a sentence commuted to transportation for 14 years. Once more, there was profit to be made; convicts were sold to contractors who shipped them to the West Indies or the southern American colonies and sold them on to plantation owners who were as welcome and kindly to them as to their black slaves. Between 1717 and 1776 over 40,000 convicts sailed from the British Isles, by which time opposition to the idea had grown in America (though happy to keep black slaves, they objected to receiving white villains from Britain). Eventually, convicts were no longer allowed to land.

Fearing that the public would react against the quickly growing population of convicts at home, the government of the day had to think of some solution. Their answer was to pass the Hulks Act, moor the wrecks of old fighting ships on the Thames and in various harbours along the south coast and use them as prison ships. The imprisoned convicts were thus conveniently placed to do such daily work as dredging silted moorings and clearing inconvenient mud-banks. The fact that the prison population grew far too quickly for this to be a convenient working solution was ignored until prison reformers got wind of the reality of life on the hulks, with men and women herded together in conditions which not only encouraged promiscuity but resulted in gaol sickness. Ordinary people living within sight and sound – and smell – of the hulks began to be terrified of disease, especially when typhus actually became endemic on many of them.

The problem became so pressing that in 1779 a special House of Commons committee was set up to examine it and rethink the question of transportation as a solution. The committee concluded that with the prison population growing at the rate of at least 1,000 a year, the problem was indeed pressing; suggestions had been made that Gambia or Gibraltar might be excellent destinations for surplus convicts, though care should be taken to retain a sufficient number in Britain to continue to be useful as a supply of free labourers for honest folk.

How did the idea occur of using New South Wales as an enormous convict hulk? The country was certainly sufficiently remote, and there was no-one of any importance living there to be annoyed by a sudden influx of villains. Charles de Brosses, Comte de Tournay, Baron de Montfalcon, a French writer on ancient history, philology and linguistics, suggested in 1756[16] that the place would be an ideal destination for criminals, a idea repeated 10 years later by a British writer, and the committee soon heard the idea being pressed.

One of the witnesses before it was Joseph Banks, the explorer and naturalist who had been to the distant continent with Cook in 1770. He firmly asserted that Botany Bay, on the coast of New Holland, was an ideal place for a convict settlement. There would be little trouble from the natives, who though treacherous and antagonistic to strangers were also extremely cowardly; the soil, though not rich, could support a colony; the grass was rich, so cattle and sheep should thrive; the water supply was excellent, and there was plenty of wood for building and fuel. He went on to make practical suggestions[17]: the first convict expedition should carry with it plenty of seeds and tools for farming, small boats, nets and fishing equipment, cattle, sheep, pigs and poultry and sufficient victuals, clothes and drink to last for twelve months. With all this, he was in no doubt that a party of criminal colonists could within a year begin to support itself without further help from England. He was also in no doubt that in future years trade could be encouraged, and there was the strong probability of considerable profit – after all, as far as could be known, New South Wales was considerably bigger than Europe, and it would be singularly stupid to suppose that all that land could remain barren.

Banks must have known that he was vastly over-estimating the possibility of any colony becoming self-sufficiently within twelve months. He had seen enough of the country around Botany Bay to know that it was in fact extremely unpromising as far as farming was concerned. Why he pressed the destination so enthusiastically and positively remains a mystery, but it is difficult not to assume that Phillip must during the coming years have cursed the committee for believing his evidence and that of some other witnesses.

The British Government was in no particular hurry to solve the problem. Yes, the overcrowding of the hulks was a difficulty, and there was public pressure, but as soon as the unfortunate War of Independence was over, no doubt America would once more be willing to receive convicts as slaves. King George II generously agreed that he would be perfectly happy to continue to send criminals to America: 'permitting them to obtain Men unworthy to remain in this Island I shall certainly consent to,' he said.

After the King had reluctantly recognised the United States, however, it rapidly became clear that the new country would remain adamantly opposed to the idea – even the reactionary planters in the south could not be persuaded to buy. Meanwhile overcrowding in the hulks was worse than ever, contagious illness – including smallpox – became more prevalent, and the people who lived on shore anywhere near a moored hulk became increasingly nervous and angry. The Lord Mayor of London wrote to the Home Office complaining at the number of convicts now escaping from the hulks, and indeed in March 1875 the convicts on a hulk in Plymouth Sound mutinied and were only subdued after eight had been killed and 36 wounded, while Plymouthians nervously barricaded themselves in their houses.

As the Government continued to consider the problem, James Maria Matra, who like Banks had also sailed with Cook (as a midshipman), came forward to support Botany Bay as a solution: 'Give them [the convicts] a few acres of ground as soon as they arrive,' he wrote. 'Let it be here remarked that they cannot fly from the country, that they have no temptation to theft, and that they must work or starve.' Moreover, 'the climate and soil are so happily adapted to produce every various and valuable production of Europe, and of both the Indies, that with good management and a few settlers, in 20 or 30 years they might cause a revolution in the whole system of European commerce and secure to England a monopoly of some part of it, and a very large share in the whole.' An eminent naval officer, Sir George Young, agreed with even more enthusiasm, and put forward a useful practical scheme for exporting convicts as ballast on ships that would go on to China to load tea.

Yet another committee was set up, and its report concentrated on the evils of the present state of things: there were perhaps as many as 100,000 prisoners in the hulks (surely a wild overestimate). These were, apart from other moral problems, schools for villainy, where the more experienced convicts taught the young all the tricks of their nefarious trades. It could not be supposed that any single prisoner would be reformed by imprisonment in such conditions. Apart from which the expense of running the hulk was enormous. Transportation was clearly the only possible practical option.

However, conditions should apply. Any colony of convicts should not contain both male and female prisoners – the thought that convicted criminals could, by going forth and multiplying, found anything like a decent society was clearly ludicrous. The prisoners must be male labourers who would work because if they did not do so, they would not be fed. There would be no alternative.

To those who suggested that an exploratory expedition might be viable in order to ensure that the country would indeed be capable of supporting a colony, William Eden, first Baron Auckland, replied that 'criminals when their lives and liberties are forfeited to justice become a forlorn hope, and have always been judged a fit subject of hazardous experiment to which it would be unjust to expose the more valuable members of a state. If there be any terrors in the prospect before the wretch who is banished to New South Wales they are no more than he expected; if the dangers of a foreign climate, or the improbability of returning to this country, be considered as nearly equivalent to death, the devoted convict naturally reflects that his crimes have drawn in this punishment, and that offended justice in consigning him to the inhospitable shore of New Holland, does not mean thereby to seat him for his life on a bed of roses.'[18]

So that was all right. The problem remained, however, of the destination of this disreputable expedition. New South Wales seemed in almost every way to be reasonable – except that another witness before the committee produced worrying figures that suggested that transporting convicts over such a distance would cost at least 30 pounds a man (perhaps £2,500 in today's currency), and that this was at least five times what it cost to send such a man to America.

In the end the committee sat firmly on the fence, agreeing in the age-old cant phrase that 'something must be done', while omitting to suggest an alternative solution to the problem, except to offer again the notion of somewhere on the west coast of Africa (which had the advantage that fever would probably decimate any colony, thus much reducing the expense of maintaining it). The discussion rambled on, to and fro, between the politicians, the unofficial and official advisors, the Home Office, the Treasury and the Admiralty.

At last, in the Speech from the Throne on 23 January 1787 it was announced that the King had approved Botany Bay as the proper place for a settlement of convicts: 'A plan has been formed by my direction, for transporting a number of convicts, in order to remove the inconvenience which arose from the crowded state of the gaols in different parts of the kingdom.' Lord Sydney, at the Treasury[19], made it known that three companies of marines and their officers would accompany the first expedition, with provisions sufficient for two years and cattle and seed to encourage the notion of complete independence. The Lords Commissioners of the Treasury were instructed to provide shipping to transfer supplies, provisions and men to Botany Bay.

In general, the idea was welcomed by all, and positively took fire with idealists, who rejoiced in the conviction that in sylvan conditions far from temptation horrid men would reform and flourish in peace and contentment. The more practical resolutely believed in the new settlement as a source of increasing trade and profit. To satisfy the public interest an opera on the subject, *Botany Bay*, opened at the Royal Circus. On the hulks the news was greeted with less enthusiasm. After all, sailing for New South Wales was not unlike setting off for the moon. As a convict balladeer sang:

*All you that's in England, and live at home at ease,*
*Be warn'd by us poor lads, that are forc'd to cross the seas,*
*That are forc'd to cross the seas, among the savages to go*
*To leave friends and relations to work at the hoe.20*

At the Home Office and the Admiralty, practical preparations were put in train. Ships must be found and crews set aboard, officers and commanders must be chosen, supplies must be bought and loaded, the convicts to be transported must be selected and a Captain General and Governor-in-Chief chosen. The choice of the latter fell on a slightly obscure naval officer at present on half-pay, and farming in the New Forest.

Speculations about Captain Arthur Phillip's selection have occupied many pages of many books and articles over the past two centuries and more. One rumour that went around at the time of his appointment, when few people outside the navy had ever heard of him, was that Captain Phillip had already had experience in running a convict ship. This idea seems to have taken root in a paragraph which appeared in the *St James Chronicle* on 2 February 1787:

> Capt. Phillip, the Commander in Chief of the Expedition to Botany-Bay, was several Years in the Portuguese Service, and obtained no small Degree of Reputation from the following Incident: Being employed about five Years since to carry out with him near 400 Criminals from Lisbon to the Brasils, during the Course of the Voyage an epidemical Disorder broke out on board his Ship, which made such Havock, that he had not Hands sufficient to navigate her; in this Dilemma he called up the most Spirited of the Transports, and told them in a few Words, his situation, and that if they would assist in conducting the Vessel, and keep their Companions in Order, he would represent their Behaviour to the Court of Lisbon, and, in short, do all in his Power to get their sentence mitigated. This Speech had the desired Effect; the Prisoners acted with Fidelity, and brought the Ship safe to Buenos Ayres, where they were delivered into the Custody of the Garrison; and on Capt. Phillip's Return to Lisbon, and representing the meritorious Conduct of

the Transports, they were not only emancipated from their servitude, but had small Portions of Land allotted them in that delightful Country.

As far as anyone has been able to discover, there is no truth in this story; it is a convenient anecdote which appeared after Phillip's appointment and bears all the signs of journalistic invention. The truth is probably that both Lord Sydney and Evan Nepean knew Phillip and his qualities, and he was in a sense an obvious choice – a tried and tested seaman perfectly capable of guiding a small fleet to the other side of the world; a man with a cool head but a firm hand, totally reliable, firm in carrying out instructions but with a talent to improvise should that become necessary. There was some slight opposition from the First Lord of the Admiralty, Lord Howe, who had his own candidate, but on consideration he told Sydney that he 'could never have thought of contesting the choice you would make of the officers to be intrusted with the conduct of [the project]. I cannot say what little knowledge I have of Captain Phillips [*sic*] would have led me to select him for a service of this complicated nature. But as you are satisfied of his ability, and I conclude he will be taken under your direction, I presume it will not be unreasonable to move the King for having his Majesty's pleasure signified to the Admiralty for these purposes.'[21] So Phillip's appointment was ratified on 2 September 1786, and he received his commission from the King on the day after his 48th birthday.

George the Third, &c., to our trusty and well-beloved Captain Arthur Phillip, greeting:-

WE, reposing especial trust and confidence in your loyalty, courage, and experience in military affairs, do, by these presents, constitute and appoint you to be Governor of our territory called New South Wales, extending from the northern cape or ex- Territorial extremity of the coast called Cape York, in the latitude of 10° 37' south, to the southern extremity of the said territory of New South Wales or South Cape, in the latitude 0' 43 ° 39' south, and of all the country inland to 'the westward as far as the one hundred and thirty -fifth degree of longitude, reckoning from the meridian of Greenwich, including all the islands adjacent in the Pacific Ocean, within the latitude aforesaid of 10° 37' south and 43 ° 391 south, and of all towns, garrisons, castles, forts, and all other fortifications or other military works, which may be hereafter erected upon this said territory or any of the said islands.

You are therefore carefully and diligently to discharge the duty of Governor in and over our said territory by doing and performing all and all manner of things thereunto belonging, and we do hereby strictly charge and command all our officers and soldiers who shall be employed within our said territory, and all others whom it may concern, to obey you as our Governor thereof; and you are to observe and follow such orders and directions from time to time as you shall receive from us, or any other your superior officer according to the rules and discipline of war, and likewise such orders and directions as we shall send you under our signet or sign manual, or by our High Treasurer or Commissioners of our Treasury for the time being, or one of our Principal Secretaries of State, in pursuance of the trust we hereby repose in you.

Given at our Court at St. James's, the twelfth day of October, 1786, in the twenty-sixth year of our reign. By his Majesty's command, SYDNEY.[22]

The Governor's salary was fixed at £1,000 a year (in the region of £80,000 today) added to his captain's pay of £500 (say, £4,000), with an allowance of £20 (£160) for stationery and five shillings a day (£2) for a secretary.

Once he had left England, he would have the authority almost of a god. Over that enormous stretch of land and sea he had ultimate power – to regulate the justice system, impose fines or more strenuous punishments and to direct armed forces 'for the resisting and withstanding of all enemies and rebels both at sea and on land'. He was to all intents and purposes to be monarch, subject only to the King himself, with 'full power and authority . . . [to] judge any offender or offenders in criminal matters or for any fine or fines and to remit all offences, fines and forfeitures treason and wilful murder only excepted in which cases you shall likewise have power upon extraordinary occasions to grant reprieves to the offenders until and to the intent our royal pleasure may be known therein.'

His orders, conveyed in the name of the King, were that 'whereas we have ordered that about 600 male and 180 female convicts now under sentence or order of transportation . . . should be removed out of the gaols and other places of confinement in this our kingdom, and be put on board of the several transport ships which have been taken up for their reception, it is our royal will and pleasure that as soon as the said convicts, the several persons composing the civil establishments, and the stores, provisions, &c., provided for their use, shall be put on board the *Supply*, tender, and the transport ships . . . and be in readiness to depart, that you do take them under your protection and proceed in the *Sirius* with the said tender and transports to the port on the coast of New South Wales, situated in the latitude of 33° 41', called by the name of Botany Bay.'[23]

Sydney wanted the convict fleet to be ready to sail by December – a hopelessly ambitious aim. If he had thought that the newly-appointed captain-general would 'get on with the business' without troubling himself too much about detail, he must soon have realised that he had backed the wrong man. Phillip's idea of 'convenient speed' did not mean racing ahead without due consideration of every aspect of the task before him. Apart from attending to the practical considerations of equipping and readying ships and appointing captains and crews he would, during the weeks before he was ready to sail, not only plan the whole venture in detail but add a theoretical, philosophical gloss. Not only would he concern himself with getting his cargo of convicts to New South Wales, but consider how to work them when they got there – how to construct a 'colony of disgracefuls' which must, in his view, become – though perhaps over many years - a colony of 'respectables'.

His destination was to be Botany Bay (though his powers certainly included the authority to alter that destination should some other area seem more promising). He was also to colonise Norfolk Island, 1,676 kilometres northeast of Sydney, the occupation of which, though it was only about eight kilometres long and three wide, was believed to be an ambition of the French. He was to have nothing to do with any French forces which might show themselves – and indeed, nothing to do with any foreign powers. On landing, he was immediately to distribute tools to the convicts and set them to work the land with the purpose of making the new colony self-sufficient in food as quickly as possible. The settlement was to be a Christian community, and religious observance should be enforced – while at the same time, on the voyage out, an eye should be kept open at any ports which were visited for any women who might care to join the expedition. As his commission put it, 'whereas, as from the great disproportion of female convicts to those of the males who are put under your superintendence, it appears advisable that a further number of the latter should be introduced into the new intended settlement, you are, whenever the *Sirius* or the tender shall touch at any of the islands in those seas, to instruct their commanders to take on board any of the women who may be disposed to accompany them to the said settlement. You will, however, take especial care that the officers who may happen to be employed upon this service do not, upon any account, exercise any compulsive measures, or make use of fallacious pretences, for bringing away any of the said women from the places of their present residence.'[24]

If this sounds like well-meaning government pimping, it is a reasonable description. It was realised that with a proportion of 100 convict women to 347 men there was bound to be sexual jealousy and violence and it was usual under such circumstances to attempt to remedy the situation by gathering extra women when this was possible. As it turned out, this proved impossible where the New South Wales settlement was concerned, with the inevitable result that there was a considerable tally of sexual assaults of one sort or another during the first years of the colony. As a realist, Phillip must have suspected that the problem would arise, and he dealt with it severely – to do otherwise would have been to tolerate sexual anarchy.

His instructions had been set down with considerable forethought and a degree of sympathetic consideration (though certainly not divorced from practical considerations). It was ordered, for instance, that every male convict who had served his time and wished to remain in the colony should be granted 20 acres of land – 30 if he were married, and another 10 for every child – and there should be no rental or other charge on him for 10 years. He should also initially be supplied with food for himself and his family, tools and home utensils and a reasonable number of cattle, sheep and pigs, together with seed for planting. Every encouragement in fact should be given to any free person, including members of the armed forces, who decided that they wanted to settle in the new colony.

All this seems to have the mark of Phillip's humanity rather than the strictly functional attitude of the authorities. The policy laid down for the colony's attitude to the Indigenous people of the country, too, was surprisingly positive. The Governor was instructed to:

> open an intercourse with the Natives, & to conciliate their Affections, enjoining all our Subjects to live in amity and kindness with them. And if any of our Subjects shall wantonly destroy them or give them any unnecessary interruption in the exercise of their several Occupations it is our will and pleasure that you do cause such offenders to be brought to punishment according to the degree of the offence. You will endeavour to procure an account of the numbers inhabiting the neighbourhood of the intended settlement, and report your opinion to one of our Secretaries of State in what manner our intercourse with these people may be turned to the advantage of this colony.[25]

This seems altogether a more constructive attitude than might have been expected of a somewhat splenetic monarch and a government not overly sympathetic to foreigners of any description. But of course His Majesty was not personally concerned with the instructions, and there is every reason to suppose that Phillip himself had some input into them, through his friends at the Home Office and Admiralty.

He will not, however, have been responsible for the continual emphasis on economy and possible profit which runs in a seam through his instructions – the emphasis on speed, for instance, which would ensure that once the convicts had been set ashore the ships could go on to Canton in time to pick up cargoes of tea before the end of the season. He was to watch carefully the quantity of stores set on board, particularly relating to the food and clothing of the convicts, and strict accounting was necessary. Once settled in New South Wales he should keep a keen eye out for the possibility of barter with the neighbouring natives[26], and he was encouraged to focus his attention, as far as the profitability of the colony was concerned, on the production of hemp, which could be used to make clothing and would also be very useful when exported to Britain. As to food, no problem was likely to arise, for 'the settlement will be amply supplied with vegetable productions, and most likely with fish' so apart from the sick and convalescent, no-one would need fresh provisions from England. Phillip would have cause to recall that paragraph with a hollow laugh, in 18 months' time.

The thoroughness of Phillip's own preparation for the task which lay ahead is reflected in a series of notes which he made during the period between his appointment and setting sail. These make up a remarkable document which in itself is an index of how fortunate the new colony was in its first Governor. Some notes record what are merely ambitions which, as he must have known when he wrote them, were unlikely to be achieved: he would for instance have seen that ships were sent ahead of the main expedition to prepare the ground for the arrival of the main force – to plant crops to sustain the colony from the first instant, to built huts to protect the free men when they arrived and prepare the allotments where the convicts would work. This was never going to happen; it would have seemed far too expensive.

Then he considered the long voyage itself, and the problems it would bring. 'During the passage,' he wrote:

when light airs or calms permit it, I shall visit the transports to see that they are kept clean and receive

the allowance ordered by Government; and at these
times shall endeavour to make [the convicts] sensible of
their situation, and that their happiness or misery is in
their own hands, – that those who behave well will be
rewarded by being allow'd to work occasionally on the
small lotts of land set apart for them, which they will
be put in possession of at the expiration of the time for
which they are transported.[27]

He was eager that at the beginning of the voyage the convicts
should be as free from disease as possible – obviously in the
crowded conditions on the transports contagion would be
almost impossible to control. So care must be taken that
convicts who left prison or prison hulks to join the transports
should be free of disease.

He gave considerable thought to the problem that a
small proportion of the convicts would be female – of those
who sailed from England, 193 were women, 579 men. The
women, he thought:

in general should possess neither virtue nor honesty.
But there may be some for thefts who still retain some
degree of virtue, and these should be permitted to keep
together, and strict orders to masters of the transport
should be given that they are not abused and insulted by
ship's company, which is said to have been the case too
often when they were sent to America.[28]

He was by no means mealy-mouthed when it came to considering
the practical problem of men and women being confined in
close quarters on the same ship, often within arm's length of
each other and separated only by improvised and sometimes
insecure bulkheads. It was a problem which merited 'great

consideration'. For the relief of tensions, he thought that it might 'be best if the most abandoned are permitted to receive the visits of the convicts in the limits allotted them at certain hours and under certain restrictions.' Those women condemned for non-sexual crimes such as stealing a few pounds of cheese, a few shillings-worth of butter or a hen should if possible be kept separate from their more licentious sisters – arrived at the colony they might after a time even marry, in which case the couple should be allowed extra time during which to work on their own small plot of land. Fruit trees and cuttings should be carried out with the expedition and fresh supplies taken on at the Cape of Good Hope – including livestock.

Not content with giving his attention to the preparations for the voyage and conditions on the transports, Phillip spent many hours considering the nature of the society he wished to create. The suggestion that no thought was given to the Indigenous people from whom the land was to be taken is mistaken; on the contrary, Phillip give the matter careful thought. Avoiding any trouble between the incomers and the natives was, he thought, 'a great point'.

> A few of [them] I shall endeavour to persuade to settle near us, and who I mean to furnish with everything that can tend to civilise them, and to give them a high opinion of the new guests, [sic], for which purpose it will be necessary to prevent the transports' crews from having any intercourse with the natives, if possible. The convicts must have none, for if they have, the arms of the natives will be very formidable in their hands, the women abused, and the natives disgusted.[29]

Phillip took an entirely realistic view of the pent-up sexuality of the convict men, and saw no problem in allowing them to

exercise it on 'the most abandoned' of the native women, though
he does not comment on how these were to be identified. The
natives might after a while allow their women to marry convict
men, and he would have no objection but would 'think it
necessary to punish with severity the man who used the women
ill.' Any man who took the life of a native should be put on trial
just as if he had killed a marine.

New South Wales was beginning to sound like an
egalitarian society, but Phillip was no starry-eyed idealist – he
believed for instance that various degrees of segregation would
be necessary in the new society. As on the voyage out, the
worst among the convicts should be kept from those who
seemed most likely to reform. The marines should not mix
with the convicts – ideally, a stream or river should separate
them – and certainly the convicts should be segregated from
any free settlers who came to the colony later:

> As I would not wish convicts to lay the foundations
> of an empire, I think they should ever remain separate
> from the garrison and other settlers that may come from
> Europe and not be allowed to mix with them, even after
> the 7 or 14 years for which they are transported may be
> expired. The laws of this country will, of course, be
> introduced in South Wales [sic], and there is one I wish
> to take place from the moment his Majesty's forces take
> possession of the country: that there can be no slavery
> in a free land, and consequently no slaves.'[30]

Again, an almost liberal note is struck, but never for a moment
did Phillip lose sight of the fact that he would have the power
of life or death over the colony – not only of the convicts, but
of the sailors and marines. The laws of Great Britain should
be introduced from the first moment of stepping on shore,

although at first they would have to be subject to military government. He believed that capital punishment would hardly ever be necessary – his own view was that the threat of death never prevented any man from 'a bad action.' His notes took a slightly wild turn here, however:

> There are two crimes that would merit death – murder and sodomy. For either of these crimes I would wish to confine the criminal till an opportunity offered of delivering him as a prisoner to the natives of New Zealand, and let them eat him. The dread of this will operate much stronger than the fear of death.[31]

This threat, uncharacteristic of everything we know about Phillip, was never carried out – later indeed he put forward a more typical notion, that an offender should be stranded on a small island and left to live or die, according to his own ingenuity and determination.

Apart from these considerations, much of Phillip's time over the seven months between his commission and the sailing was spent in communicating with the Home Office, the Treasury and the Admiralty about the practical preparation of the fleet. The authorities from the first viewed the operation as a simple one: contractors would be engaged to handle the business of providing transports, getting the convicts together and readying them for the voyage, the navy would provide armed escorts and a suitable flagship for Phillip, and all that would then be necessary would be for the provisions to be loaded and marines and convicts to embark. The transports should be ready by mid-September, and there should be no difficulty in sailing by the beginning of October.

Unsurprisingly, perhaps, this was not the case. First, there was the matter of Phillip's flagship. The Admiralty's eye had fallen on the *Berwick*. She had been a victualler built for the East India Company, but before she had been launched had caught fire and burned down to the waterline. The Government had bought what remained of her extremely cheaply, had fitted her up with bits and pieces of other ships left lying about in the dockyard, and she had staggered off on two journeys to the West Indies and America. She was seaworthy – just about – and in the Admiralty's view was thus suitable to make a voyage to the furthermost parts of the Earth. She was renamed *Sirius*; at 540 tons she could carry 160 men and 20 guns were loaded onto her so she could be classified as a warship. The fleet needed an armed tender, and Phillip got a very small craft indeed, the 170 ton *Supply*, which had been a navy transport; this had eight guns and a crew of 50 men, could carry only a small quantity of provisions and was clumsy under sail.

Five transports were originally provided – the 452 ton *Alexander*, commanded by Duncan Sinclair, *Scarborough* (418 tons, John Marshall), *Friendship* (278 tons, James Meredith), *Lady Penrhyn* (338 tons, William C. Sever) and *Charlotte* (345 tons, Thomas Gilbert). The latter two were almost as clumsy as the *Supply*. They were joined later by *The Prince of Wales*, another transport of 333 tons, commanded by John Mason and by the three store-ships, the *Borrowdale* (R. Hobson, 272 tons), *Fishbourne* (Francis Walton, 278 tons) and *Golden Grove* (L. Sharp, 331 tons). By way of comparison, the modern Sydney inner harbour vessel, the *Lady Northcott*, is of 366 tons

Something that upset Phillip considerably was the fact that he was allowed to have nothing to do with the practical arrangements for the voyage. A company called Turnbull, Macaulay and Gregory had tendered £29 8s (about £1825 today) for accommodating and feeding each convict, and guaranteed to feed the troops for 7½d a day. The Government thought this exorbitant, and declined the tender. Instead, they hired the transports for 10 shillings a ton per month, until they either returned empty to England or left New South Wales for Canton. This complicated matters, because it would be the masters of the transports who were contracted to carry the convicts; they would be formally handed over together with the necessary paperwork, and Phillip would not have responsibility for what happened to them until he had taken take over the contract from the masters.

The victualling was more satisfactorily and simply arranged. Zachariah Clark, a representative of the contractor (one William Richards Jr), actually sailed with the fleet and was responsible for the matter while at sea; when the vessels touched port, supplies became a matter for the officials of the settlement. The marine officers were responsible for the health of the convicts and for discipline, and had the right to inspect their food.

The fact that all this had been set up without any input from Phillip did not mean that he simply sat back and let events take their course. Indeed, he interfered much too much for the taste of the Government. He asked for extra six-pounder guns and for small shot, enquired why no scythes were among the implements provided and wanted the patterns of the convicts' handcuffs modified and the transports' hatchways strengthened. He required 200lb of preserved soup for use after landing, asked for a quantity of wine to be added to the medical supplies, wanted someone to stop the contractors substituting rice for flour and demanded a supply of antiscorbutics to minimise scurvy – which 'must make a great ravage amongst people naturally Indolent, & not cleanly.' Fresh air would help in that respect, but he had doubts about allowing the convicts on deck. He put forward the notion that he might himself transfer to whichever proved the fastest of the ships and press on ahead of the fleet, perhaps arriving as much as two months before the rest and thus able to construct some huts for any who might be sick, and plant vegetables which would provide them with fresh greens.

His arriving ahead of the main expedition would have other advantages – he could choose the best site for the settlement, build huts for the women and others in which supplies could be kept secure, and stockades for the cattle and other beasts. Good land could be partitioned out into equal areas for distribution and, using lists which the Government would provide showing the nature of the crimes of the convicts but also their ages and trades, it would be possible to plan in advance how the settlement could be brought to an efficient start, making it possible to plan the order in which they would be brought on shore, and how they should be accommodated. It was important to know the nature of their offences: 'The sooner the crimes and behaviour of these people are known the better, as they maybe divided, and the greatest villains particularly guarded against.'[32] He never received this information, and indeed many of his proposals fell to the ground because of government lethargy – or it may be that his continual requests caused the Navy Board such irritation that in the end their patience gave out and they simply began to ignore him. Captain George Teer indeed noted that 'Capt Phillip has from time to time so increased the Orders for Stores, implements for Botany bay, and Increased the Number of Marines from seventy four up to One Hundred & Sixty . . . [that] they will occupy upwards of Three Hund. Tons space, each day, & week, continuing to add more, that I was Obliged to put a stop to his wishes still to add.'[33]

When the convicts began to be loaded onto the transports and he was actually able in January 1787 to inspect the conditions under which they would sail, Phillip was appalled. There was already overcrowding, and many convicts had been set on board with various illnesses, to contaminate the healthy – some so weak as to be virtually unable to move. Many of them were almost completely naked, and no clothing was being provided for them: at Plymouth he ordered clothing to be provided for them from the stores on board the *Sirius*, presuming that the Navy Board would replace it (they did not). He again emphasised that it was absolutely necessary that convicts sent onto the transports should be washed and properly clothed before they left prison.

In March, he wrote to Nepean:

These complaints, my dear sir, do not come unexpected, nor were they unavoidable. I foresaw them from the beginning, and repeatedly pointed them out, when they might have been so easily prevented, at a very small expense, and with little trouble to those who have had the conducting of this business. At present the evils complained of may be redressed, and the intentions of the Government by this expedition answered. But if now neglected, it may be too late hereafter, and we may expect to see the seamen belonging to the transports run from the ships to avoid a fatal distemper, and may be refused entry into a foreign port.

The situation in which the magistrates sent the women on board the *Lady Penrhyn* stamps them with infamy – tho' almost naked, and so very filthy, that nothing but cloathing them could have prevented them from perishing, and which could not be done in time to prevent a fever which is still on board that ship, and where there are many venereal complaints, that must spread in spite of every precaution I may take hereafter, and will be fatal to themselves . . .[34]

There is a note of desperation here, and well it might be so; in March 1787 typhus broke out on the *Alexander* off Portsmouth.

Eleven prisoners died, followed by five more before the fleet sailed. This was unsurprising: the overcrowding of the transports would have appalled a modern reader. Phillip himself was disgusted. He told Nepean that the convicts really should be cleared off the *Alexander*:

> while the ship is cleaned and smoaked, and tho' I have so often solicited that essence of malt or some anti-scorbutic may be allowed, I cannot help once more repeating the necessity of it; and putting the convicts out of the question, which humanity forbids, the sending of the marines that are on board the transports such a voyage as they are going, in a worse state than ever troops were sent out of the Kingdom . . . cannot, I am sure, be the intention of his Majesty's Ministers, yet it is absolutely the case, and I have repeatedly stated this fact. The necessity of making one of the transports an hospital ship is obvious, and, I think cannot be deferred.[35]

The Government, needless to say, had no difficulty in deferring that decision, and indeed continuing to defer its response no almost all of Phillip's requests. The fleet had to convey almost one and a half thousand people, including the officers and marines, the seamen and some wives and children and the convicts, in conditions with which Phillip was from the beginning at odds. It was calculated for instance that each person — marines and seamen as well as convicts — would relate to less than three tons of ship; on a modern cruise liner, the proportion would be about 250 tons per person.[36] Phillip knew, and told the Home Office, that it would be 'very difficult to prevent the most fatal sickness among men so closely confined; on board that ship which is to receive 210 convicts there is not a space left sufficiently large for forty men to be in motion at the same time.'

The fitting out of the transports was unusual enough for Gidley King to devote considerable space to it in his journal:

The transports are fitted up for the convicts the same as for carrying troops except the security, which consists in very strong and thick bulkheads, filled with nails and run across from side to side 'tween desks abaft to the mainmast, with loopholes to fire between decks in case of irregularities. The hatches are well secured down by cross-bars, bolts, and locks, and are likewise rail'd round from deck to deck with oak stanchions. There is also a barricade of planks about 3 feet high, armed with pointed prongs of iron, on the upper deck abaft the mainmast, to present any connection between the marines and ship's company with the convicts. Centinels are placed at the different hatchways, and a guard always under arms on the quarterdeck of each transport in order to prevent any improper behaviour of the convicts, as well as to guard against any surprise.[37]

Four convicts would share a sleeping space about the size of a king-sized modern bed, and with only 1.14 meters head-room. There was no light except what sneaked in when a hatch was opened, and that was rarely enough. Candles and lanterns were not allowed for fear of fire. These nauseous spaces had been occupied on the *Scarborough* and *Lady Penrhyn* since January, the prisoners badly fed (the contractor, as a matter of course, substituted rice for flour, and in small quantities).

Through February and March more and more prisoners arrived at Portsmouth and Plymouth – the women half-naked in the winter cold. John White, the expedition's surgeon-general, arrived at Plymouth on 5 March to supervise the moving of prisoners from the hulk *Dunkirk*, the men in chains, to the

*Charlotte* and *Friendship*. He then sailed with them to Spithead, and anchored with the other transports.

White went on board all the transports and was surprised to find that on the whole the convicts were in reasonable health, though there were several staying all day and night huddled in the same space, covered with what material they could find to stave off the effects of the bitter cold, against which they had very little clothing to protect them. Others were weak as a result of their long imprisonment in the dark and cold and with only salty beef to sustain them; their spirits, White remarked, seemed 'rather low'. He wrote immediately to the Secretary of State:

> to urge the necessity of having fresh provisions served to the whole of the convicts while in port, as well as a little wine for those who were ill. Fresh provisions I dwelt most on, as being not only needful for the recovery of the sick, but otherwise essential, in order to prevent any of them commencing so long and tedious a voyage as they had before them with a scorbutic taint; a consequence that would most likely attend their living upon salt food; and which, added to their needful confinement and great numbers, would, in all probability, prove fatal to them, and thereby defeat the intention of Government.[38]

He had small victories – some fresh beef and vegetables arrived at the last moment – and when the marines complained that there would be no liquor in New South Wales (which the men considered 'indispensable for the preservation of our lives, which change of climate and the extreme fatigue we shall be necessarily exposed to may probably endanger', and 'without which we cannot expected to survive the hardships') he succeeded in persuading the authorities to supply three-year's worth of rum and wine. He managed to arrange for a small amount of tobacco, too.

Otherwise little was done, and finally the fleet sailed without any considerable quantity of extra food being supplied, or extra clothing being replaced, without any papers relating to the convicts or their convictions – even without any ammunition for the marines (that had to be kept a close-guarded secret during the voyage, for fear of encouraging the possibility of mutiny by the convicts). Government spin, however, let it be known that it had gone out of its way to 'render everything as permanently comfortable to the unhappy convicts as the nature of the case will admit . . . both as to provisions and every necessity that they may stand in need of . . . even trifles have been thought of. One instance as a proof, they now have comfortable beds.'[39] Phillip in the end had to make do with the conditions under which he found himself serving, but it is clear he was far from satisfied: apart from present troubles, he was concerned about his posterity – whether 'it may be said hereafter the officer who took charge of the expedition should have known that it was more than probable he lost half the garrison and convicts, crowded and victualled in such a manner for so long a voyage.' That it was not as bad as this was due largely to his personal efforts.

# FIVE

Apart from the provisioning of the fleet, attention was turned to the appointment of various officers – something on which Phillip could have an influence.

His second-in-command was to be Captain John Hunter, who in due time was to be the second Governor of New South Wales. Born in Scotland in 1737, he was the son of a captain in the Mercantile Marine, and there is a legend (which may be just that) that he went to sea with his father as a boy. The *Naval Chronicle* relates that it was during one of these voyages that the ship he was in was wrecked on the Norwegian coast:

> near a small fishing town, the inhabitants of which flocked to the scene of distress; amongst them was a group of women, who, when our young sailor was landed from the wreck, being then a small delicate boy, took him up in their arms and carried him home to the house of an honest fisherman, where he was taken great care of, and put to bed between two of the good man's daughters, whose care and caresses he long remembered with gratitude.[40]

Whether or not that pleasant story is true, it is certain that Hunter was educated first at Lynn and then at Edinburgh, where he briefly attended the University and studied and was fond of the classics. He left university for the Royal Navy, which he entered as a captain's servant – the rating given a boy who joined the service at about the age of twelve, before he became a midshipman. He turned into an intelligent and studious young officer, devising his own version of a quadrant because he could not afford to buy a proper one, and using it to study astronomy. But he lacked advancement, and remained a midshipman for many years, though he passed the examination for a lieutenant when he was 23. He was 49 when he was commissioned second-in-command of the *Sirius*, and Acting Governor in the cast of Phillip's illness or incapacity.

Another of Phillip's officers was to become Governor after him – a second lieutenant on the *Sirius*, Philip Gidley King. King was a Cornishman, born in Launceston, the son of a draper – a fact which prompted some of the more snobbish of his naval colleagues to consider him 'not quite a gentleman'. He joined the navy as captain's servant when he was twelve, spent some years in the East Indies, and was commissioned lieutenant in 1775 (one of his examiners exclaiming that he was 'one of the most Promising young men I have ever met'). He first encountered Phillip in the *Ariadne*, and sailed to India with him in the *Europe*. He was one of Phillip's first choices as an officer to accompany him to New South Wales.

Three important appointments were also made relatively soon after the Governor was commissioned: Robert Ross, a major in the marines, was commissioned Lieutenant-Governor, Captain David Collins was deputy judge-advocate, Richard Johnson chaplain and John White surgeon-general.

Ross was a Scot, born in about 1740, a conscientious officer who had joined the marines at 16 and served in North America at the siege of Louisburg and the capture of Quebec. Major by 1783, he had also seen action in the West Indies and the Mediterranean, and with a large family to support was eager for promotion. He did not see his new appointment as likely to offer it, however, and was consequently irritated and discontented from the first, particularly when he learned of Hunter's appointment as Deputy Governor, which seemed to weaken his own position (and indeed, the situation was a curious one). He failed to get on with Phillip from the moment they met, and was cordially disliked by many other officers – one had an 'inexpressible hatred' for him, another found him 'without exception the most disagreeable commanding officer I ever knew'.

Captain Collins, on the other hand, was generally liked. The son of a marine officer and educated at grammar school, he had entered the service at 14 and had also seen service in the American war. He volunteered to go to New South Wales with the fleet – but his appointment as deputy judge-advocate must surely have been something of a surprise to him, for he had no legal training whatsoever. A thoroughly sound, loyal man with a strong sense of duty, he was able to consider problems dispassionately and apply common-sense solutions.

It is difficult to arouse much enthusiasm for of the Moravian Methodist Reverend Richard Johnson. He was a humourless, dedicated evangelist, recommended to his post as chaplain by some of his friends in the London Eclectic Society, a group of evangelical clergy and laymen interested in mission and prison reform. Entirely unenthusiastic about the idea, he reluctantly reconciled himself to a martyr's crowd in a far-off land among moral degenerates, and put together a collection of theological munitions in the shape of no less than 4,000 books to accompany him to the antipodes – including 100 Bibles, 100 Books of Common Prayer, 100 copies of Osterwald's *Necessity for reading the Scriptures*, a dozen of Wilson's *Instructions for the Indians*, 100 of *Exhortations to Chastity* and half a dozen copies of *The Great Importance of a religious Life*.

Despite the *Exhortations*, Johnson always seemed less concerned for the morals of his convict flock than for their familiarity with scripture. He appeared to take the view that the correction of sin was less important than a thorough understanding of the Articles of Faith – he was to take great offence when Phillip suggested that a word or two on sexual moderation might be included in his sermons. His wife, who seems to have been the very model of an acid-faced puritan, accompanied him to New South Wales, where their great preoccupation became the growing of vegetables which could be sold to the needy at exorbitant prices.

John White, appointed surgeon-general to the project, went into the navy when he was about 22 as a third surgeon's mate, promoted to surgeon two years later in 1780. He sailed on the Charlotte, and was considered a conscientious and humane man, whose care of the convicts was attentive and as caring as was possible in the circumstances.

The senior officer for whom anyone reading the accounts of the voyage and the settlement must have most sympathy and fondness was Watkin Tench, who was in his late twenties when he sailed on the *Charlotte* as one of the two captain-lieutenants of the marine detachment. Born in Chester, he was the son of a dancing master who kept a boarding school. This might have led to a snobbish reaction among his fellow-officers, except that his friendly personality defeated any such idea – and in any case his father was a highly respected man, a freeman of Chester with many friends, some of them influential. Watkin joined the Marine Corps as a second lieutenant in 1776 when he was about 18, and during the War of American Independence served in ships occupied off the American coast, ending as first lieutenant in the *Maryland*. The ship was driven ashore during a storm, and Tench was captured and spent three months as a prisoner of war. Released, he was promoted captain-lieutenant in 1782, but went on half-pay in 1786 and almost immediately volunteered to join Phillip's fleet for New South Wales. He was a deservedly popular man, cheerful and positive, observant and humane. He wrote by far the best accounts of the voyage and the first years of the settlement at Botany Bay, and any book on the subject is bound to quote him at large.

Who else should we note, among Phillip's companions?

Lieutenant William Dawes was an amateur astronomer – indeed something more than an amateur, perhaps, for he had been recommended for inclusion in the expedition by the Astronomer Royal, Dr Nevil Maskelyne. He took with him a number of instruments provided by the Board of Longitude, and was particularly entrusted with instructions to observe a comet which was expected to appear during the voyage. He, like Tench, was intelligent and widely popular, though in the end he was to quarrel with Phillip and leave the colony, to devote many of his later years to the cause of the emancipation of slaves. His colleague, Lieutenant Ralph Clark, was of less use to the colony and considerably less sympathetic to the reader. Born in Edinburgh, the son of a 'gentleman's servant', he had become a second lieutenant in the marines in 1779, and in 1784 married a Devonshire girl, Betsy Alicia. He sailed on the *Friendship*, and his furious anger at the loose behaviour of the male and female convicts on board was committed to his intimate personal diary, much of which is taken up by lugubrious if understandable moanings about being parted from his young wife – despite which he was quick to take an Aboriginal mistress in New South Wales, who bore him a child.

These were some of the men who accompanied the First Fleet, not knowing how momentous a voyage it would be in the history of the country to which they were bound. Indeed, for both officers and men – apart from Phillip himself, and perhaps Gidley King, in whom he may have confided – it probably seemed no more than a slightly unusual but routine voyage, unlikely to bring any great financial reward or kudos, and to be just as uncomfortable as any other long passage. As for life in New South Wales, the year or so during which they must stay would no doubt be interesting but scarcely momentous.

And what of the cargo the fleet was to carry? What of the convicts?

They were as varied in character as those who had charge of them – varied too in occupation and in the crimes they had committed, which included everything from highway robbery to breaking and entering, grand larceny to selling stolen property, forgery to minor theft. Phillip and his officers were in no doubt about the necessity for strict surveillance during the voyage. As Watkin Tench wrote:

> an opportunity was taken, immediately on their being embarked, to convince them, in the most pointed terms, that any attempt on their side, either to contest the command, or to force their escape, should be punished with instant death; orders to this effect were given to the centinels in their presence; happily, however, for all parties, there occurred not any instance in which there was occasion to have recourse to so desperate a measure; the behavior of the convicts being in general humble, submissive, and regular: indeed I should feel myself wanting in justice to those unfortunate men, were I not to bear this public testimony of the sobriety and decency of their conduct.[41]

Tench was always rather more on the side of the convicts than not (inasmuch as that was possible); their 'sobriety and decency', he later had to admit, was not constant.

Most of them were in their twenties, though one was nine years old (little John Hudson, a chimney sweep, who had stolen some clothes and a pocket pistol and was 'snatched

from destruction' by a considerate magistrate). The oldest was
Dorothy Handland, 82, sent away for perjury. There were 119
men aged between 16 and 35, and 108 women in the same
age-group – but if that suggests a large number of strong and
active immigrants it would be a mistake, for the great number
were weak and under-nourished if not positively sick after,
sometimes, years in prison followed by months in prison hulks.
Moreover, many of them had no trade or profession – among
the total of 736, there were six carpenters, five weavers, two
brick-makers, two bricklayers, two butchers, only one baker, a
few who had been servants and one or two of slightly arcane
professions such as ivory-turners, jewellers or silk-dyers. Most
of them perhaps were an unregenerate lot; many would be
hanged, some – including Dorothy Handland – would later
commit suicide. Among them, we should remember, were the
true founders of the future state.

Officers, crews and marines now began to ready themselves
for the voyage – putting their affairs in order, paying their
debts (or not), preparing to say a long farewell to their wives,
mistresses and parents. Lieutenant Clark was distraught at the
thought of leaving his Betsy and their two year old son. He
wrote to Phillip on 3 April asking 'if ther is any impropriety
for me to take my family out with me.' Phillip did his best,
saw the Secretary of State and put Clark's case, but the answer
was no. Clark was unhappy: 'I think it a great hardship in
being debard So Small a favour when the Clergyman and every
Private Man has that indulgence granted them.' Phillip again
replied kindly – he would certainly have made no objection,
but orders were orders. Clark wrote yet again, asking for 10
days' leave 'to goe to Plymouth to Settle my Private affairs
Occasioned by the Secretary of State not permitting me to take
my family out.' Philip was unable to allow leave, either – it must
have been obvious to him by now that Clark was simply, like so

many others, unable to tear himself away from his family. The exchange is an example of the care he gave even to the smallest request made to him.[42]

Phillip – himself convinced that he would be away from England for at least three and possibly five years – continued to concern himself with the practical readiness of the fleet, which in many ways was not ready at all. The course he was to take had been laid down in January: it was anticipated that three weeks' sailing would bring the fleet to Tenerife and seven weeks more to the Cape of Good Hope, though the possibility of touching land at Rio de Janeiro for supplies was not excluded. Two months more at sea would bring them to Botany Bay. Phillip did not query this, although the passage from the Cape to New South Wales would take place in winter, with the possibility of storms and even ice. Other minor but important matters preoccupied him, particularly regarding provisions –would he be permitted to buy fresh food in any ports he touched, especially meat, and for the whole party, including the convicts? Might he buy wine, valuable in case of outbreaks of sickness? If there *were* sickness on a large scale, might he convert one of the transports into a hospital ship?

In May he travelled down from his lodgings in Suffolk Street, Haymarket, to Portsmouth, his private servant, Henry Edward Dodd, brought up with him from his New Forest farm, carefully carrying with him the *Sirius's* sextant and chronometer which Phillip had carefully checked at Portsmouth Naval Academy to be sure of its accuracy. It was then carried on board the *Sirius*, to be wound every day in the presence of Phillip, Hunter and Dawes. It was of such importance to the navigation of the vessel, and thus of the fleet, that the lieutenant on duty was to ensure that the watch should not be changed until the relieving officer was sure that the chronometer had been properly attended to: Lieutenant William Bradley noted that 'the Centinal at the Cabin door was also ordered to plant himself inside the Cabin and not to go out to be relieved until he was told or saw that the Timekeeper was wound up by one of the officers.[43]

At Portsmouth he found his secretary waiting – Andrew Miller, who, although he is rarely mentioned in books about the First Fleet and the establishment of Sydney, became a close and trusted associate of the Governor and almost a friend. Highly efficient, he was known as Secretary to the Colony, counter-signing Phillip's commissions, and was a loss when ill-health forced him to resign and return to England early in 1790, to be succeeded by Judge-Advocate Collins. He reported to Phillip that there was chaos among the seamen, who had gone on strike – they were not formally under naval command, since they were employed by the firm which had chartered the transports. Phillip had paid the crews of the *Sirius* and *Supply* two months' pay in advance, but the crews of the transports had received no pay for seven months and had no money with which to buy the clothes and other things they would need on a long voyage. They could of course buy these items from the owners' stores, at highly inflated prices, but preferred to buy them privately in Portsmouth, where they would be much cheaper. Phillip managed to sort the matter out, but he could do nothing about the fact that the clothing ordered for the marines and the women convicts had not arrived. Nor was he able to do anything about the absence of the third mate of the *Charlotte*, who had deserted, or the shortage of bread and water on the transports. He must set sail.

At last, at daybreak on 13 May, the *Sirius* led the fleet west of the Isle of Wight, past the Needles and into the Channel. Tench summarised the force:

In addition to our little armament, the *Hyena* frigate was ordered to accompany us a certain distance to the westward, by which means our number was increased to twelve sail: His Majesty's ships *Sirius, Hyena,* and *Supply,* three Victuallers with two years stores and provisions on board for the Settlement, and six Transports, with troops and convicts. In the transports were embarked four captains, twelve subalterns, twenty-four serjeants and corporals, eight drummers, and one hundred and sixty private marines, making the whole of the military force, including the Major Commandant and Staff on board the *Sirius,* to consist of two hundred and twelve persons, of whom two hundred and ten were volunteers.[44]

Once again, the optimistic Tench thought the convicts showed signs of excellent behaviour – they seemed on the whole reasonably contented:

A very few excepted, their countenances indicated a high degree of satisfaction, though in some, the pang of being severed, perhaps for ever, from their native land, could not be wholly suppressed; in general, marks of distress were more perceptible among the men than the women; for I recollect to have seen but one of those affected on the occasion, 'Some natural tears she dropp'd, but wip'd them soon.' After this the accent of sorrow was no longer heard; more genial skies and change of scene banished repining and discontent, and introduced in their stead cheerfulness and acquiescence in a lot, now not to be altered.[45]

Their cheerfulness may have taken a turn sooner rather than later, for the waves of the notoriously wayward Channel lifted to the spring breeze, and at times were so rough that in his cabin – the only private place in the ship, though miniscule –

Phillip found it difficult to sit and write his journal, and most of the convicts, in the close dark below decks, were sea-sick, giving them an early taste of the nauseating conditions to which they were to be subject for the next months. Even some of the officers suffered, though they knew that seasickness was simply something they had to put up with until it passed. The fleet pressed on down-channel. As they turned out into the Atlantic, Lieutenant Clark scribbled unevenly in his diary: 'Abreast of Falmouth and a great number of fishing Boats in Sight – I wish that one of them would come in board of use that I might send a letter on shore by her to my Betsey but I find it is in Vain to Botany Bay I must goe.'[46]

# SIX

Despite a slightly rough outset, the weather was eventually extremely kind to what was to become known in Australia's history as 'the First Fleet'. A good wind took the flotilla forward, and on 20 May the *Hyena*, an armed frigate which had accompanied them for the first 500 kilometres in case of problems with the convicts, was able to bid them farewell and return to Portsmouth.

Phillip now felt able to signal to the transports to unchain those prisoners who were in fetters. They were to be encouraged to strip off their clothes on deck during the day, when they could wash themselves, and again when they turned in at night, for cleanliness' sake. Watkin Tench, on the *Charlotte*, was characteristically pleased: 'I had great pleasure in being able to extend this humane order to the whole of those under my charge, without a single exception.'[47] Other officers on other ships were less sanguine. Lieutenant Bradley noted that 'this lenient step towards making those unhappy wretches comfortable was very ill received in the *Scarborough*', while Captain-Lieutenant James Meredith pointed out to Phillip that more than half of the convicts he was carrying on the *Friendship* had been convicted of a successful mutiny and the seizure of a transport ship some years previously. Phillip instructed him to release the men when he thought it safe, but to clap them once more in irons 'on the smallest fault' (as Lieutenant Clark put it).

On 20 May it seemed possible that real trouble was in the offing. A convict on the *Scarborough* told the officer of the watch that he had overheard some others plotting to seize the ship. Whether this was a genuine plot or the informant was settling old scores remains a question, but Phillip took the matter seriously, as he must, and protesting their innocence the men fingered were flogged and sent in irons to the *Prince of Wales*, after which, as Phillip later reported, they were 'quiet and contented, tho' there are among them some compleat villains.' The Reverend Johnson was not surprised. He preached to the convicts on the terrible evil of profane language but, not convinced that they had taken heed of his words he knelt in his cabin and prayed that God might convince them of the wickedness of their conduct, and was pleased to note that for two or three days at least they watched their language when within his hearing. He was similarly unconvinced of the holiness of the captain of the *Golden Grove*, who was taciturn and ill-natured; the Commander himself did not seem specially religious in his conduct, while his outright kindliness to the convicts under his control seemed likely only to encourage their bad behaviour. Johnson was pleased to note that some attempts at discipline were made – on 28 May, for instance, John Bennet was given 37 lashes for breaking out of his irons.

Throughout the whole journey Phillip was as relaxed about disciplining both the convicts and the marines and seamen as a Commander could afford to be, but extremely firm when firmness was required. He was strongly opposed to unjustified violence. When it was reported to him that one of the fleet's officers had flogged some crewmen without real cause, Phillip called every officer on the ship in question to the captain's cabin and told them that if he heard in future of an officer who struck a man without cause, he would break him. Moreover, no officer in future was to carry a stick with which to strike anyone.

'Those men are all we have to depend upon', he told them, 'and if we abuse the men that we have to trust to, the convicts will rise and massacre us all. Those men are our support. We have a long and severe station to go through in settling this colony; at least we cannot expect to return in less than five years. This ship and her crew is to protect and support the country and if they are ill-treated by their own officers, what support can you expect of them? They will all be dead before the voyage is half out, and who is to bring us back again?'[48]

In fact, on the whole, it was agreed that the prisoners were behaving well, and the officers felt they could relax somewhat. The crew, too, gave little trouble – although Lieutenant Clark disapproved of them: they were continually complaining about their food rations – they only wanted more, he believed, 'to give it to the damned Whores the Convict Women of whom they are very fond Since they broke through the Bulk head and had connection with them. I never could have thought that there were So many abandoned wretches in England they are ten thousand time worse than the men Convicts, and I am afraid that we will have a great deal more trouble with them.'[49] When he was not engaged in reading sentimental love stories from the pages of the *Lady* magazine, a supply of which he had brought with him, he complained regularly in his diary of the licentiousness of the women on board. It is certainly true that modesty was not a common characteristic in the transports: lust got the better of both sexes early in the voyage.

The first death, and the first birth, took place early – on 28 May Ishmael Coleman, 'worn out by lowness of spirits and debility, brought on by long and close confinement, resigned his breath without a pang'; three days later, Isabella Lawson, transported for stealing, gave birth to a baby girl. (On the same day two kids were born to a goat brought on board by John Watt, the transport agent.) There were the usual shipboard accidents – a Corporal Baker of the marines was cleaning his musket one morning when it accidentally went off and the ball shattered the bones of his right ankle before passing through a cask of beef and killing two geese. Goose for supper, then, and happily Baker was able to walk again after three months off his feet.

So life went on. And the fleet sailed on – or in some cases lumbered on. The *Lady Penrhyn* was particularly slow, and lagged far astern of the others, though the *Charlotte* was also heavy (the *Hyena* had at one point been towing her). Phillip had some difficulty in keeping the fleet together, ordering sails to be shortened so that the *Lady Penrhyn* could catch up and at night making sure all the other vessels had a sight of the light the *Sirius* carried at her mainmast.

When the weather was sufficiently calm, there was a certain amount of to and fro between the flagship and the other vessels. On 25 May, for instance, Phillip sent the naval agent, Lieutenant John Shortland, over to the transports to make a list of the trades and occupations of the convicts. Shortland was an important assistant to Phillip, with whom he worked closely and well. A man of 48, he had been in the navy since he was 16, and as agent had looked after the contracts for the transport of the convicts and planned the lower-deck designs of the ships, deciding on the relative spaces allowed to convicts, marines and officers. Phillip freely acknowledged, later, that much of the credit for the successful voyage of the First Fleet had been due to Shortland's meticulous and detailed planning. The result of his survey of the convicts (see p.000, above) was not however particularly promising. Tench reports the fleet's progress: first the Desertas were sighted off the south-east coast of Madeira, then the Salvages (now the Ilhas Selvagens) half way between Madeira and the Canary islands – which a number of mariners were surprised to see, since they did not appear even on the most modern charts of the Atlantic. And on 3 June the fleet made Tenerife, and anchored at Santa Cruz.

In his orders, it had been suggested to Phillip that 'it may happen upon your passage to New South Wales that you may find it necessary and expedient to call with the ships and vessels under your convoy at the island of Tenerife, at the Rio de Janeiro, and also at the Cape of Good Hope, for supplies of water and other refreshments for the voyage'. He might take on wine (valuable for medical reasons), but not too much. He might also try to buy seed-grain – and 'take on board any number of black cattle, sheep, goats, or hogs which you can procure, and the ships of the convoy can contain, in order to propagate the breed of these animals for the general benefit of the intended settlement.'

Phillip took advantage of what fresh food was available on Tenerife, and during the week when the fleet lay at anchor there spent some of his government money on a pound of fresh beef a day for both marines and convicts, together with rice and what vegetables and fruit were available – fruit was not in season and vegetables were scarce. He also bought a considerable amount of wine.

Meanwhile, his officers were happy to stretch their legs ashore, apart from young Clark, who spent his time mooning and moaning about absence from his Betsey, reading the *Lady* magazine and doing his best not to get involved in a dispute between Major Ross and Captain Meredith – the latter court-martialled two sergeants for 'unsoldierly behaviour', while Ross came stumping on board in a rage and ordered their release (at the same time telling them they should be hanged). The disagreement was more or less amicably resolved, but was the beginning of a mutual dislike which was later to lead to endless trouble for Phillip.

On the fleet's arrival, the latter sent Lieutenant King ashore to give the Governor of the Canary Islands, Major-General Marquis Miguel de la Grue Talamanca Brancifore, an account of the fleet and the reasons for its presence off his island,

and to apologise for not saluting the fort 'on account of our being so much cumbered with casks in the gun deck'. The Governor, Sicilian by birth, was a courteous gentleman with fine aristocratic manners and a graceful air – as White put it, 'both his appearance and manners perfectly correspond with the idea universally entertained of the dignity of a grandee of Spain.' He came on board the *Sirius* and invited Phillip and those officers who could be spared from duty to dine with him. They did so, indeed, several times during their stay, in a style (Tench wrote) 'of equal elegance and splendour', surprised in particular by the number and variety of ice-creams served for dessert, brought up by deep caves excavated for the purpose of keeping them frozen even in the hottest weather.

Santa Cruz they found rather handsome, with well-designed buildings and more sumptuous, highly ornamented churches than most of them had yet seen in one place. Tench in particular was impressed by the church's evident riches: the Bishop was said to be paid **10,000 pounds a year, while the Government only received 2,000 in taxes.** The visitors were shown whatever they wished to see and more – including the factory run by the Governor for 60 'penniless girls' and destitute women in an attempt to keep them away from the prostitution which was endemic. John White considered that 'some of the women are so abandoned and shameless, that it would be doing an injustice to the prostitutes met with in the streets of London, to say they are like them.' He added that 'the females of every degree are said to be of an amorous constitution . . . and addicted to intrigue; for which no houses could be better adapted than those in Tenerife.'[50]

Tenerife was indeed famous for the licentiousness of its prostitutes, and while the officers maintained, at least in their journals and letters, a disapproving air, no doubt the lower deck took advantage of the many brothels where the girls were said to be preternaturally adept. No wonder that the Governor oversaw two hospitals for venereal disease ('a disease that has long been, and still continues to be, very common in this island', wrote White) and one for foundlings. In more polite society, there was much to impress: the men were handsomely dressed, the women discreetly veiled – though 'such as have any claim to beauty, are far from being over careful in concealing their faces.'

The officers rode about the place on mules, escorted often by some of the English merchants of Santa Cruz; they were taken up to Laguna, the island's capital, deep in the mountains – some of them found it beautiful, others depressing, with its small population and deserted air. At Corpus Christi, on 7 June, they all attempted to show respect for the celebrations – Phillip forbade the ordinary seamen to go ashore that day in case they should in some way give offence. Captain Collins was more than a little scandalised at the 'tinsel and trappings' of the Catholic church, though he and a few other officers did their best to kneel whenever anyone else knelt, both in the churches and in the streets – as did White and his friend Lieutenant Henry Ball, the captain of the *Supply*, but with an unfortunate result:

> We fell on our knees, as we observed those around us to do; but, it unfortunately happening that the spot we knelt upon consisted of sand intermixed with small rough pebbles, the posture we were in soon became so exceedingly painful that, in order to procure a momentary ease, we only let one knee remain on the ground. This heretical act did not escape the observation of one of the holy fathers, all of whom were intent on the exact performance of every ceremonious etiquette. It procured for us a frown from him, and treatment that was not of the most civil kind; so that, in order to pacify him, we again dropped on both knees. He did

not, however, pass on, without exhibiting strong marks of ill-nature and resentment in his countenance, at this trivial and unintended breach of respectful attention to the religious rights of the country.[51]

As might be expected, the Rev. Johnson deeply disapproved of all the Popery and show; after seeing a statue of the Virgin carried through the streets he wrote to a friend in England 'Alas! Alas! What superstition and idolatry is all this – God make us thankful!'[52]

The crews, many of whom had little enough time to enjoy the flesh-pots of Tenerife, given the work they had to do in refitting and victualling, worked and behaved well. The convicts on the whole were quiet, most of them kept in chains. Of the few Phillip allowed relative freedom one, John Powers, escaped from the *Alexander*, hiding on deck as night fell and then slipping over the side into a small boat and finding his way to a Dutch East Indiaman, where he attempted to join the crew. The master was suspicious and refused him, and Powers then rode to land and hid in a cave. Meanwhile there was much alarm, especially on the part of the *Alexander's* master, who stood to be fined 40 pounds if an escaped convict was not re-taken. The empty boat was spotted, drawn up on a beach, and Powers was recaptured. Phillip clapped him in irons, but in some way he managed to ingratiate himself with the Commander and was relatively quickly released. Less fortunate was another convict, James Clark, who escaped but died of the dropsy before being recaptured. Phillip reported the state of the fleet to London in a report sent back from Santa Cruz:

| | |
|---|---|
| Marines, including officers | 197 |
| Marines' wives | 28 |
| Do. children | 17 |

Chaplain and wife ............................................................ 2
Surveyor-General ............................................................ 1
Surgeon and assistants .................................................... 5
Men convicts ............................................................... 558
Women convicts ............................................................ 192
Children .................................................................... 13
Number victualled ...................................................... 1,015

Convicts dead since they were embarked ................. 21
Convict children   do.   do. ............................................ 3
Recd.  H.M.'s pardon before the ship left England  .. 2

The fleet was now relatively well stocked with water, wine and food – water had been easily taken on board from pipes laid to a mole at the docks for that purpose. Though there had not been a great deal of fish to be got, there was plenty of poultry, and though vegetables were in short supply onions and pumpkins were freely available. Hogs and sheep were virtually unobtainable, but goats could be cheaply and readily bought. Dry wines and brandy were cheap, sweet wines more expensive. On the whole Phillip was not displeased at the result of his visit. On June 9 everyone was ordered to their post, and the fleet sailed at daybreak on 10 June. When they arrived, the famous peak had been obscured by fog – now, as they sailed away, the weather was clear and the men were astonished at its height, 'the island appearing one vast mountain with a pyramidical top.' Phillip wondered whether there might be an eruption; but the volcano had been dormant for over eight years, and did not oblige.

The voyage continued smoothly, and on 18 June the *Sirius* sighted the Cape Verde Islands. Phillip sent out a general signal that he intended to stop at one of them, and the flagship attempted to put into Port Praya Bay at St Jago, but the winds were against it. White noted in his journal that 'a great swell was running, and had wee persevered in endeavouring to get in I make no doubt but some of ye vessels might have been disabled by carrying away a bowsprit or some such accident, which would have been a severe stroke to us, as it was impossible to replace anything of that kind at this or any of the Cape de Verde.'[53]

Phillip eventually signalled to the fleet to carry on to Brazil. It was now stiflingly hot, and they were encountering some tropical storms with heavy rain. However, if fish had been short at Santa Cruz, it certainly was not in the waters they were now ploughing, and this made a good contribution to everyone's diet. Some fish, though easily caught, proved poor eating – and some were merely decorative: the porpoises for instance which accompanied the fleet like a pack of hounds, moving from ship to ship in turn. At night, White wrote, 'the sea all round the ship exhibited a most delightful sight . . . occasioned by the gambols of an incredible number of various kinds of fish who sported about us, and whose sudden turnings caused an emanation which resembled flashes of lightning darting in quick succession.'[54]

The health of the crews and convicts were a great deal better than anyone could have expected, and though there had so far been 15 deaths among the prisoners, this was far fewer than had been anticipated. The close air in the convicts' quarters of the transports had been treated by occasionally lighting fires and exploding small quantities of gunpowder, and much oil of tar had been painted over almost every exposed surface.[55] White used this freely, noting that it 'resists putrefaction, destroys vermin and insects of every kind, wherever it is applied overcomes all disagreeable smells, and is in itself both agreeable and wholesome'.[56] He also instructed that the convicts should never be allowed on deck when it was raining, for they had no way of drying their clothes, and would have to lie in them until they dried, possibly contracting rheumatic fever. His good sense played an enormous part in ensuring that very few of the prisoners suffered from serious illness during the long and uncomfortable voyage.

There were setbacks, of course, invariably the result of ships' masters ignoring or neglecting Phillip's orders. For instance, he instructed that in order such crowded vessels should not become insufferably stuffy and nauseous below deck, the bilge-water should be pumped out every day and the convicts used to carry fresh sea-water and throw it into the bilges until it came out sweet and clear. On the *Alexander* this was neglected, and when White went on board to discover why there was a sudden outbreak of sickness and the hatches were opened, the smell was so fearful that it was some time before he could go below; the air was said to be so thick that the buttons on the marines' uniforms were blackened. The sickness was due to the disobeying of Phillip's orders. He sent Lieutenant King to the *Alexander*, and order was swiftly and decisively restored.

There was now a serious shortage of water. Phillip was forced to restrict the ration to three pints a day, with an extra quart allowed for boiling peas and rice. As White points out, that was 'a quantity scarcely sufficient to supply that waste of animal spirits the body must necessarily undergo, in the torrid zone, from a constant and violent perspiration and a diet consisting of salt provisions.'[57] Lieutenant Clark had the duty of serving the water ration on the *Friendship*, according to Phillip's strict instructions:

> one half to be served in the morning and the remainder in the afternoon. A lieutenant of marines with a sergeant or corporal and two of the convicts always to be present when the water is served. That part of the hold where the water is kept is never to be opened but in the presence of those appointed to see the water served,

and the sergeant or corporal and the two convicts are to be changed every day. The water that is necessary for the stock is to be given out at the time the water is served to the people, and the quantity issued daily to be marked in the ship's log.[58]

However nauseating conditions were below decks in the transports, the water rationing was absolutely necessary. Phillip would have liked to do something about the conditions in which the convicts were now living. He knew for instance that conditions on the *Charlotte* were bad, with the heat below decks so great that the female convicts were, as White wrote, 'perfectly overcome with it, frequently fainted away, and these faintings frequently generally terminated in fits'. It is perhaps better not to attempt to envisage the sanitary arrangements, or lack thereof, but despite the fact that the convicts were almost stifling in their confinement, White could not see that it would be possible to remedy the situation: 'so predominant was the warmth of their constitutions, or the depravity of their hearts, that the hatches over the place where they were confined could not be suffered to lay off, during the night, without a promiscuous intercourse immediately taking place between them and the seamen and marines.'

Not that closing the hatches deterred the more determined of the women or indeed the crew. Lieutenant Clark, on the *Friendship*, noted on 3 July that 'men had broke through the women convicts' bulkhead again' and that he had caught four of them with the men – 'four of the Number that had gone through while we lay at the Mother Bank[59] & two of them that I had put in Irons while we lay at Tenerife for fighting. I thought as I Said before that these Damned troublesome Whores it would not be long before they got there again.' This was reported to Phillip, who ordered the four men flogged and the women put in irons – Clark said if he had been Commander he would have flogged the women too. However, punishment of a sort was yet in store; he noted three months later than two of them had told the doctor that they were pregnant.

There was no deterring 'promiscuous intercourse', and it went on throughout the entire voyage. On one day in August Cornelius Connell, a private in the marines, was given 100 lashes for 'having an improper intercourse with some of the female convicts, contrary to orders', Thomas Jones was sentenced to 300 lashes for attempting get a marine on guard to 'suffer him to go among the women' (but let off by Phillip because of previous good behaviour) and John Jones and James Reiley were highly suspected of having made their way into the women's quarters, but were released for lack of evidence.

While he never ceased to sentimentalise about his beloved Betsy and the little dog which someone had given him (it was eventually lost overboard) Clark was fierce in his hatred of the women convicts. On 5 July he noted that one of the women had been flogged for being impertinent to the captain: 'The corporal did not play with her, but laid it home, which I was very glad to see, then ordered her to be tied to the pump, she has been long fishing for it, which she has at last got, until her heart's content.' He was rather displeased when flogging the women naked was given up for reasons of decorum, and sorry that the ideas of shaving their heads had not been taken up.[60] However, despite his scorn for the prisoners, he was not averse to making use of them. Upon discovering that one was adept with a needle, he provided her with thread and some kind of material, and she made him a well-fitting pair of trousers.

On 14 July the fleet crossed the equator on a delightfully calm and bright day, with the temperature no hotter than on a fine English summer's afternoon. On some ships there were the customary celebrations, so enthusiastic on the *Lady Penrhyn* indeed that she almost collided with the *Charlotte* because the crew 'did not attend to her steerage, being deeply engaged in sluicing and ducking all those on board who had never crossed it.'[61] From then on, until they reached Rio de Janeiro, the weather continued to be moderate and pleasant – 'as delightful as it was unlooked for', Tench remarked – though the favourable winds occasionally rose to storm force.   One day the *Borrowdale's* fore-top-gallant mast carried away; on another the *Alexander* lost a man overboard and was unable to save him.   Then a boat broke free in the *Prince of Wales* and crushed a woman convict, killing her.

Still, good time was made, and at three in the afternoon of 2 August the coast was sighted.  On the 7th the fleet anchored three quarters of a mile off the coast and the city of San Sebastian.  Phillip made something of a ceremony of his entry into Rio de Janeiro, leading the fleet through the heads with flags flying and a salute from his guns – this was returned by the guns of the Viceroy, Luis de Vasconcelos e Souza, an amiable but unimpressive, plump man with a squint, who offered the Commander comfortable shore accommodation.  Hospitality did not end there; the officers were given the freedom of the city and allowed to come ashore without restriction and move about without an escort.  Phillip was always happier on board the *Sirius*, despite the restrictions of his cramped cabin, but it was politic for him to accept the Viceroy's offer, and he did so, though he found the formality irritating.  Every time he appeared there was a scurry of guardsmen instructed to salute him, and as he passed them they would lower the Viceroy's colours and place them at his feet – an enormous but embarrassing compliment.  Tench noted the very obvious general respect shown to Phillip, due no doubt to his service in the Portuguese navy, 'in consequence of which many privileges were extended to *us*, very unusual to be granted to strangers.'[62]

As at Tenerife, Phillip's preoccupation was with gathering

supplies for his fleet, in particular taking on board fresh food which would enable him to continue to look after the health of both his own men and his convict charges. While they were in port, it was possible to bring fresh meat on board – a pound of beef for every adult every day – and Phillip again bought as many loads of vegetables as he could: endive, lettuce, radishes, cabbage and yams, added to which were bananas and oranges, limes and guavas. All this was extremely cheap – Gidley King had never been in a port so useful for stocking up on all kinds of provisions.

Apart from street markets, the ships were frequently surrounded by small boats from which produce was offered. Some of the local people took to rowing out to the transports and throwing oranges to the convicts, for whom they evidently felt a great deal of sympathy. The convicts were grateful – up to a point. On one occasion, a boatman was paid with false coin, and White reported to Phillip that Thomas Barrett, an ingenious convict on the *Charlotte*, had somehow managed to forge coins from old buckles, buttons and pewter spoons. White had to admire the result, 'the impression, milling, character; in a word the whole was so inimitably executed that had their metal been a little better, the fraud I am convinced would have passed undetected.' It was impossible to discover how the forging had been done on a ship where fire was strictly forbidden below decks, and where constant inspections were carried out. As White observed, the 'adroitness, therefore, with which they must have managed, in order to complete a business that required so complicated a process, gave me a high opinion of their ingenuity, cunning, caution, and address; and I could not help wishing that these qualities had been employed to more laudable purposes.'[63] Barrett's ingenuity did not save him from 200 lashes (back at home, he would probably have been hanged).

More rum and wine was brought on board, with sugar, port, coffee, rice, tapioca and tobacco and 10,000 musket balls – at last the marines could be properly armed. Phillip also bought a quantity of very handsome wood, with a view to making furniture for his quarters on land. Lieutenant Clark completed a long letter to Betsy, enclosing some butterflies he had caught – he was able to get it and many others posted on board a Portuguese ship which was just leaving for Lisbon and would deliver letters to the English Ambassador there, who would forward them to London. Clark took the opportunity to go ashore, staggering back on board with two bunches of bananas for himself, 16 cabbages for the officers' mess and several young orange trees which he intended to plant at Botany Bay.

As at Tenerife, Phillip allowed the officers, when they were not required on board their various ships, to go ashore and explore, look about St Sebastian, enjoy the religious festivals and fireworks and very possibly engage in some 'tender attachments', though the townswomen were not nearly as licentious as those of Tenerife, perhaps to the disappointment of some of the men. They were surprised at the city's size – as large perhaps as Liverpool or Exeter, but a great deal more crowded than either. It was built on a grid plan, also unusual to the visitors, with the Viceroy's palace at its centre. It was an unimpressive, long, low building, one wing of which held the opera house, and another the prison. There were innumerable churches and convents, some of which seemed to be illuminated almost every night in honour of some saint or other. The officers were more amused than anything else by the noise made by the women who stopped in front of one of the many images of the Virgin which stood at almost every street corner to sing or simply, it seemed, shriek a prayer. The inhabitants of the city seemed to have no other occupation than religious observance – it was said that when a ship had caught fire on a particular saint's day it was allowed to burn to destruction rather than interrupt the services.

As to more gallant occupations, White got himself into trouble early on by assuming that 'every woman was a proper object for gallantry'; he had been, he wrote, 'led to this conclusion from seeing many well-dressed women in the crowd quite unattended . . . As soon as it became dark, the generality of [women] exposed themselves at their doors and windows, distinguishing, by presents of nosegays and flowers, those on whom they had no objection to bestow their favours, a distinction in which strangers shared as well as their acquaintance.'[64] Unfortunately, though White, Tench and some of their friends strolled determinedly every evening in the streets beneath the balconies of the houses, they were not honoured with a single bouquet, 'though nymphs and flowers were in equal and great abundance.'[65] White, a romantic, found the women 'when young, remarkably thin, pale, and delicately shaped; but after marriage they generally incline to be lusty . . . They have regular and better teeth than are usually observable in warm climates, where sweet productions are plentiful. They have likewise the most lovely, piercing, dark eyes, in the captivating use of which they are by no means unskilled. Upon the whole, the women of this country are very engaging; and rendered more so by their free, easy, and unrestrained manner.' When he told one of them he could hardly believe that the masses of hair piled on her head was all her own, she unloosed it so that it trailed two inches on the floor. 'I offered my service to tie it up again, which was politely accepted, and considered as a compliment . . .'[66] Just as well that her husband was also present, and obligingly cordial, but after all, as Captain Collins remarked, 'These daughters of the sun should, however, neither be censured nor wondered at, if found indulging in pleasures against which even the constitutions of colder regions are not proof. If frozen chastity be not always found among the children of ice and snow, can she be looked for among the inhabitants of climates where frost was never felt?'[67]

The officers were all impressed by the excellent police service of the city, which kept it in excellent order. Tench observed that it was now relatively rare to see someone stabbed in the street, and the Church, which in Captain Cook's day had notoriously protected offenders if offered sufficient prayer money, was now less avaricious – though in general he was offended by the ostentatious power of the priests: 'Let him who would wish to give his son a distaste to Popery,' he wrote, 'point out to him the sloth, the ignorance, and the bigotry of this place.'[68]

Phillip saw little of the town – he was engaged in making sure the ships of the fleet were in good order for the rest of the voyage to New South Wales. His own flagship was almost the least sound: she had been neglectfully fitted, and her decks were leaking so badly that caulkers had to be brought on board to mend the seams in the decking. Phillip must have wondered whether she would be capable of standing the strain of the long trip yet to come. He took time from supervising repairs to tour the transports with Major Ross and speak to the convicts, promising severe punishment if they gave any trouble. He took six women who seemed likely to be trouble-makers from the *Charlotte* and transferred them, replacing them with six well-behaved women from the *Friendship* (one of whom, to Lieutenant Clark's irritation, was his seamstress).

Before sailing, Phillip sent off another report to London listing the officers 'fit for duty', and another report on the convicts and their health – only four were suffering from fever, five from dysentery, four from venereal disease and 29 from 'scorbutic ulcers'. Once again he complained that the women were almost naked, and that the little clothing with which they had been provided was 'made of very slight material, most too small, and in general came to pieces in a few weeks.' He appealed for better material to be sent out – it would in the end be cheaper for the Government – but as usual his request was ignored. However, he had bought 100 sacks of casada,[69] and 'the sacks being of strong Russia, will be used hereafter in cloathing the convicts, many of whom are nearly naked.'

The fleet sailed at six in the morning of 4 September. The officers were farewelled at a party at the Viceroy's, seen off by huge displays of sweet-smelling flowers and shrubs with the main reception room hung with cages of singing birds with richly coloured plumage. At the last minute a Portuguese soldier was found stowing away on the *Sirius*. Phillip ordered him to be set ashore on the coast, away from the port, so that he could make his way back to his regiment with the possibility that his attempt to desert would not be discovered and he would avoid being executed. As the *Sirius* led the other vessels under Fort Santa Cruz, Phillip was saluted by a salvo of 21 guns – 'a very high and uncommon compliment, and such as is seldom paid to any foreigner.'[70] He returned the compliment, and set course for the Cape.

# SEVEN

Despite a certain amount of stormy weather, the fleet made good time to Cape Town, completing the journey in 39 days. The various diarists agreed, when the voyage was over, that it had been quiet and uneventful, with few incidents worthy of recording. Upon reading the daily entries in their journals, however, it does not seem as placid as all that. Indeed, on the *Charlotte* it began with Thomas Brown receiving twelve lashes for insolence on the very day it sailed, and on the following day Clark reported an incident on the *Friendship* which certainly belied the ship's name:

> Captain [Meredith, captain of marines] and the doctor had Some words about Some wood – the doctor told the Capt that he did not behave like a Gentleman on which the Capt Struck him which the doctor did not Return – I order them both to be Quit or I would confine them both So there the matter Stands – have Seen two friend fall out about a Small piece of Wood.[71]

Fortunately, Clark seems to have reconciled the two men, and there was no further trouble.

Two days later, Phillip rationed water again – three quarts a day per person for drinking and washing. This was not as hard on crew or convicts as it had been when they were sailing through the tropics, for every day now the weather grew colder and refraining from bathing became a positive pleasure, especially when there was no means of heating water. The weather also became wilder – the *Fishburn* had her fore-top-gallant yard carried away and on 8 September the fleet was 'taken all aback' at night in a squall. The ships rolled heavily and there was much seasickness in the crowded quarters below decks, where one of the convicts, Mary Broad, gave birth to a healthy daughter in conditions it is best not to try to imagine.

There were occasional breaks in the rough weather – between the 14th and 16th indeed it was so calm that officers could once again be rowed from ship to ship, gathering reports for the Commander on the *Sirius*. Then the equinoctial gales struck again. So did dysentery. No-one died of it, or was even seriously ill, but it did not make conditions below decks any easier or healthier – nor did the fact that in rough weather the seas washed over the decks (on one occasion carrying away Captain Meredith's dog) and inevitably a great deal of water found its way below, soaking the convicts' clothes, which they had little chance of drying properly. Attempts to do this could indeed be perilous: on the 19th, William Brown, a convict from Exeter, was collecting some washing he had hung out to dry, and fell overboard from the *Charlotte*. A lifebuoy was thrown to him, but the sea was rough, and by the time a small boat was launched he had vanished.

As on most extended voyages, conditions got worse rather than better. The food is a case in point. Though occasionally there were treats of roast pork for dinner, for the most part everyone lived on salt meat, unpalatable at the best of times and worse when it dried and hardened, so that chewing it was like trying to masticate damp wood. One way of making meals tolerable was to wash the food down with hard liquor, which sometimes exacerbated tensions in the crowded, restricted spaces shared by the officers. On at least one occasion Clark was almost driven to distraction by Captain Meredith and the doctor who, having made up their quarrel, sang bawdy songs for hours together on the Lord's Day. By now everyone's nerves were strained, and what seem minor events were blown out of all proportion: when a convict woman lost some stockings the doctor had given her to wash, Clark flew into a rage on his friend's behalf: 'There were never a greater number of Damned Bitches in one place as there is in this Ship – if they were to lose anything of mine I would cut them to pieces.'[72] At least when a child of one of the convict women died, Clark showed some slight sympathy: 'Poor thing it is much better out of this world than in it.'

There had been rumours for some time of an incipient mutiny on the *Alexander*, and on 6 October her master signalled to Phillip that he needed a conference. A boat brought him to the *Sirius* with a marine officer and the Commander learned that some members of the *Alexander's* crew had given the convicts various weapons with which they were to mutiny when the ship reached the Cape. Wisely, Phillip decided that though there was no indication that any action would be taken until then, a pre-emptive strike would be the best response, and four members of the crew, including the man who seemed to have planned the collaboration, were brought to the *Sirius*. As it turned out, the ringleader proved to be none other than John Powers, who had attempted to escape at Tenerife. This time he was put in heavy irons and stapled to the deck. The informant who had revealed the plan to the captain of the *Alexander* was sent on board the *Scarborough* for his safety.

At dawn on 13 October land was sighted, and the fleet sailed into Table Bay to drop anchor by seven in the evening. Phillip sent Gidley King ashore immediately to pay the Commander's respects to the Governor, Mynheer Cornelius Jacob van Graaf, and to ask for permission to buy supplies. The Governor was polite enough, but said that any request for supplies must go before his Council – not a good sign.  At daybreak next day the *Sirius* complimented the fort with a 13-gun salute, and the courtesy was reciprocated.  However, the situation did not seem promising a far as supplies were concerned: Phillip hastened to meet the Governor, who explained there had been a famine recently, and the Cape needed to build up its resources and had little to spare for anyone else.  It would be impossible to spare grain, flour or bread.  When he added that in any case there were others to be supplied before the British ships, Phillip realized that he must take a strong line.  According to Lieutenant Bradley, he sent the Governor a formal written message, to be copied to the authorities in Britain, to the effect that 'if he had not an immediate answer concerning the supplies for us, that he must take such steps as would enable us to proceed without them'.  The suggestion that the Cape might then be generally known as a port which refused to provision ships was enough to change the Governor's mind.

However, it was clear that profiteering was to be the order of the day: prices were inordinate compared to those at Rio or Tenerife.  Surgeon Arthur Bowes Smyth[73] of the *Lady Penrhyn* commented tersely that he could not conceive that there was 'any part of the Dutch possessions better calculated to exemplify the character of Dutch avarice than Capetown.  Every article while the fleet lay there was advanced to treble its usual price.'[74] There was no recourse other than to pay what was asked for the necessary livestock, which had to be crowded into the vessels as best could be managed – a bull, seven cows, a stallion, three mares and three colts, and miscellaneous rams, ewes, sows, boars, goats and poultry.  Phillip found room for the bulls and cows on his flagship, dismounting eight guns and putting pens in their place; the horses went to the *Lady Penrhyn* and the remainder of the livestock was divided between the *Fishbourne* and the *Friendship*. While this was going on, necessary repairs were done, and yards and topmasts had to be to be struck against the possibility of gales which sometimes struck the bay.

Phillip and most of his officers went ashore. There were no hotels or boarding houses, and they stayed in private houses, more cheaply than they at first feared The food was good, and they ate well, which was a pleasure after the deprivation of the voyage. Poor impecunious Clark, who could not afford to live on shore, seems to have had only one good meal in Cape Town when Phillip invited him to dine at his table and he fell with enthusiasm on the fresh vegetables – young peas and new potatoes – and a dish of 'Straw Berries'. Next day he was ill, his stomach rebelling against the unaccustomed luxury to which it had been treated. Otherwise he was stuck on board with a few equally bad-tempered impecunious friends, several of whom once again found comfort in the bottle. One, the second mate of the *Friendship*, fell overboard while drunk and was drowned, and Lieutenant William Faddy got drunk and insulted Clark, who wanted him court-martialled. Major Ross was understandably reluctant; there was an unofficial enquiry in which Faddy said he couldn't remember what he had said but that he was sorry for it, and an uneasy peace was restored.

Meanwhile, on shore, after the liberality and relaxed atmospheres of Tenerife and Rio, where good order seemed to have been kept with a minimum of effort by the authorities, Cape Town was a severe shock. Many of the officers were appalled at the sadistic punishment meted out to its criminals. Surgeon Bowes Smyth was sickened by the sight of a row of gallows along the shore, hung with the tatters of old bodies, and by the wheels on which the bodies of criminals were broken – gobbets of flesh were still attached to some of them. To posts nearby large nails were attached the severed hands of thieves. When Dawes, White and a few others climbed Table Mountain and saw smoke rising from what seemed inaccessible ravines, they were told it was from the fires lit by runaway black slaves who preferred to starve or freeze to death rather than put up with the everyday cruelty of their masters and the fate which awaited them should they rebel. The officers were not surprised.

Were there no pleasures? Well, there was the view from the top of Table Mountain, though the climb was so arduous in the scorching sun that those who reached the summit were happy to throw themselves down and drink from the green water of a stagnant pool. Tench walked in the East India Company's garden, in which the Governor's house stood, but it was very different to the late Princess Augusta's splendid gardens at Kew – much of it was planted out with vegetables, and that area which was devoted to flowers and shrubs was too geometrically designed to please the English taste. The celebrated zoo did not impress him – 'poorly furnished both with animals and birds; a tigger, a zebra, some fine ostriches, a cassowary, and the lovely crown-fowl, are among the most remarkable.'[75]

The officers were not impressed by the Governor's militia – it was voluntary, and when White attended one of the parades he 'could not help observing that many of them had either got intoxicated that morning or were not recovered from their over-night debauch.'[76] Phillip may perhaps have been relieved that at least he did not have to put up with the kind of determined military compliments he had received at Rio. As far as the ladies were concerned, despite the apparently puritanical air of the town, all one had to do to be successful with them was to jump on them without any nice preliminaries: 'If you wish to be a favourite with the fair, as the custom is, you must in your own defence (if I may use the expression) *grapple* the lady, and paw her in a manner that does not partake in the least of gentleness. Such a rough and uncouth conduct, together with a kiss ravished now and then in the most public manner and situations, is not only pleasing to the fair one, but even to her parents, if present; and is considered by all parties as an act of the greatest gallantry and gaiety . . . In fact, the Dutch ladies here, from a peculiar gay turn, admit of liberties that may be thought reprehensible in England.'[77]

On 1 November an English ship sailed into the bay – the *Ranger*, from London. Clark was immediately frantic with excitement – 'how my heart goes pitte patty' – in expectation of a letter from his Betsey. No doubt many other hearts were similarly energised, but alas there were only two letters from home, neither for the sad lieutenant, who relieved his feelings by watching 30 sheep loaded onto the *Friendship*, 'put in place where the women convicts were. I think we shall find them much more agreeable shipmates than they were.' His temper was not improved by the fact that 8 November was a hungry day; a storm blew up that was so severe it prevented any small boats from reaching the *Friendship* with fresh beef and bread, and since no instructions had been given to broach salt beef, neither convicts nor crew had anything to eat.

Phillip signalled the fleet from the *Sirius* in the early morning of 11 November ordering ships to prepare to sail, but the wind was against them. Major Ross came on board the *Friendship* to try to patch up a quarrel between Captain Meredith and Assistant-Surgeon Thomas Arndell, who had almost come to blows the previous evening. Unfortunately, in the process Ross swore at Meredith and succeeded only in making things worse. Nor was the atmosphere improved by the appearance of another Assistant-Surgeon, Dennis Considen, who decided in the interests of the crew's general health to pull out as many teeth as seemed to require his notice.

All in all it was probably just as well that the fleet was able to sail at midday on the 12th, giving everyone enough to do to prevent any more squabbling. Encouraged no doubt by Phillip, many of the officers were busy looking after the animals they had bought privately as their own property, 'not merely for the purpose of living upon during the passage, but with a view to stocking their little farms in the country to which we were going, every person in the fleet was with that view determined to live wholly upon salt provisions in order that as much live-stock as possible might be landed.[78] Unfortunately, when the winds rose many of the chickens kept on deck were simply blown away – many were lost both on the *Borrowdale* and the *Friendship*, though Clark managed to secure his own pair (the only property he had acquired to take to Botany Bay).

On 16 November, Phillip decided to leave the *Sirius* and move to the *Supply*, a faster vessel Eight months later he explained his reasons in his first dispatch from Sydney to London: he had moved, he said, 'in order to precede the transports, in hopes of gaining a sufficient time to examine Botany Bay, and fix on the most eligible situation for the colony.' The *Alexander* and *Friendship* were to follow as closely as possible, as Philip 'wished to make some preparation for landing the stores and provisions, which the convicts on board those ships would enable me to do, if they arrived soon after the Supply, and before the other ships, as I had reason to expect.'[79]

This brief note does not tell the full story. With him to the *Supply* Phillip took lieutenants King and Dawes and several other officers. He had also gathered together a number of convicts who would be useful in establishing a foothold in New South Wales. His diligent enquiries had uncovered a very few more artisans than at first were supposed to be along the prisoners, including a gardener and a cabinet-maker (who had been employed by Clark in making him a tea-caddy for his wife, which he lamented would probably now never be finished). After getting everything in order – including putting Shortland, the naval agent, in charge of the three transports in case they lagged behind, and leaving Captain Hunter in command of the remainder of the fleet – Phillip drove ahead in *Supply*, leaving the rest of the fleet behind. He was out of sight by the 27th.

Hunter, on board the *Sirius,* had to rely on his own watch to determine his position, as Phillip had taken the timekeeper with him. Fortunately the watch was a good one. He was not convinced by Phillip's plan; had the Commander decided on the action at Rio, he would have had a very good chance of reaching New South Wales a considerable time before the rest of the fleet. As it was, no-one but himself seemed to believe that he would manage to establish a really useful lead – as indeed turned out to be the case.

Two months of sailing was still ahead of the two sections of the fleet. Their course was the same – far to the south, almost as far as the Antarctic Circle, east until they reached the South Cape of Tasmania (or Van Diemen's Land as it was then called), and then north to Botany Bay. The great stretches of ocean were bleak and utterly abandoned. The chances of seeing another friendly – or indeed unfriendly – sail were negligible. No spaceman leaving Earth for a distant planet would be as completely cut off from any evidence of human life.

One would have no idea of the difficulties, the horrors, of that journey if the only evidence was the account by Watkin Tench. In Chapter VII of his first book, dealing with 'The Passage from the Cape of Good Hope to Botany Bay', the voyage itself is dealt with in a bare three lines: 'From this time [of leaving the Cape] a succession of fair winds and pleasant weather corresponded to our eager desires, and on the 7th of January 1788, the long wished for shore of Van Diemen gratified our sight'. There is considerably more to say of the journey than that.

First, there was disease – though as with the whole long expedition, this was kept remarkably under control. However, as early as 17 November, the day after leaving the Cape, Hunter had to deal with an outbreak of dysentery 'which very soon made its way among the marines, and prevailed with violence and obstinacy until about Christmas, when it was got under by an unremitting attention to cleanliness, and every other method proper and essential for the removal and prevention of contagion.' Only one man died – 'Daniel Cresswell, one of the troops intended for the garrison, who was seized on the 19th of November and died the 30th of the same month, the eleventh day of his illness. From the commencement of his disorder, he was in the most acute agonizing pain I ever was witness to; nor was it in the power of medicine to procure him the shortest interval of ease.'

Then, on the 20th, White went on board the *Prince of Wales*, 'where I found some of the female convicts with evident symptoms of the scurvy, brought on by the damp and cold weather we had lately experienced. . .' Then 'the scurvy began to show itself in the *Charlotte*, mostly among those who had the dysentery to a violent degree; but I was pretty well able to keep it under by a liberal use of the essence of malt and some good wine . . . For the latter we were indebted to the humanity of Lord Sydney and Mr. Nepean, principal and under secretaries of state.'[80]

The weather varied almost from day to day – sometimes the becalmed ships rolled sickeningly, before a fair wind would send them scurrying along. One day the *Friendship* covered 166 miles, and a seaman was blown from the topsail yard of the *Prince of Wales* at night and drowned in the black sea. The storms could be vicious – Clark had to get up at night and fight to keep his belongings from crashing about all over the small space of his cabin. King, now on the *Supply*, found his new ship far less stable than the *Sirius*, and was uncomfortable as she wallowed about. He was relieved when better weather made her a little more stable – and drier: 'The latter part of the day [28 November] was very pleasant and serene weather, which in a vessel of this kind is a valuable circumstance if it were only to dry one's things, as the sea yesterday made fair breaches over her, and many of them wetted the head of the foresail.'[81]

On calm days there were at least some new sights to be seen: albatrosses and petrels and strange fish. One day the look-out on the *Supply* anxiously reported rocks ahead – but they turned out to be two very large whales, so close to the vessel that one could have stepped from the deck onto their backs.

Water was now rationed to three pints per person per day, and Clark began to do a brisk business in rum; somehow he managed to gain access to a bottle or two, and gave some to the boatswain and carpenter 'for things they have done for me.' Meanwhile he lamented having, for the first time in his life, to drink his tea without sugar.

Come December the cold struck, numbing not only the limbs but the brain – the helmsman on the *Supply* had to be relieved in the middle of his watch as he appeared to have lost his senses. At last the crowded conditions in which the convicts sailed had an advantage – body warmth. This led to a certain amount of sexual activity, which much exercised the mind of Surgeon Bowes, who was surprised and pleased at how well their health was standing up to the conditions, but was less delighted by their morals:

I believe I may venture to say there was never a more abandoned set of wretches collected in one place at any period than are now to be met with in this ship in particular and I am credibly informed the comparison holds with respect to all the Convicts in the fleet. The greater part of them are so totally abandoned and calloused to all sense of shame and even common decency that it frequently becomes indispensable necessary to inflict corporal punishment upon them . . .

every day furnished proof of their being more hardened in their wickedness – nor do I conceive it possible to adopt any plan to induce them to behave like rational or even human beings . . .[82]

Christmas was not celebrated with any panache on the *Sirius*, for the supply of wine had run out. The cold got even worse – Clark wore his greatcoat all day over a flannel waistcoat. Between the 18th and Christmas Eve the seas ran so high that the *Supply* was running almost under water; everyone on board was wet, cold and even frozen. Captain Walton killed a pig, but Christmas Day was nevertheless gloomy. Collins recorded that on the *Sirius* the officers and men 'complied as far as was in our power with the good old English custom, and partook of a better dinner this day than usual, but the weather was too rough to admit of much social engagement.'[83] There was a tot of rum for the crew on the *Lady Penrhyn*, 'to cheer their hearts and to distinguish this day as being the most remarkable in the year and which generally brings with it Mirth and Glee to the Hearts of all except the truly Miserable.' The women prisoners got a small ration of sugar and sago. A week later, on the last day of the year, the sea was so rough that many of them were washed out of their berths. The night was 'a dreadful night indeed.' New Year's Day was no better: Clark wrote unsteadily in his journal: 'It is now 1 o'clock and I am going to sit down to the Poorest dinner that ever I Sat down too on a New Years day a piece of hard Salt Beef and a few musty Pancakes.'[84]

On 4 January, to everyone's delight, the *Friendship* sighted Van Dieman's Land. There were another 800 miles yet to sail, but the very sight of land was a relief. The euphoria, in any case moderate, did not last long on the *Sirius* – there was another violent quarrel between Captain Meredith and Lieutenant Faddy, over nothing much. Clark was thoroughly bored with the latter, 'the most selfish grumbling and bad hearted man I was ever shipmates with.' But by now almost everyone disliked the sight of everyone else. On the *Lady Penrhyn* the officers found some claret and drank to their own sighting of land, though it looked thoroughly inhospitable. Hunter named one rock the Mewstone, because it so closely resembled the original Mewstone off Plymouth.

We have no record of what Phillip was thinking, a little way ahead. His mind was likely on what he was to do on landing, how he was to prepare for the arrival of the transports, how dispose the convicts, how begin to lay the foundations of a new society. What we know of him does not suggest a particularly gregarious man, or indeed one specially swayed by circumstance; he will have been as cold as the rest of the members of the expedition, but it would be surprising if he allowed himself to be quite so slow-witted, dull and pessimistic. To him, too, however, the relatively brief sight of the coast of Van Dieman's Land must have been encouraging.

It was on 18 January that the *Supply* sighted Botany Bay — by which time the second division of the fleet was only two days behind, so Phillip would not, as he had hoped, have any time to make real preparations for their arrival. As they came towards the land, they saw a number of natives on the shore — so many in fact that Tench thought that the country must be much more highly populated than Captain Cook had supposed. At one place, there were at least 40 men, all shouting and making 'uncouth signs and gestures.' Phillip, thinking caution advisable, landed on the north side of the bay, where there were only six men. As he was rowed ashore, the 'Indians', as Tench called them — for some time no-one decided just how they were to refer to the Indigenous people — walked along opposite the boat. Phillip was pleased when one of his officers gestured that they wanted a drink and was instantly understood, and a place was pointed out where they assumed there would be a stream.

There was not a great deal of what might be called conversation, but (Tench wrote later) 'the conduct of both parties pleased each other so much that the strangers returned to their ships with a much better opinion of the natives than they had landed with. Meanwhile, the natives seemed highly entertained with their new acquaintances, from which they condescended to accept of a looking glass, some beads, and other toys.'[85]

The fog which had impeded the *Supply* during the last two days now impeded the following vessels, which had to communicate by gunfire rather than flags. The last few miles were no easier – there was such a shortage of food for the beasts that they were weak and many died; the winds from time to time mounted to almost storm force, on one occasion splitting the main stay-sail of the *Friendship*, on another smashing in the cabin windows of the *Golden Grove*. The *Charlotte's* mainsail and the main-yard of the *Prince of Wales* were both carried away. During one gust the boatswain of the *Fishburn* fell from the topsail yard and died despite White's efforts. One or two convicts succumbed – Edward Thomson, for instance, 'worn out with melancholy and long confinement.'

At 7.50 on the morning of 20 January the *Sirius* dropped anchor in Botany Bay, next to the *Supply*, the *Alexander*, *Scarborough* and *Friendship*. Tench, setting down his thought some years later, was thoroughly realistic:

> Thus, after a passage of exactly thirty-six weeks from Portsmouth, we happily effected our arduous undertaking, with such a train of unexampled blessings as hardly ever attended a fleet in a like predicament. Of two hundred and twelve marines we lost only one; and of seven hundred and seventy-five convicts, put on board in England, but twenty-four perished in our route. To

what cause are we to attribute this unhoped for success? I wish I could answer to the liberal manner in which the government supplied the expedition. But when the reader is told, that some of the necessary articles allowed to ships on a common passage to West Indies, were withheld from us; that portable soup, wheat, and pickled vegetables were not allowed; and that an inadequate quantity of essence of malt was the only antiscorbutic supplied, his surprise will redouble at the result of the voyage. For it must be remembered that the people thus sent out were not a ship's company starting with every advantage of health and good living which a state of freedom produces; but the major part a miserable set of convicts, emaciated from confinement, and in want to clothes and almost every convenience to render so long a passage tolerable.[86]

Nevertheless, 'joy sparkled in every countenance and congratulations issued from every mouth. Ithaca itself was scarcely more longed for by Ulysses than Botany Bay by the adventurers who had traversed so many thousand miles to take possession of it.'[87] There was one notable exception: Lieutenant Clark's immediate reaction on seeing land was 'I cannot Say from the appearance of the Shore that I will, like it.'

Captain Collins ignored the negatives and celebrated with justifiable pride the extraordinary accomplishment of the First Fleet:

Thus, under the blessing of God, was happily completed, in eight months and one week, a voyage which, before it was undertaken, the mind hardly dared venture to contemplate . . . we had sailed five thousand the twenty one leagues; had touched at the American and African continents; and had at last rested within a few days sail of the antipodes of our native country, without meeting any accident in a fleet of eleven sail, nine of which were merchantmen that had never before sailed in that distant and unexplored ocean: and when it is considered, that there was on board a large body of convicts, many of whom were embarked in a very sickly state, we might be deemed peculiarly fortunate, that of the whole number of all descriptions of persons coming to form the new settlement, only thirty two had died since their leaving England.[88]

All that was undoubtedly true. What no single diarist mentioned, however, though they must surely have known it, is that the good condition of the convicts and the well-being of the crews was the result of the care, thought and forward planning (when that was possible) of one man – the man who now stepped ashore in New South Wales faced with an even greater task: Governor General Arthur Phillip.

# EIGHT

Before he even went ashore, Phillip was not pleased with Botany Bay – the greater part of it was so shallow that the smallest ship in the fleet had to anchor near the entrance, rolling about in the heavy sea that rose when the wind blew hard from the east. And when he made a serious survey with Major Ross, lieutenants Dawes, Long and King and a party of marines, the situation ashore was no more promising – there was fresh water, certainly, but it turned much of the land to swamp, and they could see no solid ground of any dimensions on which a settlement could be built. They discovered only two small fresh-water springs, at one of which Captain Cook had presumably refreshed himself and his crew; beside one they had the first meal eaten by the first settlers in New South Wales – salt beef and a glass of porter, in which they drank the health of old friends in England.

There was a remote possibility of firm land, they decided later, near Sutherland Point – so named by Captain Cook during his visit in 1770, in memory of a crew member, a Scotsman called Forby Sutherland who had died of tuberculosis during their eight day stay and been buried on the shore. The soil was good, and the grass grew thickly, but even there the ground was spongy and the ships could not come close enough to unload without difficulty. Half of the party – which had separated into two – had a brush with some unfriendly Aborigines who made signs for the invaders to go away, and were unimpressed by the tawdry gifts they were offered. One threw a spear with some force, though it simply stuck into the ground. When another was shown, King ordered a blank shot fired, at which the 'natives' ran away. When King reported the incident to Phillip, the Governor insisted on being taken to the spot. He landed alone, carrying some presents, and his lack of fear evidently impressed the Aborigines, who seemed this time to be friendly.

Later the same day – 20 January – King went back to meet them again, and from his rowboat offered them a glass of wine, which they immediately spat out. He started attempting to discover something about their language. They seemed uncertain of the visitors' sex, pointing at their genitals, puzzled by the fact that though they seemed to be men, they had no beards. King, to disabuse them of the idea that the marines were women, ordered one of them to stand up in the boat and lower his trousers:

> when they made a great shout of admiration and pointing to the shore, which was but ten yards from us, we saw a great number of women and girls, with infant children on their shoulders, make their appearance on the beach, all *in puris naturalibus – pas même la feuille de figueur* . . .[89] I [showed] a handkerchief which I offered to one of the women, pointing her out. She immediately put her child down and came alongside the boat, and suffered me to apply the handkerchief where Eve did ye figleaf. The natives then set up another very great shout and my female visitors returned on shore.[90]

On 21 January Phillip ordered Major Ross to supervise the clearing of some ground near Sutherland Point, in case he could not find a more promising situation for the settlement, and to make arrangements for the possible disembarkation of the prisoners. As he had written in his notes the previous year, it might well be extremely dangerous not to get the convicts ashore as quickly as possible – after so long a voyage they would be desperate to escape their close quarters on the transports, it would be difficult to explain why they should not do so – open rebellion might follow. He then set out in three open boats with captains Hunter and Collins, a lieutenant and a small party of marines, to see what he could see. As they made out to sea, natives gathered along the coast crying, '*Warra warra warra!*' and making gestures which seemed to suggest that they were very pleased to see the backs of the white men.

As they rowed up the coast, Phillip was at first despondent – it looked as though Captain Cook might have been right, and there was to be nothing to be found other than another small inlet large enough to shelter only one or two ships. What he saw when they passed through the heads was Port Jackson, and an astounding sight it must have been; as he put it in his first report to Lord Sydney, 'the finest harbour in the world, in which a thousand sail of the line may ride in the most perfect security.' Hunter agreed that this was the place where a settlement must be established. They rowed up the harbour, past astonishingly bright green banks of vegetation interspersed with rocks – some the size of small houses – and with beaches of bright clean sand.

As Jacob Nagle (one of the rowers) remembered, 'it coming on dark, we landed on a beach on the south side and there pitched our tents for the night. This was called Camp Cove.' The marines were put on their posts and the others fished for their supper; the party was able to sit down to a good meal before turning in for the night. They were up again at four in the morning, ate some cold fish while sitting in the loaded boats, and then rowed on. 'The Governor', Nagle wrote, 'was anxious to get to the head of the harbour, but we could not, but we got as far as where the town is now called Sydney Cove, about seven miles from the entrance of the harbour. We landed on the west side of the cove. Along shore was all bushes, but a small distance at the head of the cove was level and large trees, but scattering and no underwood worth mentioning and a fresh run of water running down into the centre of the cove . . .'[91]

While the officers went ashore to study the lay of the land, Nagle and the others fished. He caught a large bream for their lunch, and Phillip told him to remember that he was 'the first white man that ever caught a fish in Sydney Cove where the town is to be built.' The Governor had decided that this was to be the site where the fleet should unload the first white citizens of New South Wales, and he had already named it Sydney, after the Home Secretary Thomas Townsend, 1st Viscount Sydney.

The boats returned to Botany Bay, Phillip with a sense of having made a firm and significant decision. He signalled all masters to prepare to sail for Port Jackson on the following morning. While Phillip had been away Tench had taken the opportunity of seeing just how positive a relationship he could strike up with the Aborigines. He took ashore with him a small boy of about seven years old, probably the son of a marine, and walked along the beach holding his hand. A dozen men approached him, 'naked as at the moment of their birth'. They were armed with spears, and Tench carried a gun. Though wary of each other both parties seemed friendly enough, but one of the seamen in the party thought 'it appeared as though they did not approve of our visit.' The Aborigines were astonished at the white skin of the child, and even more astonished by his clothes; what could the hat actually be *for*? Eventually the men crowded round; Tench produced more presents, but they did not seem particularly interested in anything other than the looking-glasses (for one of which one man exchanged a club 'with a head large enough to fell an ox'). After almost an hour, the party broke up, but during the following few days at Botany Bay there were several more meetings with the

Aborigines 'which ended in so friendly a manner, that we began to entertain strong hopes of bringing about a connection with them.' There were one or two mistakes, as when John White fired his pistol, which terrified the men, but they did not run away, and eventually came near and were astonished at the hole the ball had made in the target. White said that one of them, 'by signs and gestures, seemed to ask if the pistol would make a hole through him, and on being made sensible that it would, he showed not the smallest signs of fear; on the contrary he endeavoured, as we construed his motions, to impress us with an idea of the superiority of his own arms, which he applied to his breast, and by staggering, and a show of falling, seemed to wish us to understand that the force and effect of them was mortal, and not to be resisted.'[92]

That evening surgeon Bowes went ashore with some of the ship's company from the *Lady Penrhyn*, hauled in a seine they had laid, and found it had caught a great many fish. He was disappointed that though the whole place looked green and lush and promising, when one got down to examining the soil was really no more than shallow black sand. There also seemed an infinite number of ants, ranging from small black creatures to enormous red ones.

On the day after Phillip's return to the fleet with the good news of Port Jackson, Sgt Henry Brewer, a middle-aged midshipman and Phillip's clerk and servant, rushed down to Tench's cabin as he was dressing and breathlessly reported that there was a ship off shore. At first Tench laughed, but then went on deck and indeed there were two sails in sight off the bay. There was some confused idea that they might be supply ships from England, but they turned out to be two French frigates – the *Boussole* and *Astrolabe*, commanded by Count Jean-François de Galoup de Lapérouse, on a voyage of discovery. His presence was not entirely innocent – he had been instructed by the French government to call at Botany Bay and discover just what the English were up to. Lapérouse told Judge-Advocate Collins that he had expected to find a town with a flourishing market. He was disappointed. However, he paid Phillip courtesy, and since he had enough stores on board for three years but was on his way back to France, and since the voyage would take only 15 months, said he would happily make him a gift of anything which might be useful.

The French ships having sailed, Phillip immediately set out again for Port Jackson, this time in the *Supply*. He had had no intention of divulging to the French commander the extent and value of the splendid harbour, and when the French vessels reappeared, not long after he had sailed, a boat was sent out to one of them with a lieutenant to offer advice on where in Botany Bay it would be safest for them to drop anchor.

Phillip meanwhile had taken with him the carpenters, builders and few other artisans as he had been able to identify, and instructed Captain Hunter to follow with the transports and store-ships at his earliest convenience. There was a little tangle as the fleet left Botany Bay, the wind being adverse; the *Friendship* ran first into the *Prince of Wales*, losing her jib boom, and then into the *Charlotte*, terrifying Lieutenant Clark. However, they had an easy run up and into Port Jackson, passing through the heads in the fresh light of a beautiful early evening, the crews crowding on deck to admire the generous green of the shore set against the brilliant blue of the water, and the astonishing extent of the harbour. So overcome was midshipman Daniel Southwell that he described the scene as thought it were the *décor* for a Drury Lane pantomime:

> Nothing can be conceived more picturesque than the appearance of the country while running up this extraordinary harbour. The land on all sides is high, and

covered with an exuberance of trees; towards the water, craggy rocks and vast declivities are every where to be seen. The scene is beautifully heightened by a number of small islands that are dispers'd here and there, on which may be seen charming seats, superb buildings, the grand ruins of stately edifices etc, etc. which as we passed were visible, but at intervals the view being pr'ty agreeably interrupted by the intervention of some proud eminence, or lost in the labyrinth of the enchanting glens that so abound in this fascinating scenery.[93]

At six in the evening the whole fleet anchored off Sydney Cove – known in later years as Circular Quay – a place where the harbour was so deep, so close in-shore, that the largest vessel would have no difficulty in approach close enough to land to make disembarkation of men and supplies as easy as might be. A small patch of open ground had been cleared near where a stream ran through a very thick wood into the harbour; otherwise the marines stepped from the boats either onto rocks or directly into a wood. Work began immediately to clear more ground, and later in the evening of that day, 26 January, in the words of Judge-Advocate Collins:

the whole party that came round in the *Supply* were assembled at the point where they had first landed in the morning, and on which a flagstaff had been purposely erected and a Union Jack displayed, when the marines fired several volleys, between which the Governor and the officers who accompanied him drank the healths of his Majesty and the Royal Family, and success to the new colony.[94]

Sydney had been 'crisned', as one marine put it.

Next day, a Sunday, some of the more trustworthy convicts

were brought shore and set to help the marines clear more ground for the settlement. Phillip had already decided that the stream which ran down into the bay[95] should make a boundary between his own residence on the east side, with his staff, a guard and a small number of convicts nearby under his eye, and the remainder of the marines and prisoners to the west. A strict boundary was set to the camp, and even before the whole body of convicts came ashore, a guard – two subalterns, two sergeants, four corporals, two drummers and 42 privates, under a captain's orders – was mounted to keep order and to make sure no one set foot outside the boundary. The Governor wasted no time in setting everyone to work. Conscious that food supply was going to be a major issue he sent a fishing party out, which returned with a good catch (a small party of Aborigines had apparently been helpful, pointing out an area where fish should be found, and even helping to drag the catch ashore).

Now, at last, it was time to release the convicts. They had been growing more and more restive, still penned below decks, and it is not surprising that they were in high spirits when they found themselves in the fresh air, their feet at last on solid ground. The male prisoners came ashore on 27 and 28 January with the remainder of the marines: 'I never saw so much confusion in all the course of my life,' Lieutenant Clark wrote in his journal. 'Thank God they [the convicts] are all out of the ship; hope in God that I will have nothing to do with them any more.' A vain hope if ever there was one.

Cattle were landed and penned – though only a few had survived – and Government House was set up on a site near the present-day Macquarie Place. It was a tent which had cost the Government £130 and, though flimsy, served Phillip for many months as both office and residence. The marine officers had less serviceable tents and marquees, and the convicts were simply given pieces of old canvas from Portsmouth Dockyard and told to do what they could with them. Phillip's quarters were neither wind nor waterproof – nor were the others strong enough to put up with the tumultuous rainstorms that were to batter them. The convicts began clearing more ground and cutting down timber to build log houses for the officers and soldiers on the west side of the stream. Nine marines were told off to work with those of the dozen carpenters among the convicts who were not sick, and the carpenter of the *Sirius* was put in charge of the small party which was instructed to set up storehouses, quarters for Phillip's staff, barracks for the marines and huts for the convicts – and all this on land covered with tangled and intractable bush. It was a big ask, and progress was at a crawl.

The good health of the convicts, about which Phillip was justifiably proud, was not as sound as he believed. On the 29th Collins began setting up sick tents on the west side of the stream, with an extra tent as a laboratory, and these were soon filled with men and women suffering from dysentery and scurvy. 'More pitiable objects were perhaps never seen,' he wrote; 'not a comfort or convenience could be got for them, besides the very few we had with us.' Phillip instructed that a special plot of land should be set aside to raise vegetables for the sick, but though at first the seeds seemed to shoot well, they quickly died – they were sown at the wrong season. Fortunately some wild celery, spinach and parsley grew nearby, which was a help. Collins and the Governor decided a hospital must be a priority, and land was set aside for a building.

Captains Bradley and Hunter had meanwhile been sent off to survey the harbour, as far as that could realistically be done without their being absent too long. It was they who began to make a serious study of the Aborigines, and attempt to make some real contact with them. There seemed to be a mixture of friendliness and suspicion – as yet little real antagonism.

On the first morning of their excursion, they went into what they called Spring Cove (between Manly and the north head), and were met by three canoes, which followed them to the beach and were joined by a dozen more, some of the men in them wearing trinkets Phillip had handed out a week before. The seamen who accompanied the officers mixed with the Aboriginal men and all was perfectly friendly – the Aborigines seemed to welcome them with little dance movements. The seamen produced combs and combed the hair of the natives, which amused them greatly.

Bradley and Hunter took the opportunity of examining the canoes, which they thought on the whole were the worst they had ever seen, though they later saw fishermen standing up in them to spear fish and keeping their balance perfectly; in some cases they also actually lit fires in the canoes, presumably to cook fish – though the two captains could never discover just how this was done.

By now some women could be seen at a distance, peeping out of the thickets. Hunter made signs that he would like to give them some gifts, but the men made it quite clear that they were unwilling for the women to come anywhere near the white men. If Hunter gave them the gifts, they would take them to the women. Hunter refused, and an old man who seemed to have some authority finally signalled to them to come forward. They seemed to be fairly young, 'well-made' and completely naked, but happy for the white men to 'decorate' them with coloured rags and beads, at which they became almost hysterical with laughter.

They were followed from the woods by about 20 men carrying shields and spears, or 'lances' as Hunter called them, also naked but with their bodies and faces painted – some of them, he said condescendingly, 'with some degree of taste'. At a distance, he thought, the white marks on the black bodies made them look exactly like dancing skeletons, 'a most shocking appearance.' They drew up in a line, almost a military formation, the officers thought, evidently ready to protect the women should any problem arise. The officers also noticed two well-armed men had been stationed near the visitors' boats, no doubt for the same reason.

Newton Fowell, a midshipman from Devon on the *Sirius*, paid special attention to the spears, and was allowed to examine them. The wood of which they were made was especially strong, and extremely sharp at the point – war spears, Fowell thought. Though they were heavy and about twelve feet long, the men could throw them at least 70 yards. Other spears had four prongs, and were clearly for fishing – at the end of each prong was a fish's tooth, firmly fixed with some kind of gum, and at the other end was a shell which they explained, in mime, they used for scraping the spear and opening oysters.

As February began, the Governor was not satisfied with the way the prisoners applied themselves to the major task of clearing the ground for the settlement. He complained in his first report to London that 'the convicts, naturally indolent, having none to attend them but overseers drawn from amongst themselves, and who fear to exert any authority, makes this work go on very slowly.'[96] The problem was yet another which had its origin in the lack of real thought on the part of the Government at home – though it must be admitted that Phillip himself seems to have missed spotting it: no plans had been made for overseers to discipline the convict workers. He complained to Lord Sydney that he had asked officers occasionally to encourage convicts they saw to be working well, and point out for punishment those who were idle or sloped off into the woods to avoid work. 'This was all I desired,' he said, 'but the officers did not understand that any interference with the convicts was expected, and that they were not sent out to do more than the duty of soldiers.

The consequences must be obvious to your Lordship.'[97] The fact was that the marines considered themselves to be military men whose duty was to protect the colony; they were not to be used to supervise workers, and simply declined to do so, and Phillip felt that in the face of the splenetic Major Ross it would be highly impolitic for him to attempt to issue orders. In view of this, the only solution was to attempt to choose reliable overseers from the convicts themselves, but it was a highly imperfect system.

The tension between Phillip and Ross was echoed by the mistrust felt by the marines towards their Governor. This stemmed in no small degree from Philip's sympathetic attitude to and treatment of the Aborigines. Arthur Bowes summed this up in his journal:

This Government (if a Government it can be called) is a scene of anarchy and confusion; an evident discontent prevails among the different officers throughout the settlement. The marines and sailors are punished with the utmost severity for the most trivial offences, whilst the convicts are pardoned (or at least punished in a very slight manner) for crimes of the blackest die. I do not even except stealing, which the Governor himself assured them would be punished capitally. What may be the result of such a very inconsistent and partial mode of acting, time (and I may venture to say a very short time) will shew.[98]

Captain Campbell complained in much the same vein: 'I know not why, or whether it was so intended by administration that the only difference between the allowance of provisions served to the officer & served to the convict, be only half a pint (per day) of vile Rio spirits, so offensive both in taste & smell that he must be fond of drinking indeed that can use it – but such is the fact.'[99]

No-one was as comfortable on shore as they had been on the ships – despite the fact that they had, at least, more room in which to move about. Lieutenant Clark had to crawl naked out of his tent one night to re-secure it to the tent-poles, and remarked in his journal, 'in all the course of my life I never slept worse . . . what with the hard cold ground, Spiders, ants and every vermin you can think of crauling over me.'[100] If the convicts had hoped for better, they were disappointed, and a number of them even managed to escape and make their way back to Botany Bay, where they went to the French ships still anchored there and offered themselves as crew. Pérousse sent them packing, with sufficient provisions to last them back to Sydney cove.

On 3 February Reverend Johnson preached his first sermon in the New World, under a tree, with marines, seamen and convicts drawn up in front of him. He chose the text 'What shall I render unto the Lord for all his benefits towards me?'[101] He also performed the first baptism in New South Wales – of little James Thomas, the son of Private Samuel and Ann Thomas. Johnson did his best, no doubt, to be positive; but he had already observed signs that the largely illiterate convicts had learned nothing about morality from the books he had freely distributed, and was not optimistic about the likelihood of reform. His pessimism was to be confirmed two days later when at five in the morning the women convicts began to disembark. That evening the crew of the *Lady Penrhyn* asked Captain William Sever for an extra ration of rum with which to 'make merry upon the women quitting the ship.' If Sever thought that they would be content with drinking, he learned a lesson. The women had gone ashore, some of them surprisingly well-dressed, having occupied their time making new clothes from whatever material they could lay their hands on. The sailors followed them and were no doubt joined by those from other ships, some of them marines.

A typical Sydney storm then blew up – 'the most tremendous thunder and lightning, with heavy rain, I ever remember to have seen,' Collins recorded. Five sheep were killed by lightning under a large tree which was rent from top to bottom. The pouring rain did nothing to cool the spirits either of the men or the women: before long a saturnalia was in progress. Tench reports that 'Licentiousness was the unavoidable consequence, and the old habits of depravity were beginning to recur,'[102] while Arthur Bowes, the surgeon, was more frank: 'It is beyond my abilities to give a just description of the Scene of Debauchery and Riot that ensured during the night.'[103] One rather touching incident recalled the legend of Hero and Leander: a young seaman swam ashore to see the woman with whom he had been living, caught a chill, and died.

Next day, the exhausted citizens of the new colony had to pull themselves together, for the Governor had ordered a grand muster. The marines, no doubt more or less hung-over, formed a ring within which the male and female convicts were seated on the ground. In the middle stood a table on which were two red dispatch-cases containing Phillip's commissions. The drums and fifes of the marine band played a march and the colours were lowered as the Governor, Lieutenant-Governor Ross, Judge-Advocate Collins and the other officers entered the circle. Collins read the two commissions and the Act of Parliament setting up a court of civil jurisdiction, and the letters patent constituting the vice-admiralty court. The marines then fired three volleys interspersing the verses of the national anthem.

The Governor addressed the company. He did not preserve the text of his speech – it may have been extempore, but as members of his audience remembered it, the main thrust was to convince the convicts that if they behaved well they would be encouraged and well treated; if they behaved ill, they would receive the punishment they deserved. George Worgan, the surgeon on the *Sirius*, reported that he went on to tell the convicts:

> he was convinced that there were a Number of good Men among them, who, unfortunately, from falling into bad Company, from the Influence of bad Women, and in the rash Moment of Intoxication, had been led to violate the Laws of their Country, by committing Crimes which in the serious Moments of Reflection, they thought of with Horrour & Shame, and of which now, they sincerely repented, and would be glad by a future Conduct to retrieve their Characters; but sorry was he to add, that he feared there were some Men & Women among them, so thoroughly abandoned in their Wickedness, as to have lost every good Principle: Therefore, from henceforth, he declared, that however it might distress his Feelings, every Crime, from the smallest to the greatest Magnitude should meet its Punishment, which the Law inflicted. He observed likewise that many of them, since they had been disembarked, instead of assisting in the necessary Work of forming the Settlement, were found skulking in the Woods, and came to the Camp only at the appointed times for the serving of their Provisions to them, for the Future, all such Idlers, as were found beyond the Limits, the Provost Martial, and the Patrol received Orders to take up and Imprison, & that in Case of their running from the Patrol, they would be fired at with Ball: Moreover, He assured them, that those who would not Work, should not Eat, for, the *good* Men, he promised, should not be Slaves for the *Bad*, their daily Labour should be much easier, on account of the Warmth of the Climate

than the Common Labourer's in England, but *That*, they should perform, or *Starve*, — He gave very good Advice & Encouragement to the Women, telling them, as well as the Men, & promised that good Behaviour should never go unrewarded by Him. They had his Permission to Marry, and proper times would be allowed for the making up their little Agreements amongst each other, but after a certain hour in the Evening, any Man seen in the Woman's Camp, the Sentry would have orders to fire at with Ball, & in all indiscriminate Intercourse with the Women, the Offenders should be severely punished.[104]

The officers heard for the first time of the powers with which Phillip had been invested, and some of them were shocked; even the well-balanced Tench observed that the Government had 'armed the Governor with plenitude of power' and that 'no mention is made of a council to be appointed, so that he is left to act entirely from his own judgement', while Clark had 'never heard of any one single person having so great a power invested in him as the Governor has by his Commission.' These sentences, though only mildly critical, hint at a problem which was to become not just an irritation but to some degree an obstruction to Phillip during his time in New South Wales.

When the company had been dismissed, Phillip hosted a cold luncheon for his officers at the canvas Government House, where many additional toasts were drunk (alcohol may have been a pleasant distraction from the food, for Lieutenant Clark noted that the cold mutton was crawling with maggots).

On the Sunday after the assembly, the 10th, Mr Johnson married 14 couples, so it seemed that at least some of the convicts followed the Governor's advice, no doubt aware of the advantage this would bring in the way of allowing them a little land to cultivate. Clark, as usual, did his best to see the dark side of things – several of the grooms, he said, had left wives and families back in England (can Johnson have known this? – was it, indeed, true?) – and went into another of his emotional spasms: 'Good God what a scene of whoredom is going on there in the woman's camp; no sooner has one man gone in with a woman but another goes in with her. I hope the almighty will keep me free from them as he has hitherto done . . .' The Almighty clearly at some stage looked the other way, for Clark later had a daughter with Mary Burnham, sent to Botany Bay for stealing clothes.

There was something of an emphasis on religion during the following week, for the Governor had to swear on the Bible that he did not believe in transubstantiation, thus ensuring the settlement, under his guidance, would be properly Protestant, and George III the only lawful sovereign. This was particularly important, since among the convicts 83 were Irish, known Catholics and therefore probably trouble-makers.

On Saturday the first court-martial sat – Clark was one of the members – and sentenced marine Thomas Bramwell to 200 lashes for assaulting one of the convict women 'because she would not go up into the woods with him.' On the following Monday Bramwell received 100 lashes, and his back being cut to ribbons was sent to the hospital to recover before receiving the other hundred. That day the criminal court sat for the first time – three senior officers and three military officers in full uniform with side-arms. 21-year-old John Tenhel (a.k.a. James Tenhel and Thomas Hill) was charged with stealing two pence worth of bread from another convict. He pleaded, simply, that he had taken it because he was hungry. Clark wrote to the Judge-Advocate pleading for leniency: Tenhel had served with him on the *Friendship* and had always been peaceable, obedient and of good behaviour. Tenhel avoided the lash, serving a week's solitary confinement on bread-and-water on 'a small rocky island near the entrance of the cove' – now known as Fort Denison or, more tellingly, Pinchgut.

Clark, though one is often amused by his puritanical frenzies, was nevertheless right about the convicts' predilection for whoring – anarchy ruled for much of the time where the women's camp was concerned – indeed on the Tuesday following the weddings a sailor, a cabin-boy and the carpenter from the *Prince of Wales* were caught in the women's tents. The band played the 'Rogue's March' as they were drummed through the camp with their hands tied behind them, the boy dressed in petticoats. Bowes, looking on, echoed Clark's view – 'the anarchy and confusion which prevails throughout the camp and the audacity of the convicts, both men and women, is arrived at such a pitch as is not to be equalled, I believe, by any set of villains in any other sport upon the globe.'[105]

It is difficult to gauge Phillip's attitude to all this – he certainly refrains from complaining about the convicts' behaviour in his dispatches – but he would not have wanted to advertise this to the people at the Home Office. Having delegated the keeping of order to the officers and courts, he did not interfere except in the most difficult or critical cases, such as the last court of appeal against a death sentence.

In the meantime, he turned his attention to the matter of Norfolk Island. In his commission he had been instructed 'as soon as circumstances will admit of it, to send a small establishment thither to secure the same to us, and prevent it being occupied by the subjects of any other European power.' The man he decided to send on this mission was Lieutenant Gidley King, the single officer he knew best and could trust utterly. On 12 February he wrote a commission instructing King, on landing on the island to turn his attention immediately to the cultivation of the flax plant, which he believed would be found growing freely there,[106] and also to planting the seeds of cotton, corn and other grain, which he was to take with him on the *Supply*. He could use part of the corn to feed himself and those accompanying him, but always 'with the greatest economy, and as the corn, flax, cotton, and other grains are the property of the Crown, and are as such to be accounted for, you are to keep an exact account of the increase, and you will, in future, receive directions for the disposal thereof.'

He was to be given provisions for six months, but they were not to be generous, for there was no doubt that plenty of fish and vegetables would be available. As to the convicts he took with him, he was to 'take particular notice of their general good or bad behaviour, that they may hereafter be employed or rewarded according to their different merits.' Certain precautions were also to be taken: he was to take only one four-oared boat with him, 'and you are not on any consideration to build or to permit the building of any vessel or boat whatever that is decked, or of any boat or vessel that is not decked, whose length of keel exceeds twenty feet; and if by any accident any vessel or boat that exceeds twenty feet keel should be driven on the island, you are immediately to cause such boat or vessel to be scuttled, or otherwise rendered unserviceable, letting her remain in that state until you receive further directions from me.' The chance that a mass escape might be planned was not to be taken.

Finally, he was 'not to permit any intercourse or trade with any ships, or vessels that may stop at the island, whether English or of any other nation, unless such ships or vessels are in distress, in which case you are to afford them such assistance as may be in your power.' He was also to read prayers on Sunday 'with all due solemnity', and to enforce a due observance of religion and good order.'[107]

His commission in his pocket, King set off in the *Supply* on the morning of the 15th, accompanied by the surgeon's mate of the

*Sirius*, Mr Jamison, a petty officer, Mr Cunningham, also of the *Sirius*, two privates, two men who had convinced the Governor that they knew all about flax, nine male and six female convicts who had proved well-behaved and some provisions.

King was to have no easier a time than he probably expected. The *Supply* arrived at Norfolk Island on 29 February, and on 9 March, after a religious service, King read his commission and then mirrored Phillip's previous speech to the convicts: he would reward virtue and punish vice. At first the convicts behaved well, and set to work with a will to clear ground and sow corn and potatoes. But gradually discipline began to slip, and very soon there was no better behaviour among them than with their brothers and sisters in New South Wales.

# NINE

Conforming to his instructions that the colony should be established from the first as a Christian community, the Governor took communion on Sunday, 17 February. Lieutenant Clark, whose marquee was used for the purpose, said he would keep his table for as long as he lived, 'for it is the first Table that ever the Lord's Supper was eat of in this country. My tooth pains me very much.'(The following day a surgeon pulled out the offending tooth, breaking Clark's jaw as he did so.)

Meanwhile, the officers were showing some interest in the natural life of the country – in particular, of course, with regards to the kangaroo. Captain John Shea seems to have been the first man to shoot one and bring it to the camp – 'the most extraordinary animal that ever I saw', Clark said, and everyone wondered at its size and vigour, its astonishing leap and its strength. In due course more were caught and cooked, but the meat was not admired: it was compared sometimes to veal, sometimes to mutton, even venison, but once the novelty had worn off it was not prized.

Though not extreme, the heat was now sorely trying to everyone, and there was regular heavy rain. The convicts predictably had the worst of things, either huddled under rotten canvas, too old and torn to be used by anyone else, or in huts built of pieces of wood, clay and mud – clay and mud which was quickly washed away, leaving them open to the elements. The ground on which they slept had at first been too hard for comfort, now it was too wet and soggy. Housing was going to be a problem for some time. Getting decent wood for building was difficult, as the tools provided by government agents were almost incapable of dealing with iron-hard trees and branches, while shortage of lime made it difficult to make cement. Gradually, enough huts were built to house almost everyone – huts the outline of which might have been drawn by a child; simple square buildings about nine feet by twelve with a central door on one side and a window each side of it. Ironwood provided excellent beams and girders, but was hard to cut and harder to work. Cabbage-tree palms provided material that could be worked – the trunks were soft in texture, easy to fell and roughly consistent in size; unfortunately every cabbage-tree in the vicinity of the settlement had soon been cut down. The first roof-shingles were made of wood from the casuarina, known popularly as 'Botany Bay wood'.

The problem of the tools was a highly irritating one for Phillip. On the face of it, the list he had been given of tools to be supplied had suggested that there would be more than enough to be going on with – including as it did 700 axes, another 700 hatchets, 700 spades, 700 shovels, 12 ploughs, 175 hammers, 175 handsaws and so on. It soon became clear, however, that almost all of them were of appalling quality; they bent, they broke, and their edges were easily dulled and damaged. It was another case of Government contractors feathering their nests at the expense of people who would be too far away to be able to complain.

Sawpits were quickly dug, to which were hauled tree-trunks trimmed into logs; these were sawn into planks by two men, one working above, one below the trunk – arduous work in the heat of midday. Women were sent to what became known as Rushcutter's Bay to collect reeds for thatch – a somewhat dangerous occupation, for the Aborigines clearly regarded the area as their own, and two rush-cutter women were speared and killed.

The accommodation devised was temporary but acceptable,

even if the moment heavy rain caused the mud with which the mimosa-wood walls were daubed began to wash away. Wattle and daub persisted for some time, however – the first church in the settlement was built of that material some years later in 1793, even though bricks and tiles were by then available. The Government refused to allot money for a church, so Mr Johnson began work on his own account, and eventually constructed (with some help) a church 15 feet wide and t-shaped, 73 feet in one direction and 65 in the other. In good time he presented the Government with a bill for £67 12s 11½d.

Work on better accommodation for the major figures of the colony began almost immediately, and Phillip put James Bloodworth, one of the convict brick-makers, in charge of finding suitable clay and supervising teams of men who would tread clay and water into a malleable mess, mould it into bricks and fire them. Oyster shells were ground into a paste to make lime. Bloodworth, who had been sentenced in 1785 to seven years' transportation for some un-named crime, was a man of parts – Collins said, in a few years' time, that there was not a house in Sydney town that did not owe something to him. He was emancipated in 1790 as a reward for his services, and the *Sydney Gazette*, the colony's first newspaper, founded in 1803, was to write of him that most of the public buildings of Sydney had been erected under him. He died as official Superintendent of Buildings.

Naturally, the first brick house to be built was for the Governor. It would be a symbol of authority, and indeed of permanence – important because Phillip suspected that a large number of convicts harboured the ambition to return, one day, to England – an ambition which would only be fulfilled for a minute minority. Work started on the more solid replacement for the canvas Government House on 15 May, when the first stone was laid and a plaque later set up:

His Excellency
Arthur Phillip, Esq.,
Governor-in-Chief and Captain-General
in and over the Territory of New South Wales,
landed in this Cove,
with the first Settlers of this Country,
the 24th Day of January, 1788;
and on the 15th Day of May
in the same Year,
being the 28th of the Reign of His present Majesty
George the Third,
The First of these Stones was laid.

The house was at first planned as a three-bedroom bungalow, but since lime-bonded walls proved satisfactory an upper story was added with three more rooms. The façade of the building was attractive, if severe; it had stone foundations (traces of which can still be seen in the forecourt of the Sydney Museum today) and brick walls with stone corner pieces, and it was the only building with interior walls cemented with lime mortar, made from ground-up shells. Its façade was 53 feet long, and the two ground floor rooms were 16 feet and six inches deep, and 30 and 20 feet wide, respectively.

Gradually, the town was to have, under Bloodworth's supervision, many brick buildings. He supervised the building of soldiers' barracks on the west side of the Tank Stream and swiftly constructed brick houses for the Reverend Johnson, the Surveyor-General and the Judge-Advocate. Eventually, he set up brick-works under a convict called Wheeler, at which 22 men and two boys produced 40,000 bricks and tiles each month These were hauled by 24 men harnessed to carriages over rough tracks to where they were needed. There were smaller brick-works, too, producing rather fewer bricks —

from them carts emerged carrying 250 bricks at a time - still a significant burden. Work, however hard, had to be done on a weekly ration of seven pounds of bread, a pound of flour, seven pounds of beef or four pounds of pork, three pints of dried peas and six ounces of butter a week. Convicts, privates and officers – and Phillip himself – had the same ration; the female convicts and the few wives in the settlement were given two-thirds of the men's ration.

Not unnaturally, this led to food theft, and on 27 March four convicts – John Ryan, Henry Lavell, Thomas Barrett and Joseph Hall were brought before the criminal court charged with stealing butter, peas and pork from the stores. Ryan, a silk weaver, was sentenced to receive 300 lashes; the others, to death. At five o'clock the same day all the convicts were mustered around a large tree between the men's and women's camps. As Lavell, Hall and Barrett were brought to the tree, Major Ross, in command of the large number of marines also gathered (and the supervisor of the ceremony), received a message from the Governor. Phillip had delayed the execution of the former two for 24 hours, presumably to examine their records more closely. Barrett was deemed by common consensus 'a most vile character', and his execution was to go ahead.

There was a delay, however, when the convict who had volunteered for the job of executioner refused to perform it. Ross had to order the marines to threaten to shoot him before he complied, and Barrett climbed the ladder and was 'turned off' – in the cant phrase – making a show of the event with a long speech confessing the wickedness of his life. He was 17 years old.

Next day, when once again a rainstorm startled everyone with its vehemence, the convicts were mustered again and Hall and Barrett were brought to the tree-gibbet. Another last-minute message from the Governor pardoned them just as they were climbing the ladder – he had received an appeal for clemency signed or marked by almost every convict in the settlement. The two were sent off to Pinchgut on short rations.

Phillip, despite expressing the view that death never prevented any man from 'a bad action', found it impossible not to employ the ultimate sanction (he was proved right: in the hungriest of months the choice, after all, came down to probable death by starvation or possible death by the rope). We cannot know what brought him to the decision to succumb so early to the temptation to use the gibbet – it may be that pressure from his officers, and maybe particularly the splenetic Major Ross, was an element. If so, he was not entirely convinced, for he made fairly free use of his prerogative to commute the sentences.

Nevertheless, the first execution having taken place on the 27th, it seemed likely that another would follow within a week. The court sat in the morning of the 29th to try Daniel Gordon, John Williams and George Whitaker with stealing 18 bottles of wine. Whitaker was discharged, but Gordon and Williams, both black men, were sentenced to death. Then came William Sherman and James Freeman, both convicted of stealing flour – enough to satisfy 15 men for a week. Freeman was sentenced to death, Sherman to 300 lashes.

Once more the ceremony of mustering the convicts, once more the condemned men marched to the gibbet with halters about their necks and once more the Reverend Mr Johnson prayed with and over them. Then, as they stood at the foot of the ladder, Major Ross read the Governor's message pardoning the two black convicts on condition that they were to be 'banished', and forgiving Sherman his beating. Freeman was pardoned on condition that he agreed to become the public hangman. Gordon and Williams were put on Pinchgut in chains; Phillip said that he intended, when it was possible, to put them ashore in Tasmania and leave them to their own devices.

Meanwhile, relations between the settlers and the Aborigines remained friendly. Bowes, for instance, rowed across to the north shore in the *Sirius's* pinnace on the 28th, and was greeted freely by men, women and children who were 'very social', helped the white men to fish and even made a fire and cooked some of the catch to share with them. Captain Hunter thought that there should be no problem about maintaining friendly relations; although the natives seemed always to go armed with spears, whenever the white men lay down their arms the others followed suit, 'with spirit and a degree of confidence scarcely to be expected.' He was convinced that in time they would understand that the newcomers were not their enemies and the two races would live perfectly peaceably together.

Less sanguine, David Collins, the Judge-Advocate, feared that when (rather than if) the black men realized that the white men intended to remain on their land for ever, there would be trouble. The convicts were now collecting 'souvenirs' from the natives at a great rate – spears, shields, fishing lines and so on – in a way which amounted to theft, and that did not auger well. He had also heard that La Pérousse, or his men, had fired on some of the Aborigines at Botany Bay, and though he personally believed that this had only been done from necessity of some kind, it could not be expected that the natives would not consider Governor Phillip's people as likely to fire on them as Lapérouse's.

It was now March, and gradually the harbour was being more fully explored. On the second day of the month the Governor, with Lieutenant Bradley and a few others (including Nagle and some marines) set out in two six-oar cutters on an expedition to an area of the coast eight miles north of Port Jackson, which had been mentioned by Captain Cook. When they landed to spend the night on shore – probably at Pearl Bay – they were met by a considerable number of Aborigines, the men heavily armed with spears, clubs, stone hatchets and wooden staves. Nevertheless they were, as Phillip remarked, very friendly.

The next day they pressed on, spending their second night in the neighbourhood of what is now Woy Woy, then on to Broken Bay, where a thunderstorm forced them to moor for the duration. The heavy rain continued next day – an old Aboriginal man signalled to them to land, pointing to a cave, but Bradley in particular suspected a trap, so the white men stayed out in the storm. As Phillip himself put it, 'this was rather unfortunate, for it rained hard and the cave was the next day found to be sufficiently large to have contained us all, which he [the old man] certainly took great pains to make them understand.' He was very impressed by the south side of Broken Bay, which he thought 'the finest piece of water I ever saw. And which I honoured with the name of Pitt Water. It is, as well as the south-west branch [of the bay] of sufficient extent to contain all the Navy of Great Britain.'[108]

On the 7th, a Saturday, they again encountered the old Aboriginal who, said Phillip, 'met us with a dance and a song of joy', but when it was dark stole a spade. The Governor, to show he was displeased, gave him 'two or three slight slaps on the shoulder with the open hand, and pointed at the spade.' This seems mild enough, but was a mistake – the old man picked up a spear and seemed about to use it, when he was dissuaded by some of his friends. Next day he waved the party off in a perfectly friendly way, as though nothing had happened, and the cutters were rowed back to Sydney.

Meanwhile, the *Supply* had returned from Norfolk Island with news that not a single flax plant could be found there, though the information had been that it grew freely. Everyone, however, had been impressed by the height and splendour of the pine-trees. On her way back, the ship had discovered a new island – uninhabited, but populated by very large colonies of turtles, which would surely be a splendid source of food for the colony. Lieutenant Ball had named it Lord Howe Island.[109]

On May 6 the *Supply* was sent off directly to Howe Island for turtles, but returned without having seen any; the season was wrong. This was a serious blow, for fresh provisions were now growing scarce – as scarce, Tench remarked, as in a town under blockade. The livestock situation was increasingly desperate – two bulls, five cows, 29 sheep, 19 goats, 49 hogs, 25 pigs, five rabbits, 18 turkeys, 29 geese, 35 ducks, 122 fowl and 87 chickens comprised the animal population – and it was far more important to try to breed from these than to slaughter them. Goodness knows, they died quickly enough of natural causes. Fish were increasingly difficult to catch and, Tench tells us, 'had it not been for a stray kangaroo, which fortune now and then threw in our way, we should have been utter strangers to the taste of food.'[110]

No sooner had Governor Phillip settled back into his daily routine after his excursion than trouble arose with Major Ross. A marine, Joseph Hunt, was court-martialled for striking a colleague, William Dempsey. Dempsey was going to the cookhouse with a pot to boil, when he saw Jane Fitzgerald, a convict, talking to another marine. She said good-day, and they had a desultory conversation, at which Hunt came up and hit him with a stick. Dempsey asked why, and Hunt replied that he had no right to speak to a woman from his, Hunt's, ship. Another marine, Jones, came up and asked what was going on, whereat Hunt called him 'a Portsmouth rascal!' and told him to 'Get out of my sight!'

Jones gave evidence, and yet another marine, Wedman, said he had seen Dempsey 'show some dissatisfaction' at being hit with the stick, 'upon which Hunt struck him twice on the head with his fist, and on being told by the prosecutor that he would complain of him, the prisoner said that if he pleas'd he was welcome to do so.'

Hunt admitted striking Dempsey, but said he 'was not in

earnest in it, and did it not with the intention of hurting him.'

It was a storm in a tea-cup – a simple quarrel about Fitzgerald, with whom Hunt had probably had a relationship on the *Charlotte*. There were strict unwritten rules by which the women on board one ship were forbidden to associate with men who had arrived on another, and in addition there was considerable jealousy and ill-feeling between the marines from Portsmouth and those from Plymouth, so it was far from unusual for quarrels of this sort to flare up. This they often did, though they rarely came to the official notice of the authorities – if they came to the Governor's notice, he left his officers to deal with them.

The court consisted of lieutenants Tench, Robert Kellow, John Poulden, Davey and Timins. Poulden and Timins knew Hunt and spoke well of him, and though he was found guilty of the charge a lenient if eccentric sentence was passed: the prisoner was 'either to ask public pardon before the battalion of William Dempsey, the soldier whom he struck and injur'd, or to receive 100 lashes on his bare back, by the drummers of the detachment.'

Major Ross, hearing the sentence, was furious – to give a prisoner a choice of punishments was absurd. He instructed his adjutant to write to Tench, as President of the Court, and 'having pass'd a sentence by no means consistent with the martial law . . . proceed to passing a sentence without the choice of two sentences.' Tench declined to do so. Ross's adjutant wrote again, insisting that 'you do immediately proceed to finish the court-martial that you were in orders for, by passing only one sentence for one crime.' The reply was signed by all five officers, and reiterated simply that they 'were not prepared to alter a judgment which we gave after the most impartial enquiry and most mature deliberation.'

This impertinence (the sentence *was* eccentric) was one

result of the dislike with which most of his officers regarded Ross, whose response was as quick as it was intemperate: he put all the officers under arrest. Phillip knew of the affair, and had almost certainly been advising the officers – his relationship with Ross had always been prickly, and though surely he must have privately agreed that the sentence was a ludicrous one, he was not about to take the Major's side. Now he received a formal letter from the five officers, complaining that 'the treatment we have received [is] so violent, and our present disgraceful situation so notorious, that we cannot, without injustice to our feelings, consent to have the arrest we now suffer under taken off until a public reparation should have been made for the indignity we have been used with.'

Major Ross also sent the Governor a formal letter, complaining that by the actions of the officers he had been forced 'to resign all authority into their hands, and give up the command of the detachment entrusted to my care' (which was clearly ridiculous) and that he had no alternative but to arrest them for disobedience to orders 'til such time as the opinion of more competent judges than either them or myself might be had thereupon. Your Excellency will therefore please to take such steps in this disagreeable business as may appear to you most proper for the establishment of good order and military discipline, so indispensable and absolutely necessary in our present critical situation.'[111]

Phillip did not need to be told his duty as to 'good order and discipline', but he was tactful in his response, simply pointing out that it was impracticable to keep five officers under arrest when there were only four captains and two lieutenants in the detachment, two of whom were already ill and unable to perform their duties. He suggested the arrested officers should be released, and the matter settled in some manner less damaging to the morale and practical running of the settlement. In the meantime he had sent the papers in the matter to the Judge-Advocate; the officers could be court-martialled if absolutely necessary, at some convenient time in the future. Tench and his fellow officers wrote a general declaration that 'whenever Major Ross shall think proper to bring the merits or demerits of our conduct to a legal decision we are ready to meet the charge, and we once more repeat that a general court-martial only can bring the matter to a proper issue.'

And there the rather silly affair subsided, the matter never to be raised again. Silly, but significant as far as the relationship between Phillip and Ross as concerned – they were very different personalities. (The peace was to be broken again, and fairly soon.) Meanwhile, Phillip was no doubt pleased to get away, which he did on 1 April, on an expedition which crossed over to Manly and pressed inland for some distance, finding and admiring some rocks on which the Aborigines had cut patterns and figures, and getting a glimpse of a black swan. Examining what is now Curl-Curl creek they failed, they believed, to reach its source, although when they camped out near a swamp they were in fact at the head of the creek. At the head of Middle Harbour they turned west into what seemed 'an endless wood' and penetrated a further 15 miles inland, climbing the 'mountains' where they could in order to spy out the land as best they might. Phillip named several of them – the Carmarthen Hills, the Lansdowne Hills, Richmond Hill . . . He thought the lay of the land argued in favour of a considerable river, but failed to find one. He set out again on 22 April, but found that the landscape was intractable. His report to London, in his first dispatch, has passages very like some of those in the journals of the first explorers, many years later:

I believe no country can be more difficult to penetrate into than this is, tho' we always found pools of water that had remained after the rainy season, yet, as that could

'*Arthur Phillip Esq., Captain General and Commander in Chief in & over the territory of New South Wales.*' Engraving based on a miniature by Francis Wheatley, c.1786. Original copy owned by the National Library of Australia (pic-an 9846227).

I

An early woodcut showing the '*Sirius* and *Supply*' in Jacksons Bay, with Government House in the background. Original copy owned by the National Library of Australia (pic-an 9576706).

'*The melancholy loss of H.M.S Sirius off Norfolk Island March 19th 1790*', c. 1791. Original copy owned by the National Library of Australia (pic-an 21511971).

'*Bennelong, a native of New Holland*', engraved by Samuel John Neele,
probably when he was in London in 1793. Original copy owned by the
National Library of Australia (pic-an 9353133).

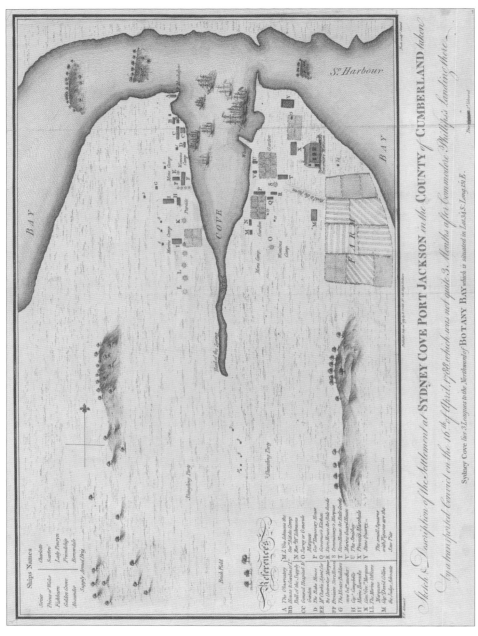

Sydney Cove, April 1788. Attributed to convict Francis Fowkes, transported for stealing a pair of boots. The map shows the 'Governor's Mansion', the marine barracks and men's and women's camps. Original copy owned by the National Library of Australia (nla.map-nk276).

not be depended on, the water necessary for the day was always carried, which, with the provisions, arms, and a couple of tents, obliged every officer and man to carry a very heavy load.[112]

Unfortunately, after he had slept for several nights on the wet ground, Phillip began to suffer from severe pains in his side. Surgeon White (who accompanied him) believed these to be brought on by cold, damp and exhaustion. They had to return prematurely to Sydney.

There he faced another problem: venereal disease was spreading among both convicts and marines. It had been, Captain Collins said, 'the anxious care of everyone who could prevent it, that [it] might not be introduced into the settlement.' That was no doubt always a vain hope, and it was now spreading quickly. Phillip ordered that anyone who had contracted it and failed to declare it should receive corporal punishment and be put on short rations for a considerable time. Predictably, this did no good at all, and it was not long before it inevitably spread to the Aborigines. Initially, Surgeon Worgan had thought this unlikely:

what with the stinking Fish-Oil with which they seem to besmear their Bodies, & this mixed with the Soot which is collected on their Skins from continually setting over the Fires, and then in addition to those sweet Odours, the constant appearance of the Excrementitious Matter of the Nose which is collected on the upper pouting Lip, in rich Clusters of dry Bubbles, and is kept up by fresh Drippings; I say, from all these personal Graces & Embellishments, every Inclination for an Affair of Gallantry, as well as every idea of fond endearing Intercourse, which the nakedness of these Damssels might excite one to, is banished and I can assure you

145

there is in some of them a proportion, a softness, a roundness and plumpness in their limbs and bodies, were they but cleanly, that would excite Tender and Amorous Sensations even in the frigid breast of a Philosopher.[113]

The convict men presumably lacked his sophisticated tastes, exercising freely their 'Tender and Amorous Sensations'. At all events, venereal disease was to wreak havoc among the Aboriginal population of New South Wales, with the most horrifying of results.

At the beginning of May the *Charlotte*, *Lady Penrhyn* and *Scarborough* sailed for China, and there were some melancholy farewells: the master of the *Scarborough* reluctantly left his Newfoundland dog Hector behind him, in the care of one of the officers. Worgan, walking it a day or two later, visited the colony's official farm for the first time, and was heartened to find that the cows, bulls and horses were thriving, though several sheep had died. As to cultivation, almost 10 acres of land had now been cleared and ploughed, and there was talk of planting corn very soon. The effort involved should not be underestimated: what with inefficient tools and the fact that restricted rations had weakened the men, convicts could take as long as five days to chop down, cut up and then uproot a single tree.

Phillip had originally set up a garden near the hospital in an attempt to provide fresh vegetables of some sort for the sick. He followed this by setting aside six acres for cultivation near Government House and encouraged the crews of the *Sirius* and *Supply* to cultivate their own plots. The officers were allowed two acres each, and there were allotments for the marines and convicts. These plots thrived, at least to the extent that the plants and fruit-trees did well, as did some vegetables, and six acres of wheat and eight of barley were flourishing at Farm Cove under the care of Henry Dodd. A nagging problem was theft;

the officers' gardens – tended by convicts – were continually raided. Lieutenant Clark had established his on a small island – still known as Clark's Island – but when he went there one afternoon he found that someone had landed by boat and dug up his onion patch, stealing all the vegetables. 'It is impossible for any body to attempt to raise any Garden stuff here, before it comes to perfection they will steal it,' he wrote dispiritedly in his journal.[114] Phillip suggested that the 'official' garden should be planted on another island, 300 yards from shore, but though very few convicts or marines were ingenious enough to land on Garden Island, the soil was so poor there that the vegetables grown there were skimpy and weak.

Towards the end of May there were disconcerting signs that the Aborigines were growing restive and even antagonistic. On the 23rd convict William Ayres who had been picking herbs in the woods staggered naked back into the camp with a spear stuck into his loins. After it had been removed by Surgeon White – with difficulty, because the barb was extremely efficient – Ayres said that three natives had come up behind him, beaten him severely, stripped him then speared him. As he was making his way back, he saw a group of Aborigines carrying off the body of another convict, Peter Burn. Burn's clothes were found later, but he was never seen again. A week later a 19-year-old convict, William Okey, was killed while cutting rushes, stuck with several spears and his skull stove in. The body of his companion Samuel Davis was found nearby; he was thought to have died of fright. When Phillip had an enquiry made he was told that the two men had, a few days before, stolen a canoe from some Aborigines; he assumed, probably correctly, that their deaths were revenge killings.

On the following day the Governor, with Surgeon-General White and some marines, was walking not far from Botany Bay, when they came upon a large number of Aborigines – he thought about 300 – who when they saw the white men all got to their feet and armed themselves with spears. Phillip, as was his practice, counselled calm and ordered the marines to fix bayonets, but he himself walked towards the Aborigines unarmed and with his hands open. At this they seemed placated, and accepted a few gifts of fish-hooks, beads and the usual pieces of looking-glass. There was no trouble, but when he returned to Sydney the Governor ordered that no unarmed party of six or fewer men was to go into the woods without protection.

The King's birthday was celebrated traditionally on 4 June, the *Sirius* and *Supply* firing royal salutes at sunrise, midday and sunset. The marines marched out with colours flying and fired three volleys, then returned to enjoy a pint of porter each. The convicts were given half a pint of rum each, four of them who had been in chains for some time on Pinchgut were freed and the officers had the rare pleasure of a glass of wine at two-o'clock lunch with the Governor. Worgan was surprised at the varied fare – mutton, pork, duck, chicken, fish and kangaroo, with salads, pies and preserved fruit, accompanied by port, Madeira and 'good old English porter'.[115] There would have been lamb, but someone had stolen the beast which had been carefully fattened for the occasion. Phillip offered a reward of full emancipation to anyone who would inform against the thief; no one did. After dinner, toasts were drunk to His Majesty, and to the Prince of Wales, the Queen and members of the Government. It was a happy and relaxed party, though the Governor was clearly unwell and in severe pain, despite taking great pains to disguise the fact. It appears almost as though he suffered from a stone in the kidneys, but no medical records have been found to disclose the nature of his recurring illness.

After the party broke up, the officers walked out to see the bonfires the convicts had built for the occasion, around which they were singing and dancing. On Phillip's appearance they gave him three cheers and sang 'God save the King'. He announced that he had pardoned several convicts, and was confident that there was 'not a single heavy heart in that part of the King's dominions.' That statement may have been perhaps a little over-confident, but the occasion was an enjoyable one. Next day, it was found that the colony's prize bull, Gorgon, along with four cows had somehow escaped from their pen and ambled off into the bush.[116] White reported that the officers were 'astonished at the number of thefts which had been committed during the general festivities.' Samuel Peyton and Edward Cormick, in their early twenties, were hanged together for the theft of shirts and stockings from officers' tents; White was intrigued that 'in the agonizing moments of the separation of the soul from the body [they] seemed to embrace each other.' Other convicts inflicted punishment on themselves – one by making his whole week's supply of flour into 18 cakes and eating them all. He died the following day.

Phillip was increasingly unable to avoid inflicting capital punishment. As both convicts and others grew more and more hungry stock was being illegally killed and provisions stolen from huts and tents. The convicts in particular tended to eat almost all their week's rations on the day they received them, and then after a day or two found themselves starving. One or two of the more intelligent among them watched carefully what the Aborigines ate, and found that wild figs and even the flower of the banksias were nourishing. As far as provisions were concerned, things were steadily getting worse. On 4 July Surgeon White wrote formally to the Governor to warn him that 'among the troops, their wives and children, as well as among the convicts who have been ill, the want of necessaries to aid the operation of medicine has been most materially and sensibly felt. My duty leads me to mention this circumstance to your Excellency in order that you may use such means for their procurement as may seem most expedient.' He needed blankets and sheets, sugar, barley, rice, oatmeal, currants, soup and tamarinds to supplement the diet of the sick. Major Ross also insisted that the marines were in need of greatcoats, shoes, needles and thread, scissors and material for making shirts and trousers.

What did they expect Phillip to do? He was not a magician. He could and did appeal to Nepean and Sydney, but even if the Government decided to be generous, it would be some time before goods would reach the country. He sent his dispatches and letters via one of the transports, for on 14 July the *Alexander,* *Borrowdale* and *Friendship* sailed for England, carrying letters from anyone who wished to send them. Everyone in the colony had been busy scribbling. Apart from the official report in his dispatch, Phillip's appeals to Sydney and Nepean were for clothing, good tools and some kitchen equipment – including something from which the convicts could eat – for 171 men and women only 700 wooden bowls and platters had been provided, and most of these were already damaged and unusable.

It was also very important to send to the colony men to oversee the convicts, and if possible a small number of professional carpenters and bricklayers. Without proper surveillance it was impossible to get good work from the convicts, many of whom were indolent, quite apart from those who were now too old, frail or sick to work. Phillip also had the problem, not having been given the details he had so often requested, of having no histories of the convicts, their crimes and sentences, so he did not know how many had years of imprisonment still to serve, or might be due for release within months. He did not say so, but the incompetence of the Home Office had resulted in a number of convicts being sent to New South Wales who were due for release almost before they got there.

Major Ross also wrote a private letter to Nepean on 10 July, complaining about everything, including the Governor: 'I came out without any orders or instructions from your office with respect to the intentions of Government, so I am still ignorant of it, for the Governor has never told me, neither has he ever advised or consulted with me on the subject, and I believe everybody else are in the dark as well as myself, Should his Lordship [Lord Sydney] expect letters from me, I hope you will think the above a sufficient excuse, for I cannot see how I could write without informing him of the manner in which the Governor treats me as Lieut-Governor; and as to the detachment, they have just the same cause for complaint that I have.'

He really did not want to complain, he went on, but Nepean could take his word for it that 'there is not a man in this place but wishes to return home, and indeed they have no less than cause, for I believe there never was a set of people so much upon the parish as this garrison is, and what little wee want, even to a single nail, we must not send to the commissary for it, but must apply to his Excellency, and when we do he always says there is but little come out, and of course it is but little we get, and what we are obliged to take as a mark of favor.' He was utterly pessimistic about the possibility of the settlement ever becoming self-sufficient, for thought corn might grow in New South Wales, he believed it would be at least 100 years before the place could exist without generous support from London, and so 'it will be cheaper to feed the convicts on turtle and venison at the London Tavern than be at the expense of sending them here.'[117]

Ross was also furious that he and the officers received food which was no better than that given the convicts. 'Could I possibly have imagined,' he wrote to a secretary at the Admiralty, 'that I was to be served with, for instance, no more butter than any of the convicts . . . I most certainly would not have left England without supplying myself with that article.' Lieutenant Clark wrote to a friend in Plymouth that 'Major Ross and the

Governor are not on the best of terms. Nor is the former with several of us; he is without exception the most disagreeable commanding officer I ever knew.'

However, it must be admitted that Ross was not the only man to have his doubts about the Governor. Captain James Campbell,[118] a friend and confidant of Ross, told a friend in England:

> 7I do not think your three kingdoms could produce another man, in my opinion, so totally unqualified for the business he has taken in hand, as this man is . . . there is hardly a day in which the orders of the preceding are not contradicted, men are taken from one piece of work before it is well begun and sent to another which is again left in the same state – I must here except such things as are actually carrying on for himself, which are never suffered to be interfered with. Everything that can be got hold of is appropriated to his own use. He is selfish beyond measure, in so much that even the public stores sent out, as we suppose, for the benefit of the colony at large, are, as far as possible by this strange character, looked upon as private property . . .[119]

Both Ross and Campbell particularly disliked what they saw as Phillip's secretiveness, though he had made an effort to disclose to Ross his thinking about the settlement and its future. Ross clearly thought he should be privy to every turn of the Governor's mind, and that was never going to happen.

# TEN

In his first dispatch to Lord Sydney,[120] Phillip showed that he had been giving some time to the planning of the future town of Sydney. Life in the colony was still extremely uncomfortable, but the Governor knew that conditions would improve – they must – and he instructed his Surveyor-General, Augustus Alt, to work with him on a scheme for the future design of the town.

Young Arthur Bowes assisted by sketching a map of its present layout. This still exists, dated July 1788 – the first real map of Sydney. It shows the vestigial town as it then was, with Bowes' observatory marked (at the spot where its successor now stands, near the south end of the bridge), and ground set aside for 'a small house for the Governor' and for Government House itself. It also shows a house for the Lieutenant Governor, for storehouses, a hospital, a church, a nine-acre farm (in Farm Cove) and temporary barracks and huts. Bowes also marks 'ground intended for buildings hereafter', more or less on the present site of George Street, and the line of 'the principal street' a little to the west.

There was a long way to go, but the Governor assured Lord Sydney that good bricks were now available so that building could go ahead, and that he intended to work to a firm plan. 'I have endeavoured to place all public buildings', he wrote, 'in situations that will be eligible hereafter, and to give a sufficient share of ground for the stores, hospitals, &c, to be enlarged, as may be necessary in the future. The principal streets are placed so as to admit a free circulation of air, and are two hundred feet wide . . . and as the ground that runs to the southward is nearly level, and a very good situation for buildings, streets will be laid out in such a manner as to afford a free air, and when the houses are built . . . the land will be granted with a clause that will for ever prevent more than one house being built on the allotment, which will be sixty feet in front and 150 feet in depth. This will preserve uniformity in the buildings, prevent narrow streets, and the many inconveniences which the increase of inhabitants would otherwise occasion hereafter.' This excellent plan nevertheless collapsed not long after Phillip left Sydney, when the association between town planning and greed became irresistible.

The Governor proposed that the main streets should run to the south-east, allowing the prevailing winds to aerate the city. The main street as shown in Bowes' plan was to begin at the south-west end of the marines' parade-ground, near the present-day corner of George and Bridge streets, and run for 550 feet to meet another street at right angles near the northern end of what is now Wynyard Street. Phillip intended the Governor's house and the criminal court to be built here, looking down the main street. Another street was planned to run from near that spot to the water's edge at Darling Harbour, with yet another intersecting it near the east end of Barrack Street. A church was planned for a site at the border of the parade ground, roughly at the intersection of the present Harrington and Argyle streets.

Meanwhile with winter approaching more practical matters were pressing: the housing situation remained to be seriously addressed. It was impossible at the moment to think seriously of Sydney as more than a camp. As an anonymous convict woman wrote to a friend in England:

We have now two streets, if four rows of the most miserable huts you can possibly conceive of deserve that name. Windows they have none, as from the Governor's house etc. now finished, no glass could be spared, so that lattices of twigs are made by our people to supply their place. At the extremity of the lines, where since our arrival the dead are buried, there is a place called the church yard; but we hear as soon as a sufficient number of bricks can be made a church is to be built and named St Phillip after the Governor.[121]

Public buildings of a sort were in fact rising fairly quickly – by March Alt had already designed and built a wharf on the east point of Sydney Cove and landed some ordnance there; he had also seen to the erection of a large storehouse – 100 by 25 feet, with a thatched roof. This was a calculated risk: no one had given a thought to the combustible quality of thatch until in July when the roof of the blacksmith's shop caught fire and many valuable tools were lost. A law was then passed making it illegal to have a chimney in any house with a thatched roof. This did not contribute to the comfort of any home, especially as the winter was a cold and particularly blustery one, with the temperature sometimes falling to 10° at noon. Phillip wrote to Nepean requesting leather for shoes and material for clothes: 'Shooes here last but a very short time, and the want of these materials, and thread to mend the cloathing, will render it impossible to make them serve more than half the time for which they were intended. This country requires warm cloathing in the winter; the rains are frequent and the nights very cold.'[122]

August started with rain-storms so severe that all work had to stop for some days. The brick-kiln fell in under the torrent and a large number of bricks was destroyed. The rain did not, however, dampen the spirits of two assistant surgeons, White and Balmain, who drank the health of the Prince of Wales too freely on His Royal Highness's birthday, quarrelled, went out into the dark night and fired five rounds of shot in each other's general direction, the only result being a slight flesh wound to Balmain's thigh. Phillip, intervened (at some risk) and told them to concentrate on bleeding their patients rather than each other.

The end of the month was enlivened by another farcical incident. While Phillip was away on one of his expeditions in the area, a convict, James Daley, violently excited the colony by claiming that he had found gold, producing a lump of earth which indeed seemed to have veins of gold running through it. Questioned by Captain Campbell he said he would be pleased to disclose the site of the alleged gold-mine on condition that he received free pardons for himself and the woman with whom he was living. Campbell believed him, and Daly led the captain and a party of marines across the harbour and into the bush. He then retired behind some trees 'to do his business', doubled back, took the boat and returned to Sydney where he reported that the captain had been astonished by the richness of the vein of gold and had sent him back to secure a stronger guard.

Phillip would surely have been suspicious had he been there, but Daly was generally believed, and was just setting out with more marines when Campbell and the first guard returned having tramped back overland. Seeing them approaching, Daly took off into the bush again, but was driven back by hunger and was arrested. When Phillip returned he sent Daly with another lieutenant to the place where the convict said he had found the gold. There was nothing to be seen, and Daly confessed that he had made the 'gold' himself by melting down some old brass buckles. He was given 300 lashes and made to wear a coat branded with a large 'R' for Rogue. No one could fathom why he had invented so ludicrous a story, and he kept mum even some months later when he was hanged for burglary. The incident does illustrate how important Phillip's common sense was to the colony.

Aside from these minor incidents, which Phillip may have

regarded as light relief, he was increasingly preoccupied with the problem not only of housing but of feeding and clothing the colony. At the end of September 1788 the commissary contained only 15 weeks' ration of rice, and though there was enough pork for 128 weeks the beef stock would last for only 43 weeks, and there was scarcely sufficient flour for a year. There was no news of the prospect of any further rations from England. On 2 October he sent the *Sirius* off to the Cape of Good Hope with instructions to buy flour, and on the same day the *Golden Grove* set out for Norfolk Island with a number of convicts on board: fewer mouths to feed at Sydney – more for Tench, overseas. In his dispatch to England in July the Governor emphasised again what he had said before – that 'a regular supply of provisions from England will be necessary for four or five years, as the crops for two years to come cannot be depended on for more than what will be necessary for seed, and what the *Sirius* may procure can only be to breed from. Should necessity oblige us to make use of what that ship may be able to procure, I do not apprehend that the live stock she will bring in twelve months will be more than a month's provision for the colony.'[123]

In the meantime, he sought out land where crops might grow rather better than they did in Sydney cove. At the beginning of November he and a number of officers went up to the east end of the harbour and on up a river to a hill which was surrounded by clear, only sparsely wooded land the soil of which seemed promising. Moreover it was, as Captain Collins noticed, 'free from that rock which everywhere covered the surface at Sydney Cove, and unobstructed by underwood.' Phillip named the hill Rose Hill, after an official at the Treasury in London.[124] He decided to start up a settlement there, initially with 10 convicts, mainly those who had shown an interest in and talent for cultivating the land, and with Captain Campbell in charge.

But in his letters to Nepean in particular, Phillip begins to sound almost desperate about food supplies: when he says in a letter to Nepean that 'I make no doubt but that supplies will arrive in time, and on which alone I depend', it is difficult to believe that he was really convinced that his appeal would receive a speedy response. Speed, in any case, was relative where voyages between England and the antipodes were concerned. Phillip also confided in Nepean that there was a shortage of decent clothing: much of that which had been supplied and brought out on the transports had proved too small for the average man or woman and they had no needles or thread with which to alter them. Warm clothing really was a prerequisite: the nights were now very cold. Surely Nepean would agree that some kind of clothing was desirable for the children?

He began to take unusual measures. He gave the convicts Saturdays off in order that they could forage for food where they might find it. This was in fact rather dangerous, for relations with the Aborigines were getting steadily worse – exacerbated by the convicts stealing fish, fishing lines, canoes and anything else they fancied. There had been a number of particularly vicious murders – convict Cooper Handley had been attacked while collecting wild vegetables and 'murdered and mutilated in a shocking manner'. Altogether, eleven male and one female convicts had vanished since they landed; it was more than likely that they had been killed. Others had been stripped and severely beaten. Hunger persuaded even the most fearful to take their chance, and not allowed to carry arms several took the precaution of shaping sticks like muskets and using them to frighten off attackers. Phillip remained sturdily of the view that the convicts were probably responsible for their own deaths. The extent to which he took the part of the Aborigines against the convicts is a tribute to his real attempt to respect the original occupants of the land, even when it was seriously strained.

When two rush-cutting men had been killed, in May, he was sure that their deaths had been in some way the result of their own actions, but thought it well to establish contact if possible with the responsible tribe, if only to try to recover the rush-cutters' tools, which had been taken. The day after the killings he went with a small party of marines to the spot where the incident had occurred, but marched for 20 miles without seeing a single native – their talent for concealment may simply have meant that they were observing him without being seen. The party slept on the beach just north of Botany Bay. Next morning they found 20 canoes drawn up on the beach, but not a soul in sight. They began to return towards Sydney, and suddenly came across an assembly of Aborigines.

'I had barely time to order the party to halt before numbers appeared in arms,' Phillip wrote, 'and the foremost of them, as he advanced, made signs for us to retire, but upon my going up to him, making signs of friendship, he gave his spear to another, and in less than three minutes we were surrounded by two hundred and twelve men, numbers of women and children were at a small distance, and whether by their superiority of numbers, for we were only twelve, or from their not being accustomed to act with treachery, the moment friendship I offered was accepted on their side they joined us, most of them laying down their spears and stone hatchets with the greatest confidence, and afterwards brought down some of their women to receive the little articles we had to give them. I saw noting to induce me to believe these people had been concerned in the murther which had been committed.'[125]

Once again Phillip's confidence and bravery had resulted in avoiding a confrontation; as he himself supposed, had he marched his men towards the group of Aborigines violence would almost certainly have been the result. He was more than ever convinced of 'the necessity of placing a confidence in these people as the only means of avoiding a dispute.' His view had always been that it should be possible to establish a perfectly amiable relationship with the people whose land he had been instructed to appropriate, and if this now seems to us surprising we must see it in the context of the expansionist era to which he belonged, and give him the credit for his attitude. His approach may have been paternal, but it was entirely positive. Moreover, from the start he actually *liked* the Aborigines he met – he trusted them, and did his best to get them to trust him. Certainly sometimes this was rather naive, as when noticing that several of the men had had a tooth knocked out in the centre of their jaw, he opened his own mouth to show that he too had a tooth missing, believing that this would in some way show him to be one of them.

Most of his officers, on the other hand, tended to regard the Aborigines either as sources of gentle amusement or as interesting specimens of a previously unknown genus, to be studied as one might study a fossil. The exception was the intelligent Watkin Tench, who managed to an extent to combine Phillip's view with his own, which was that the Aborigines were a species of human being the only bar to whose adaptation to 'civilised behaviour' was that they had previously had no one to teach them their manners. Again, we must take this in the context of the times. When he remarked on the 'hideousness' of their appearance, the ugliness of their wearing a fish-bone stuck through their nose, their inability to build even the roughest huts in which to live and the 'despicable' design of their canoes it was because he was genuinely appalled that a race of human beings should have failed to evolve into a more civilised state. This made him unable to share the Governor's more optimistic view, and to a degree he was right.

By December 1788, many of the marines and some of the officers had come seriously to mistrust the natives, while the convicts had become almost hysterical. On the 18th, for instance, when a crowd of them approached Sydney, someone rushed to Government House to tell Phillip that 2,000 Aborigines were about to attack. Someone else followed to report the appearance of 400. Finally, it turned out that about 50 had approached the brick-kilns, but had run away when the convicts working there pointed their shovels at them like guns.

It was just after Christmas that Phillip decided to capture one of the Aborigines in order that he and some of his officers might learn to speak the native language. On 30 December he sent off two boats under the marine lieutenants Ball and Johnson, with instructions to them to capture two or three natives. They rowed over to Manly, where they approached a small group of Aborigines, distributed a few paltry presents and then seized two men. The rest ran away, but then returned desperate to rescue their friends. One got away, but the other was carried off, the boats rowed away under a hail of spears, stones and anything else that could be thrown at them. The captive was tied to the thwarts of the boat, shrieking loudly at first, but then quietened by a little cooked fish which was offered him.

When he was landed at Sydney and immediately surrounded by a curious crowd, his agitation returned, but when some order had been restored he quietened down again and it was noticed that he was curious at all he saw, and was particularly courteous to the women who spoke to him. He was taken to Government House, terrified at the sound of the door-bell, astonished at the upper storey, enabling men to walk about on top of each other, and fascinated (Watkin Tench says) by the life-size portrait of the Duchess of Cumberland, pointing to it and exclaiming 'woman!'

At dinner Phillip sat his captive down at a side-table, where he ate fish and duck with an appetite, was highly suspicious of bread and salt, and rejected any form of alcohol.

Discouraged from wiping his hands on the seat of his chair, he used a napkin 'with great cleanliness and decency.' In the afternoon the Governor had his prisoner's hair cut, which he would not accept until he had seen someone else subjected to it, but was then rather pleased at the operation – eating with enthusiasm, until dissuaded, the nits and lice which emerged from the hair cuttings. He was less delighted to be immersed in a tub of hot water and thoroughly washed. Tench assisted at the operation, 'in order that I mighty ascertain the real colour of skin of these people.' He reckoned that they were as black as the lighter African negroes (and indeed when the Aborigines caught sight of the negro prisoners they thought they must be of their own tribes).

Clean, and reluctantly wearing a shirt, jacket and pair of trousers, the prisoner was now tethered by a handcuff and a rope fastened to his wrist. Touchingly, he at first was delighted with what he thought an honour, but then swiftly became furious when he realised it was to restrain his movement. Though led by a convict he was given considerable freedom of movement, and at night, given his own hut, he settled down with what appeared to be resignation, and slept.

The Governor and most of the officers celebrated the coming of 1789 by lunching on fish and pork, entertained by music played in a neighbouring room, after which (Tench tells us) one of the company sang several songs 'in a very soft and superior style.' The single member of the company who did not appreciate the entertainment was the captured Aboriginal – whom Phillip had named Manly, but who was later known as Arabanoo, an approximation to his Aboriginal name. He nevertheless enjoyed the meal, though he was inclined to throw his plate out of the window when he had finished. Dissuaded, he sighed, lay down on the top of a chest, put his hat under his head, and fell asleep. Later, he was wakened and rowed over to Manly, where he saw several of his friends. The intention was that he should convince them that no violence had been done to him and that he had been treated well. The marines with him did not understand what was said, but he talked to his friends for some time, and was sad and depressed when he was returned to Sydney. However, he had recovered by dinner time, when he ate two kangaroo rats each the size of a rabbit, and three pounds of fish.

Never a man to allow imagination or day-dreaming to affect him, Phillip had few hopes for the coming year other than that at some time fresh supplies of food and clothing might arrive from England. He meant in the meantime to concentrate on improving the home production of food, particularly at Rose Hill, and exploring the so far unknown country around the settlements. In Sydney itself life continued very much as usual, except that there was a considerable increase in crime. Much of this was naturally connected with the shortage of food and clothing. In January alone Rebecca Holmes was given 50 lashes for stealing a shirt while her friend and accomplice Mary Marshall suffered the ignominy of being stripped and led behind a cart. George Legg received 100 lashes for stealing two chickens, and Thomas Sanderson was hanged for robbing the storehouse. While he was being hanged, another convict was lashed for an assault on a woman. All this took place in the first 10 days of the new year, and before January was over John Russell received 300 lashes for assaulting two women, Thomas Tennant was given 200 for stealing a shirt and Tamasin Allen 50 for buying it from him. Two convicts were lashed for being drunk, another received 300 lashes for stealing beans from the farm and another 75 for being drunk on a Sunday.

Some of this treatment seems out of key with Phillip's former attitude to crime and punishment, but he had gradually convinced himself that there was no alternative to strictness if the colony was to be kept under control, and he set out a number of rules which may seem unusual – for instance, making it a punishable offence to buy or sell anything, arguing that 'those who sell their own provisions must support themselves by stealing from others'. Incidentally, Arabanoo was horrified at the spectacle of men being whipped so severely on their bare backs that not only were they literally skinned, but the muscle and in the worst cases even the bone was exposed: he understood that this was a punishment, but could not understand the cruelty of it, and (Tench says) 'display'd symptoms of disgust and terror.'

It was not only the convicts who were driven to theft by hunger. At the end of March six marines were hanged for robbing the public stores of flour, meat, spirits, tobacco and other things. They had got hold of and copied keys to three different doors, and arranged among themselves that when one of them was on sentry duty at the stores, two or more others would come and help themselves. The sentry would lock the door behind them, so that if there was an inspection it would appear as if everything were secure. Unfortunately for them, one member of the gang was greedy, and when on duty opened the store himself; he was disturbed, and in his panic broke the key in the lock. The gang attempted to get a blacksmith to mend the lock, but he recognised the key as belonging to one of the group, Hunt, who in turn betrayed the others in exchange for clemency. The six men were hanged together, with 'hardly a marine present but what shed tears, officers and men.'[126]

At least now the summer weather had eased the clothing problem – there was little need for any, and some of the convicts went almost as naked as the Aborigines. The marines, however, were forced to remain in uniform, and with the temperature rarely below 25° (on one day it reached 40° at midday) they were extremely uncomfortable. The convicts who had to try to till the ground using hoes and picks (they had no ploughs) worked sluggishly, unaware that the season was quite wrong for cultivation, the dry earth dusty and crumbling. The heat was uncomfortable too for those who were sick, and there were several deaths in the hospital, including that of Captain Shea. Major Ross reported the death to the Governor, who assumed that the senior lieutenant, First-Lieutenant George Johnson, then Phillip's adjutant, would take over Shea's detachment.

Whether he said anything about this to Ross is an open question, but Ross immediately offered the detachment to Captain Collins. This can only have been done to annoy Phillip, for if Collins had accepted the post he would have had to resign his position as Judge-Advocate, which would have put the Governor in an extremely awkward position. Fortunately, Collins, who was a supporter of the Governor (though a testy one), declined Ross' offer, but the incident added to the already irritated relationship between the Governor and the marine commander.

Another and terrible problem arose in April. Hearing that an Aboriginal family was ill, Phillip and a small party which included Arabanoo himself rowed to the cove where they lay. They found a dead woman and little girl, with an old man and a boy still alive. These were carried back to the settlement and placed in a hut near the hospital, where the old man almost immediately died. The boy recovered, and was adopted by the Surgeon-General, John White. Arabanoo nursed the old man and boy so devotedly that Phillip decided that he should be set free of his shackles. But not for long: in May he himself died of the smallpox. A rather remarkable relationship had grown up between himself and Phillip: the Governor ordered that Arabanoo, who had been particularly attentive when Phillip himself was in pain, as he frequently was – should be buried in his own garden, and he attended the funeral. Tench may to an extent have seen the Aboriginal through rose-coloured spectacles, for he was one of those few who really desired a good

relationship between the settlers and the natives, but he saw
Arabanoo as a man who also desired such a relationship: 'His
fidelity and gratitude particularly to his friend the Governor were
constant and undeviating, and deserve to be recorded. Although
of a gentle and placable nature, we early discovered that he was
impatient of indignity, and allowed of no superiority on our part
. . . If the slightest insult were offered to him, he would return it
with interest. At retaliation of merriment he was often happy;
and frequently turned the laugh against his antagonist.'[127]

Most of the people in the colony thought that the smallpox
must be, as Gidley King put it, 'a distemper natural to the
country.' However there is no doubt that it was brought to New
South Wales by someone from England, and within a relatively
short time it killed almost half the Indigenous population of
the area. Tench records how 'repeated accounts were brought
by our boats of finding bodies of the Indians in all the coves
and inlets of the harbour', and many were found floating on
the tide or left unburied in rock shelters. It is said that by
the end of 1791 only three members of the Cadigal people
remained alive. The damage done by smallpox, together with
that inflicted by venereal disease and other serious infections
such as influenza and typhoid, and later alcohol, was of course
entirely unconscious, but none the less one of the most terrible
effects of the coming of the white people to New South Wales.
Though Phillip mentions it nowhere in his dispatches, he was
too intelligent a man not to have been conscious of the fact.

Meanwhile, once again the tension between himself and
Major Ross was building to a climax. At the trial of the six
marines, evidence had been given by a convict woman, Mary
Turner. It was suspected that she perjured herself, but the Judge-
Advocate decided that there was not sufficient evidence to prove
this, and released her. Seeing her at liberty, Captain Campbell
remonstrated. Collins told him that if he felt strongly about

the matter, he should prosecute her himself. Outraged at what he considered an insult, Campbell wrote to Collins formally refusing to sit on any criminal court in future, with a copy to his friend Major Ross. Ross immediately convened a meeting of marine officers and, as Phillip put it in a dispatch, addressed them 'in a manner calculated to induce them to join Capt. Campbell in declining the duty of the criminal courts, saying that he had told the Governor that both he and the officers at large considered that service as what they had volunteer'd, not as a duty; that the Governor's conduct in calling on Capt. Campbell or on officers for that service was oppressive, and that he thought it hard officers should be obliged to sit as members of the criminal court, and oppressive to the highest degree.'[128]

Placed in a difficult position, Phillip persuaded Collins to apologise and wrote to the officers pointing out that it was their duty to assist the court, but agreed to Ross's demand that there should be a proper enquiry into whether there was a legal requirement for his officers to sit as members of a criminal court. This was long and tedious, and the transcript was sent to London for a final decision. A reply did not arrive in Sydney until July 1791, when a successor to Lord Sydney (who had by then retired) gave his opinion that officers serving in New South Wales *were* legally required to sit as members of the criminal court when summoned to do so, and that they would be guilty of a misdemeanour if they refused. 'The proceedings of Maj. Ross according to your representation appear to have been in many instances but ill-calculated to promote . . . good understanding,' Lord Grenville added. Phillip and Collins were vindicated, but at the expense of worsening relationships with Ross and Campbell.

In the evening of 8 May, the *Sirius* anchored off Sydney, returned from the Cape with 127,000 pounds of flour for the settlement and enough stores to feed her crew for a year, though on short commons. Lieutenant Bradley, looking out from the deck as the ship sailed in, was surprised and appalled to see 'the great number of dead natives in every part of the harbour.' Captain Hunter invited the Governor to dine on board, and he was accompanied by Arabanoo on what was probably his last excursion. The captain was naturally interested to see how the colony had fared during an absence of over 18 months, and was impressed by the little settlement at Rose Hill. More land had been cultivated than he had expected and there seemed every prospect of success, though the lack of a regular water supply might make for difficulties.

On 2 June, the King's Birthday was celebrated with volleys from the marines, 21 gun salutes from the ships in the harbour, and dinner at Government House – into which Phillip had very recently moved. There was also a remarkable event – the production of the first play to be seen in New South Wales. Sadly, we know virtually nothing about the production or who was involved in it, but we can make a few guesses: for instance, perhaps the single piano brought to the colony – owned and played by Surgeon Worgan – was carefully carried down to the hut where the performance took place in order to add its voice to those of the actors. As to the play itself, though it may seem a little surprising that the text of George Farquahar's *The Recruiting Officer* had found its way to New South Wales in the first place, we can make a guess at its provenance. We know that Lieutenant Clark spent much time reading while on the voyage out, and though his choice of reading matter was rather Catholic (he enjoyed the stories in copies of a women's magazine) he certainly possessed a copy of *Lady Jane Grey* by Nicholas Rowe, first produced in 1715,[129] so it is by no means unlikely that he also had a copy of Farquhar's play.

In any case, *The Recruiting Officer* was a piece which will have commended itself to the more literate convicts – first produced in 1806, it is a story about a press gang's visit to a country town, and the author clearly knew something about the procedure. Captain Plume makes love to the women in order to secure their followers as recruits and outdo his rival, Captain Brazen, while Sergeant Kite poses as an astrologer for the same purpose. Sadly, we have practically no details about the production – not the single name of an actor or actress, no idea who was responsible for the production. Captain Collins simply tells us that 'in the evening some of the convicts were permitted to perform Farquhar's comedy of the Recruiting Officer, in a hut fitted up for the occasion. They professed no higher aim than humbly to excite a smile, and their efforts to please were not unattended with applause.'[130] Tench is a little more forthcoming:

The anniversary of His Majesty's birth-day was celebrated, as heretofore, at the government-house, with loyal festivity. In the evening, the play of *The Recruiting Officer* was performed by a party of convicts, and honoured by the presence of his excellency, and the officers of the garrison. That every opportunity of escape from the dreariness and dejection of our situation should be eagerly embraced, will not be wondered at. The exhilarating effect of a splendid theatre is well-known: and I am not ashamed to confess, that the proper distribution of three or four yards of stained paper, and a dozen farthing candles stuck around the mud walls of a convict-hut, failed not to diffuse general complacency on the countenances of sixty persons, of various descriptions, who were assembled to applaud the representation. Some of the actors acquitted themselves with great spirit, and received the praises of the audience: a prologue and an epilogue, written by one of the performers, were also spoke on the occasion;

which, although not worth inserting here, contained some tolerable allusions to the situation of the parties, and the novelty of a stage-representation in New South Wales.[131]

Sadly, the prologue and epilogue did not survive, although for many years it was believed that it did, and some lines supposed to be from it became famous:

*From distant climes o'er wide-spread seas we come,*
*Though not with much éclat or beat of drum,*
*True patriots all; for be it understood,*
*We left our country for our country's good;*
*No private views disgrac'd our generous zeal,*
*What urg'd our travels was our country's weal,*
*And none will doubt but that our emigration*
*Has prov'd most useful to the British nation.*

The story was put about in London that these patronizing lines had been spoken before the play, by George Barrington, a famous pick-pocket, who was not even in the colony at the time. They were written in fact by a journalist, Henry Carter, considerably after the event.

Meanwhile, Phillip had to see to other practical matters, including the repair of the *Sirius*, which had run into a serious gale on her voyage back from the Cape and been severely damaged. The Governor ordered her to be taken to Elbow Cove to be careened for repairs. Elbow Cove, on the north shore, later became Careening Cove, then Sirius Bay, and still later was renamed Mosman Bay. One or two Aborigines were seen as she came in, but this was one of the areas where the smallpox had done its fatal work, and there were very few still alive. A temporary wharf was built, some sawpits dug, and a piece of ground was levelled to make working easier. The cleaning of the *Sirius's* bottom, removal of barnacles and replacing of damaged woodwork took from June to November.

Weighed down as he was by the problems of the settlement, Phillip took the opportunity, during 1789, to make or order a number of expeditions. These were infuriatingly described by Major Ross as 'parties of pleasure,' which was spectacularly far from the truth. What they were, in fact, was a series of attempts to find land more suitable for farming than what was so far known. The Governor had hoped for some time to discover a large river around which pastoral land might lie, and this year he was to find it. He set out on 6 June with Captain Collins and a party which included Hunter, Captain Johnstone, Worgan and a large troop of marines. They were rowed across to Manly, and walked to Broken Bay, sending the boats on ahead in the care of Captain Keltie to meet them at Pittwater.

A few natives were fishing from the shore as the party landed, but all made off except for one 'poor naked creature' – a young girl who was trying to conceal herself in the long, wet grass. Using a few phrases they had learned from Arabanoo they managed to quiet her fears. They lit a fire and warmed her, then shot some birds, roasted them and made her eat. She had vanished by morning, but next evening, when they returned from exploring around Pittwater, they found her again, cowering in a small makeshift hut and nursing a child. They did their best to make the hut watertight and built another fire for her and the baby. By this time she was confident that they meant her no harm, and showed gratitude for what was done for her. All this we can be fairly sure was mainly encouraged by Phillip, who now almost alone retained his conviction that kindness and friendliness would bring about good relationships with the Aborigines.

Next day the party set off again and spent several days in and around Broken Bay, finding one opening which looked like evidence of a river. They rowed up-river for some 20 miles, with the land around shelved between the water and 'immense perpendicular hills of barren, rocky lands with trees growing from between the rocky cliffs.'[132] By this time provisions were running so low that they had to retrace their journey and return to Sydney, to set out again on 28 June and return to the river. On reaching Richmond Hill they climbed it to see a long range of mountains below which, in front of them, was a valley through which Phillip believed an extensive river must surely run, though they had again to return to Sydney without reaching it (Phillip was later to name it the Hawkesbury, after a minister in the Government back in London).

The expedition ended on 14 July, when the party reached Middle Harbour but had no means of taking to the water. They did find two Aboriginal canoes, in which they thought two men might make their way around to Elbow Bay, but the flimsy vessels collapsed as soon as the men got into them. Phillip then proposed that they should simply march on, but several of the party were in no state to do so, and Captain Hunter was barefoot, his shoes having fallen to pieces. Two of the marines volunteered to swim, possibly from Clontarf to the Spit – about 400 yards – and after drinking a dram of spirits they plunged in. An hour and a half later they reached the *Sirius*, and a boat was sent to pick up the Governor and the rest of the party.

By coincidence, Captain Tench was at the same time making his way towards the Hawkesbury, or a branch of it, which Phillip was to name the Nepean. Tench had been appointed commander of the settlement at Rose Hill and was disappointed not to have been able to accompany Phillip in his expedition. Finding that the settlement could go on working perfectly well without him, he set out on 26 June with Assistant-Surgeon Thomas Arndell, Assistant-Surgeon Lowes (surgeon's mate on the *Sirius*), two marines and a single convict, to see what new landscape he could discover. His expedition was at first not especially rewarding – 'trackless immeasurable desert, in awful silence . . . Save that a melancholy crow now and then flew croaking overhead or a kangaroo was seen to bound at a distance, the picture of solitude was complete and undisturbed.'[133] On the following day, however, they quite suddenly found themselves on the bank of a fine river, 'nearly as broad as the Thames at Putney, and apparently of great depth.' Though they saw no Aborigines, there was obviously a large population, for there were signs of them everywhere – huts, snares, decoys and canoes.

There was one more major attempt at exploration during 1789 – in December Phillip sent a party under lieutenants Dawes and Johnston to cross the Nepean and to try to reach the Carmarthen mountains. Lowes led the party in Tench's footsteps from Rose Hill to the river, which they managed to cross, then struggled onward through trying country in fearful heat, managing only to make about 15 miles a day. Eventually, though they managed to get further inland than anyone previously (just over 50 miles from the sea), they gave up and returned to Sydney.

One of the problems now preoccupying Phillip was the one which he had suspected would arise: a number of convicts, having quite naturally kept careful records of time passing, came to him and argued that they had served their sentence and should be made free men. Despite his best attempts, the Governor had not been given the records of the convicts that sailed with him. The only thing he felt he could do was to direct the Judge-Advocate to take affidavits from the men and women concerned, swearing that they had served the term prescribed by the law. He advised them that the best thing they could do was to 'work for the public until some information was received from the government' – this was satisfactory to none.

Meanwhile the stealing of food and clothing went on unabated, as did the punishments: William Boggis took 100 lashes on his bare buttocks for stealing a shirt (he was also made to work in irons, and labelled with the word 'thief'); Carolina Laycock was to be 'publicly whipped with 50 lashes on her bare body' for aiding and abetting him. Two men endured 150 lashes for buying 'necessaries' from a marine, while another received 100 lashes for selling fish which he had caught for the hospital. All this took place within only two days.

On a more positive note, the Governor had approved the rebuilding of Dawes's tented observatory in stone, so that the young amateur astronomer could further his observations.

With August came the establishment of what in effect was the first police force in New South Wales. The proposal came from a convict, William Harris, who went to Phillip and proposed that a 'night-watch' should be set up, selected from among the more dependable convicts. The Judge-Advocate rather reluctantly assented: it might have been wished to make up the watch from free men, he said, rather than from 'a body of men in whose eyes, it could not be denied, the property of individuals had never before been sacred. But there was not any choice. . . It might, however, be supposed, that among the convicts there must be many who would feel a pride in being distinguished from their fellows, and a pride that might give birth to a returning principle of honesty. It was hoped that the convicts whom we had chosen were of this description.'

Phillip concurred, and he and the Judge-Advocate between them drew up the regulations. There would be twelve watchmen, divided into four parties, to patrol throughout the night and take up anyone suspected of nefarious intent, detaining anyone seen about the settlement after tattoo had been beaten. The convicts' quarters were divided into sections, each of which was allotted to one watchman, and any person who had been robbed should report the robbery to the watchman responsible for his area. We can suspect that Phillip was responsible for the clause which states that watchmen are never to receive any fee or gratuity from any individual whatever – 'but their diligence and good behaviour will be rewarded by the Governor.'

Major Ross and the marines, as may be guessed, were appalled at the idea, but Phillip insisted, and in the end even the Judge-Advocate agreed that the night-watch was 'of infinite utility . . . they were instrumental in bringing forward for punishment several offenders who would otherwise have escaped.' If they were hated by the marines, they were of course equally loathed by their fellow-convicts, which itself was a tribute to their honesty and assiduity. In fact, Collins thought that London was not better guarded than Sydney, and as Phillip pointed out to Lord Sydney in February, three months after the watch was set up, not a single robbery occurred.

The establishment of the police force came at the right time: more food was being stolen or wrongfully bought and sold than ever before – the consequence of the Governor reducing the weekly rations – from eight pounds of flour a week per person to five pounds five ounces, from five pounds of salt pork to three pounds five ounces, and from three pints of peas to two. Butter had now run out completely (no great loss, Collins thought; it had never been very good). Phillip believed that with these reduced rations, the settlement could now hold out until June 1790.

His spirits would have lifted had he known that on 12 September HMS *Guardian* set sail from England with supplies for the colony, including 2,250 pounds of dried soup, 3,000 pounds of brown sugar, 3,000 pounds of currants, 4,433 pounds of pearl barley, 900 pairs of men's and 600 pairs of women's shoes, 1,500 pounds of leather for soling shoes, 600 pairs of women's stockings, 900 men's hats, 225 hammocks and 600 *pallaisses* and other goods and medicines. Of course he could not know this was coming, and on 1 November reduced the rations for men again – officers, marines, sailors and convicts – by two-thirds. The women's ration was not reduced – they were already on two-thirds of the men's ration, and many of them were either nursing babies, or had children who would have been quite capable of eating their mother's rations as well as their own.

Not only were some food supplies dangerously near to running out altogether but there was now a giant problem with rats – at one point they destroyed eight whole casks of flour. The colony now had a number of dogs, including, it appears, some domesticated dingoes, which were a help in keeping the rat population down in the area of the stores – but the vermin simply turned their attention to the gardens and farm, where they very much enjoyed the growing corn.

Collins sympathised with the Governor, of whom he said that 'his humanity was at all times conspicuous', but the shortening of rations yet again resulted in complaints from a good number of officers and men who suspected that he had quietly stockpiled food for himself and his favourites – Ross, of course, took this and every other opportunity to irritate and annoy the Governor. When, for instance, a convict came to him to inform him that his time had expired, the Major replied: 'Would to God my time was expired too.' On that occasion Phillip did somewhat lose his patience, and wrote to Ross asking that he 'would be so good as to be a little more guarded in your expressions, for I am certain you will think on reflection that the answer you gave to the convict . . . was not calculated to make him satisfied with his situation.'[134]

Ross's continual sniping at the Governor was not the result of excessive zeal alone, though he was certainly sufficiently zealous, and from that point of view an excellent if unprepossessing officer. His fuse, however, was far too short, and explosions were frequent – as when in early November the watch unlawfully (in the Major's opinion) arrested a marine who had been wandering about after dark, and according to practice put him in the guard-house until morning. Ross immediately sent his adjutant to the Judge-Advocate to protest that 'he considered a soldier being stopped, when not committing any unlawful act, as an insult offered to the corps, and that they would not suffer themselves to be treated in that manner, or be controuled by the convicts, while they had bayonets in their hands.'

As soon as Phillip heard of the protest, he sent for Ross to point out that it was entirely proper for the watch to stop a sailor or soldier found at night in the convicts' camp or some other suspicious place, and pointed to an article in the regulations which stated unequivocally that 'any soldier or seaman found straggling after the tattoo has beat, or who may be found in the convicts' huts, is to be detained.' He also emphasised that the frequent robberies which had previously been a problem had now stopped, and that most of them had in fact been carried out by soldiers. Ross simply repeated that the incident was an insult to the corps, and that if the Governor had anything else to say he must say it to him next day, in the presence of two officers. Phillip cannily replied that Ross should perhaps bring all his officers with him – knowing perfectly well that the majority of the Major's officers regarded him with less than affection. Ross immediately caved in, and nothing more was heard of the matter, but it was another needless irritation for the hard-pressed Governor to endure.[135]

The situation was really very difficult: there were only 18 officers in the corps, and in February one was on duty at Norfolk Island, another seemed to be permanently attached to Major Ross and to do nothing in particular, five had been put under arrest and were performing their duties under the threat of a court-martial and another two were temporarily suspended, accused of 'unofficerlike behaviour'. The adjutant and quarter-master disliked Ross, who equally disliked them both; the Major had complained of the Judge-Advocate's conduct, who had complained to Phillip of being publicly denigrated by Ross and wished to resign his post. Captain Hunter, who acted as an assistant to the Judge-Advocate when needed, thought himself so badly treated by Major Ross that he too had made an official complaint to the Governor and asked to be excused duty. Ross, meanwhile, had accused Phillip of absenting himself from Sydney to go on 'parties of pleasure' into the country – his description of the Governor's expeditions of exploration or visits to Rose Hill.

Phillip was understandably driven to complain bitterly to Nepean of the Lieutenant-Governor's attitude to him. He wrote pointing out that as to his visits to Rose Hill, he 'should have been better pleased to remain in my bed than have gone to Rose Hill to sleep on the boards in a hut belonging to the man who has the direction of the convicts.' Apart from anything else, the continual pain in his side made his expeditions anything but pleasurable – indeed they were 'parties in which nothing but a sense of duty and necessity would make me engage; and in fact they are such parties that they have lately been declined by most of those who were at first induced to engage in them from motives of curiosity.'

Major Ross was continually complaining about being 'kept in the dark' about plans and regulations at the settlement. On the contrary, Phillip had again and again sent for him to explain what he planned and how it was to be carried out. He had carefully read to him every part of his instructions relating to the settlement, and had been grateful for Ross's assurances of support and help, but 'a warmth of temper, which has been the source of many discontents, has obliged me for some time past to avoid, as far as the service permits, calling on the Lieutenant-Governor otherwise than as the commandant of the detachment. At the same time no order has ever been given which might in any shape or form restrict his authority. So far from it that from the time we landed to the present time it has been understood by everyone in the settlement that all orders given by the Lieutenant-Governor are to have the same effect as if given by me.'[136]

Nothing, however, would enable the two men to work amicably together.

On 25 November 1790 Phillip decided that it was time another attempt was made to kidnap some more Aborigines, with the same motive as before – to attempt to learn the language of 'the natives', to find out more about their way of life and – particularly important – to find out 'whether or not the country possessed any resources by which life might be prolonged.'[137] One of the black convicts had in fact escaped with the idea of living with the Aborigines, but had never been accepted by them, and hunger drove him back to the settlement. Nanbaree, the boy who had been adopted by John White (see p.000), and Abaroo, a young girl similarly recovered from smallpox and adopted by Mrs Johnson, the clergyman's wife, were living more or less happily among the white settlers, but were too young to have more than a small knowledge of the language or customs of their people.

So Phillip sent Lieutenant Bradley on this mission, with two petty officers and a rowing crew. They came upon two men fishing, Bradley showed them some fish he had in the boat, and when they came to examine it, carried them off, an iron ring on one of their legs and a rope tied to a thwart. The Governor made a point of having Abaroo and Nanbaree meet the two captured adults when they arrived at Sydney – and the children obviously knew something of them, because they immediately called them by their names, Bennelong and Colbee. The result was not promising – both men seemed sullen and unlikely to be co-operative – Bennelong, who seemed to be about 26 years old, had 'a bold intrepid countenance which bespoke violence and revenge'[138], while Colbee, perhaps a little older, was only a little less sullen.

Phillip issued strict orders that the two were to be treated well – though also carefully guarded. Colbee at least was not guarded carefully enough, for within a week he has escaped, with the iron ring still on his leg, and wearing his European clothes. It seems possible that Bennelong may not by then have been quite so interested in escaping as his companion. Unlike Arabanoo, he particularly enjoyed alcohol, and (Tench remarks) 'would drink the strongest liquors, not simply without reluctance, but with eager marks of delight and enjoyment.'[139] He was clearly an intelligent man: he picked up the rudiments of the English language and of acceptable polite behaviour remarkably quickly, and seemed to enjoy telling his captors all about his life and history. Love and war, Tench remarks, were Bennelong's favourite pursuits, and he eagerly explained how he had got the various scars which decorated his body, including those he had received when trying to carry off an unwilling young woman. He was a real character, and a strange but strong *rapport* almost immediately grew up between him and the Governor.

As December ended, and the Governor was occasionally able to forget his troubles in the company of his new Aboriginal guest, leagues away the crew of the *Guardian* were throwing overboard almost all the supplies with which she had been making for New South Wales. Twelve days after leaving the Cape of Good Hope, she had run onto ice, lost her rudder and sprung a leak. Seven horses, 16 cows, two bulls and numbers of sheep, goats and deer were slaughtered and thrown overboard, but the hastily lightened ship was clearly impossible to save. 20 men volunteered to stay on board and try to save her; the rest took to the boats. Only one of them was ever seen again – the longboat was saved, and the survivors taken to Cape Town. Against all the odds, the *Guardian* tottered into harbour there some weeks later, only 75 barrels of flour saved from all the supplies with which she had been laden.

# ELEVEN

As 1790 began, the entire population of Sydney and Rose Hill had one hope for the year ahead: that a ship, or preferably ships, would arrive from England, bearing not only supplies but letters and news. They had now been completely isolated for two years. They knew nothing of the fall of the Bastille, the declaration of the Rights of Man or the election of President George Washington, and they had no idea whether their wives, husbands, parents or children were alive or dead. Also, increasingly, they were starving and – the convicts at least – almost reduced to nakedness.

Much of everyone's time was spent looking out for a ship and speculating about when one might appear. Every time a shot was heard for which there was no ready explanation, they thought it must signal a sighting. Even a clap of thunder was mistaken for a ship's gun signalling its approach. In January, Captain Hunter detailed some men from the *Sirius* to build a look-out house and flagstaff at the South Head, from which news of a sighting could be rapidly signalled to the settlement. The seamen lived in a tent for 10 days while building a substantial small house from which 'on the summit of the hill every morning from daylight until the sun sunk,' Tench writes, 'did we sweep the horizon, in hope of seeing a sail. At every fleeting speck which arose from the bosom of the sea, the heart pounded, and the telescope was lifted to the eye.' Midshipman Daniel Southwell's eyes were often deceived by a low cloud into believing that he saw a ship making towards Port Jackson.[140]

Phillip himself often went up to the flagstaff, frequently with Bennelong, but was always disappointed.

Meanwhile, he had decided on an almost desperate measure. On 14 January he ordered the *Sirius* and *Supply* to be prepared for sea. He would send them to China for supplies, *via* Norfolk Island, where he had decided to send Major Ross to replace Lieutenant Gidley King. While the *Supply* went on to China, the *Sirius* would bring King back to New South Wales and then follow her. King, the man above all whom Phillip could trust, would go on to England with dispatches, and do his best to convince the Government of the true situation of the colony and the desperate need for regular and generous supplies. Meanwhile the irascible Major would be out of the Governor's hair: in future, he could hope that by the time Ross's complaints reached his ears, it would be too late to do anything practical about them. The two ships sailed out of Port Jackson together on 5 March, carrying Ross, Lieutenant Clark, two companies of marines and 116 male and 67 women convicts.

The *Supply* actually headed for Batavia[141], to buy from the Dutch whatever food was possible – ideally provisioning the ship for eight months – then buying for the colony 200,000 pounds of flour, 80,000 pounds of beef, 60,000 pounds of pork and 70,000 pounds of rice. Phillip handed the captain Lidgbird Ball a letter addressed to Lord Sydney, to be sent on to London by whatever means he could contrive. It is a slightly odd letter – carefully optimistic on the one hand, dispirited on the other, and showing that the Governor's view of the degeneracy of the convicts had not altered in the past months.

> As the settlement is now fixed, whenever his Majesty's service permits, permits, I shall be glad to return to England, where I have reason to suppose my private affairs may make my presence necessary; but which I

do not ask in any publick letters, nor should I mention a desire of leaving this country at this moment but that more than a year must pass before it can possibly take place, and I make no doubt but that every inconveniency now felt in this colony will be done away before this letter reaches your Lordship. I am sorry to say that nine-tenths of us merit every little inconveniency we now feel.[142]

At the same time he wrote to Nepean, mentioning his letter to Sydney and adding that he had only appealed for leave because he believed that 'the inconveniencies under which the colony now labours will be done away long before my letters can reach England.' His estranged wife, he says, ' was supposed to be dying when I left England', and should she have died there would be important financial business to be done. He adds, and underlines, '*I should have no objection to return here* . . . but to come to England for a twelve month is what I wish, for many reasons.'

One can discern signs of resignation in these letters, but he is still remarkably upbeat, considering the circumstances; though 'dismal accounts' would no doubt be given in England about the problems in New South Wales, 'we shall not starve, though seven-eighth of the colony deserve nothing better; the present want will be done away by the first ship that arrives.'[143] Phillip and Tench went up to the flagstaff lookout on 5 March and watched the *Supply* until she disappeared over the horizon.

The population of Sydney was now considerably attenuated. Phillip took the opportunity to call the remaining convicts together and address them. He was redistributing the huts and gardens of those who had left, he said, and trusted that the men and women who remained in Sydney would cultivate them assiduously. He explained that the fact that the population of the town was now reduced could not mean that there would be extra rations, for much food had had to be sent with the ships to support the growing population of Norfolk Island. Nevertheless he was convinced that relief was on its way – he never appeared, in public, to doubt that support would eventually arrive.

On 5 April, Tench heard a rumour that a ship had been sighted from the lookout, and indeed when he went up to the observatory and looked through the telescope there, he saw that a flag was flying from the flagstaff. He and the Governor made their way down to the harbour and saw a boat rowing towards the landing-place. As it approached, they recognised Captain Lidgbird Ball, the commander of the *Supply*, who was gesturing in a manner that Tench thought boded ill. He turned to Philip and said: 'Sir, prepare yourself for bad news.'

When Ball landed, it was to tell the Governor that the *Sirius* had been lost – wrecked on Norfolk Island on 19 March, though without loss of life. The news was so calamitous that the Governor summoned the first general council ever to be held at Sydney, and rendered an account of the provisions still remaining. There was enough salt beef to last only until the beginning of July, flour until 20 August and rice or peas until 1 October. Once more the rations must be reduced – to two pounds of pork, two and a half pounds of flour and two pounds of rice or a quart of peas a week for adults and children over 18 months old. Children under 18 months were to receive the same amount of rice and flour, and one pound of pork.

This sounds bad enough, but in fact matters were worse, for as Tench points out, 'The pork and rice were brought with us from England: the pork had been salted between three and four years, and every grain of rice was a moving body, from the inhabitants lodged within it. We soon left off boiling the pork, as it had become so old and dry, that it shrunk one half in its dimensions when so dressed.'[144]

Phillip instructed that every man in the settlement, including the surgeons and the Reverend Johnson, must go fishing on alternate nights, with all fish caught to go to a common hoard. The best marksmen must go out every day in search of kangaroos, which should also be delivered to the commissary. A reward of 60 pounds of flour was offered for information about anyone who thieved from a garden, and the penalties for pilfering food were now extreme. One convict who was caught stealing 20 ounces of potatoes from Mr Johnson's garden was given 300 lashes and ordered to be chained for six months to two other convicts and to have his allowance of flour stopped for six months. Another who had lifted three pounds of potatoes received 1,000 lashes. A sailor from the *Sirius* was shot and wounded as he tried to steal vegetables, but was nevertheless given 425 lashes. In April, William Lane noticed the lock on a store-house was broken, went in, and stole some biscuit. He was ordered 2,000 lashes – the most severe punishment of its kind yet inflicted.[145] Convict Thomas Tarsley was given 60 pounds of flour for catching a man stealing vegetables – it was a reward, Tench remarked, 'more tempting than the ore of Peru or Potosi.'

There were several deaths from starvation, and everyone was in such a state of lethargy from lack of food that work almost came to a complete standstill. Phillip handed over to the general store 300 pounds of flour which were his private property, but the only result was that he was accused of having hoarded it. He recognised that no one was now in a condition to work normal hours, and these were reduced to those between sunrise and midday – in the afternoon the men and women should tend their gardens. It was the time to ready the ground for sowing, but no one had the energy to do much about it. The marines were as badly off as the convicts, and as for clothing, everyone was in an equally bad way. The marines' uniforms had mostly fallen to pieces, and on parade there were sometimes more of them barefoot than in the tattered remnants of shoes. The women became immensely ingenious in mending clothing and contriving to keep themselves more or less decently covered, but lack of resources made real needlework next to impossible.

The stock of salt now ran out and the Governor ordered two large boilers to be set up in which sea-water could be evaporated. Surgeon Worgan, with little enough energy or indeed to inclination to play his piano, commended the use of a dog, rat or crow – if either could be got – to augment the two ounces of pork which must last for 48 hours.

Most people now sat around for much of the time so enervated that they had not the energy to contrive a form of amusement, let alone work. Phillip could not bear inaction on his own account, and worked daily with Bennelong, with whose help he and Collins were working to compile a basic dictionary of the language of his tribe: *boorana*, a bird; *birrang*, the stars; *Dyennibbe*, laughter; *nangara*, to sleep – and so on.

Bennelong seemed happy enough, but on 3 May, in his room upstairs in the Governor's house in the middle of the night, he pretended to be ill, went downstairs and outside, jumped over the fence and vanished. Everyone had tried to keep the true state of the colony from him, for fear that he might tell his tribe of the weakness of the marines and convicts, and provoke an attack, but this certainly did not happen, and it was the general view that he had escaped in order to visit one of the Aboriginal women he had frequently spoken about.

June began with blustery weather – heavy rain and strong wind with which no one was in the mood to cope. Then, on the 3rd, a Thursday, Tench was sitting in his hut at three in the afternoon when he heard an uproar from outside and found men, women and children running to and fro in wild excitement. He ran to the top of a hill with a neighbour, a brother officer, and with his spyglass saw that the flag was flying from the look-out. The two men wrung each other's hands, tears streaming down their faces, while women ran to and fro with children in their arms, kissing and hugging each other. Tench and his friend, with Phillip, who had been sent for, got into a boat and were rowed down the harbour, battling against wind and waves and rain. At last they saw 'a large ship, with English colours flying, working in between the heads which form the entrance of the harbour.' The wind and weather were so bad – the ship had made an attempt to enter harbour two days previously, but had been beaten back – that for a time they feared that she might be wrecked on the North Head. The strong southerly blew her perilously near the rocks, but happily moderated, and with the help of the tide disaster was averted.

When the officers saw she was safe Phillip had himself rowed back to Sydney to prepare to receiver her, while Tench and the rest went on. At last they saw the word *London* on her stern. She was the *Lady Juliana*. 'Pull away, my lads!' Tench cried to the oarsmen. 'She is from old England! A few strokes more, and we shall be aboard! Hurrah for a belly-full, and news from our friends!'[146]

Once the *Lady Juliana* had docked the settlement was almost overwhelmed with news – it 'burst upon us like meridian splendour on a blind man', Tench commented. They heard of the madness of King George III and of his recovery, of the wreck of the *Guardian* and of the French Revolution ('that wonderful and unexpected event', Tench called it) – and they had news of friends and families. Their pleasure was only modified by the fact that the ship carried relatively little in the way of supplies: there were 222 female convicts on board, and the only food was what was intended for them – and of the flour, much of it was spoiled by the sea-water that had made its way through the old ship's infirm timbers. Collins commented that 'it was not a little mortifying to find a cargo so unnecessary and so unprofitable as 222 females, instead of a cargo of provisions.'[147]

Phillip had a celebratory dinner that evening, though with little enough to celebrate other than the recovery of the King, which was toasted with all the enthusiasm of those who had not had an excuse for celebratory toasts for many months. The flour ration was increased to five and a half pounds of flour a week for the next three months, and the Governor forgave every convict who was awaiting a lashing. His clemency did not extend however to Robert Abel and John Jeffries, who received 200 lashes each for stealing sugar from the *Lady Juliana*.

The news that Phillip welcomed most was that a newly raised New South Wales Corps consisting of 300 men was on its way to the colony. It consisted of a Commandant, 13 commissioned officers, a chaplain and a surgeon, a surgeon's mate, 24 non-commissioned officers, eight drummers and 268 privates. This would mean that the hard-pressed, exhausted marines who had served since the arrival of the First Fleet could be relieved and go home if they wished; they would be offered the opportunity to resign and remain as private citizens with the right to settle and farm. Every single NCO would be entitled to 130 acres, and if married to 150. Every private soldier would be allotted 80 acres if single, 100 if married, with an extra 10 acres for every child, and after five years they would be entitled to double the quantity of land. There was also a small bonus of three pounds to any soldier who decided to stay, with an allowance of clothing, seed and grain.

If this was in general rather cheering, on 11 June there was the dispiriting sight of the women convicts being disembarked from the *Lady Juliana*, many of them old and tottering. In one of them, Governor Phillip eventually took a particular interest. A letter from Sir Joseph Banks, the distinguished botanist who had visited New South Wales with Cook, asked him to take care of a young woman called Mary Rose, who had been sentenced to seven years transportation for thieving. She was the daughter of a Lincolnshire farming family who had eloped with an officer who a few weeks later was posted abroad and left her alone in Lincoln. Her landlady accused her of stealing clothes – it is assumed in order to get her hands on some money her lover had left with Mary. The girl was tried at Lincoln assizes, found guilty, and sentenced. She spent 18 months in gaol, but somehow managed to interest Banks in her plight, and while she was on board the *Lady Juliana* on her way to New South Wales Banks and the girl's relatives discovered the truth, the landlady was arrested, and with one of the vessels of the Second Fleet a free pardon was sent after Mary Rose.

Phillip, according to anecdote, offered the young woman a room at Government House, treated her as a lady and at last arranged for her a marriage with 'one of the best men in the colony', John Trace, a Devon man 20 years older than Mary Rose, but already an established farmer.

Nine days after the arrival of the *Lady Juliana* the store-ship *Justinian* entered harbour, having made good time from Falmouth – a voyage of only five months. Everyone was put back on full rations, and in addition there was food to be bought, for the opportunistic master of the *Justinian*, Benjamin Maitland, opened a shop on shore, selling groceries, millinery, even perfume and stationery, all at exorbitant prices. In this case, Maitland happily caught a cold, for virtually no one could afford his prices – indeed few people could afford to buy anything from him at any price.

On 26 June the transport *Surprize* came into the harbour, followed on 28 June by the *Neptune* and *Scarborough*. The *Surprize* carried male and female convicts, together with a number of officers, non-commissioned officers and privates of the New South Wales Corps. More of these came in on the *Neptune*, together with male and female convicts; the *Scarborough* carried only male convicts.

If some of the women landed from the *Lady Juliana* had looked sick, those who struggled ashore from the other ships were in an infinitely worse case. Under Phillip's command, only 24 people had died on all the vessels of the First Fleet, and on the *Lady Juliana* only five women had died. The Second Fleet lost a total of 273 – 163 of them on the *Neptune*, which landed only 97 healthy convicts, and some of these were to join the 269 sick men and women who struggled or were almost thrown ashore. The other two ships did rather better: on the *Surprize* there had been 42 deaths, 121 of the convicts were sick and 89 relatively healthy. Of 250 embarked on the *Scarborough*, 68 had died on the passage and 96 were sick. Collins described the situation as follows:

> a scene truly distressing and miserable; upwards of thirty tents were pitched in front of the hospital, the portable one not being yet put up; all of which, as well as the hospital and the adjacent huts, were filled with people, many of whom were labouring under the complicated diseases of scurvy and the dysentery, and others in the last stage of either of those terrible disorders, or yielding to the attacks of an infectious fever.
>
> The appearance of those who did not require medical assistance was lean and emaciated. Several of these miserable people died in the boats as they were rowing on shore, or on the wharf as they were lifting out of the boats; both the living and the dead exhibiting more horrid spectacles than had ever been witnessed in this country. All this was to be attributed to confinement, and that of the worst species, confinement in a small space and in irons, not put on singly, but many of them chained together . . . the [ships'] masters, who had the entire direction of the prisoners, never suffered them

to be at large on deck, and but few at a time were permitted there. This consequently gave birth to many diseases. It was said, that on board the *Neptune* several had died in irons; and what added to the horror of such a circumstance was, that their deaths were concealed, for the purpose of sharing their allowance of provisions, until chance, and the offensiveness of a corpse, directed the surgeon, or some one who had authority in the ship, to the spot where it lay.[148]

The Reverend Mr Johnson was moved by the physical state of the convicts to a horror previously reserved to moral degenerates. He wrote a lengthy and moving letter to a friend, describing how on the *Surprize* he could scarcely bear the stench of the naked or half-naked lice-ridden wretches, lying on bare decks without bed or bedding, unable even to turn over. Conditions on the *Neptune* were, if anything, even worse; many dead bodies had been thrown from her deck as the ship entered harbour, and could be seen lying naked on the rocks (Johnson immediately spoke to Phillip about this, and parties were sent to collect the bodies and give them decent burial on the north shore). The master of the *Scarborough* physically prevented Johnson from going down into the convicts' quarters, presumably for fear of what he would see there. Johnson watched with increasing horror as members of the ship's crew detailed to help the convicts ashore slung men and women overboard 'in the same manner as they would sling a cask, a box, or anything of that nature. Some died upon deck, and others in the boat before they reached the shore. When come on shore many were not able to walk, to stand, or to stir themselves in the least . . . Some creeped upon their hands and knees, and some were carried on the backs of others.'

A 'portable hospital' – a number of small tents – had been

brought out on the *Justinian* and was hurriedly erected; soon the scenes within them were almost as terrible as anything on the transports. Many of the sick had only rags of clothing, and when these were cut off they were found to be infested with innumerable lice, which immediately took refuge in the bed-clothes – if the sick man or woman was fortunate enough to lie on bed-clothes rather than the dried grass which served most of them for a bed.

The complaints the Governor heard from those convicts capable of speaking to him bore witness to conscious and constant ill-treatment on the voyage out. They – including the obviously sick – had been chained hand and foot for days at a time, sometimes up to their waists in sea water. If they were not hardened criminals when they left England, hardship taught them well – their behaviour in the hospital sickened Mr Johnson: they would hide their clothes, complain that they were naked, and persuade him to get them jackets or trousers, with the end result that they would end up with several sets of clothes to barter or sell. The moment a man or woman died, the clothing would be stripped from the body and hidden. In the cold of the night the strongest patients would steal the blankets from the weakest. The living would steal the extra food and drink given to the dying, 'saying with an oath that it would be of no service to them.' The clergyman was torn between pity and disgust.[149]

Governor Phillip was aghast. The circumstances on board the three transports contradicted all his ideas of decent behaviour and every humane instinct. He summoned the three masters to Government House and by all accounts addressed them in terms which could not be mistaken for anything but the most serious rebuke. He intended, he said, to make a full report of the circumstances to London; their callous treatment of the prisoners was tantamount to murder. He did not mince words in a private letter of 13 July to Lord Grenville, who had succeeded Lord Sydney at the Home Office:

> I will, not, sir, dwell on the scene of misery which the hospitals and tents exhibited when those people were landed, but it would be a want of duty not to say that it was occasioned by the contractors having crowded too many on board those ships, and of their being too much confined during the passage. The convicts having the liberty of the deck depended on the agent and the masters of the ships; the agent died on the passage, and the masters say it was granted so far as was consistent with their own safety. And that many of the convicts were sick when sent from the hulks.
>
> I believe, sir, while the masters of the transports think their own safety depends on admitting few convicts on deck at a time, and most of them with irons on, which prevents any kind of exercise, numbers must always perish on so long a voyage, and many of those now received are in such a condition from old complaints, and so emaciated from what they have suffered on the voyage, that they never will be capable of any labour.[150]

Two days later he wrote an official dispatch, quoting first from the report of one of the surgeons who had inspected the allegedly healthy men and women among the newly arrived convicts: 'After a careful examination of the convicts, I find upwards of one hundred who must ever be a burden to the settlement, not being able to do any kind of labour, from old age and chronical diseases of long standing. Amongst the females there is one who has lost the use of her limbs upwards of three years, and amongst the males two who are perfect idiots.'[151] Then the Governor allowed himself to indulge in some plain speaking:

Such are the people sent from the different gaols and from the hulks, where it is said the healthy and the artificers are retained. The sending out the disordered and helpless clears the gaols, and may ease the parishes from which they are sent; but, sir, it is obvious that this settlement, instead of being a colony which is to support itself, will, if the practice is continued, remain for years a burthen to the mother country. The desire of giving you a full and clear information on this head has made me enter into this detail. Of the nine hundred and thirty males sent out by the last ships, two hundred and sixty-one died on board, and fifty have died since landing. The number of sick this day is four hundred and fifty; and many who are not reckoned as sick have barely strength to attend to themselves.[152]

By the time this dispatch had reached the Home Secretary, the Third Fleet had sailed for Sydney, carrying 1,864 convicts, one in 10 of whom would die before reaching New South Wales, the rest arriving so gaunt and weak as to be incapable of work.

The likelihood that the Government at home would be equally appalled was open to question, for there had been a total failure to supervise the Second Fleet which made the attention to the First Fleet seem, in comparison, almost admirable. The contractors would have made a perfectly decent profit at the 17 pounds a head the Government allowed for the transport of the convicts, but greed took hold, and every means of making additional money was firmly grasped. To take only one instance, the reason why Captain Maitland could sell provisions at his shop was that he had stolen them from the convicts. As for Captain Donald Trail of the *Neptune*, he had clearly taken the view that a dead prisoner was more profitable than a live one, and his abdication of care was criminal (it was on the *Neptune* that there had been cases of bodies left to rot, the men chained nearby being so hungry that they tolerated the smell of the corpse rather than lose the dead man's ration).

After spending twelve months longing for the arrival of a ship from England, four had now arrived, but if anything they had made the situation worse than before. A profound depression settled over the colony. The only moment of levity was when Hector, the Newfoundland dog left behind by Captain Marshall, the master of the *Scarborough,* in May 1788, swam to the ship, jumped on board and instantly greeted his old master, and as Collins writes 'manifested, in every manner suitable to his nature, his Joy at seeing him; nor could the animal be persuaded to quit him again, accompanying him always when he went on shore, and returning with him on board.'

Nine days were spent setting up the 'portable hospital' which had come out on one of the ships. Collins noted wryly that it was advertised as having been erected, in London, in a few hours. It was finally inhabitable on 7 July and was instantly filled with patients. That day they buried 30 convicts. The settlement also lost a midshipman and two sailors in a freak accident on the 23rd. John Ferguson was fishing with three marines when a huge whale started frolicking with the small boat they were in, eventually coming up beneath it and throwing it over. Ferguson and two marines were drowned; the third swam a mile to the north shore (having, he said, ridden on the monster's back for some minutes). More was to be heard of the whale later.

By the beginning of August, despite the general pessimism, the health of the convicts appeared to be improving somewhat. Phillip was able to report to Nepean that the number of sick had declined considerably. There were now just over 200 – only 89 people had died since 27 June. More or less normal rations, and even normal working conditions, now gave Sydney an air of relative stability, and the attitude of many of the officers and marines to their Governor had softened somewhat. Accusations that he was hoarding food for his own use were no longer heard, and invitations to Government Houser were accepted in the knowledge that it was no longer necessary to 'bring your own bread', as had been the case during the starvation month. The Governor was pleased that a number of assiduous gardeners at last seemed to have got the measure of the land and the climate, and were producing food in quite reasonable quantities. The Reverend Johnson (for whom, as a clergyman, Phillip had very little time) had grown 'cucumbers' (surely he meant vegetable marrows?) 16 or 18 inches long and a foot or more in circumference, sweetly-flavoured melons, pumpkins, oranges, limes and lemons, guavas and strawberries (Johnson had kindly given the Governor a root of the latter, and he himself had an excellent bed). In the Government House garden there were vines, and Phillip had been able to serve his guests grapes and 'as fine figs as ever I tasted in Spain or Portugal.' Up at Rose Hill someone had managed to produce a cabbage weighting 26 pounds.

The best gardener in the colony was the Cornishman James Ruse, who had spent five dreadful years in a prison hulk at Plymouth, but on arrival in New South Wales speedily convinced the Governor that he deserved to be trusted. He claimed his freedom in August 1789 (in the first dispatch Phillip received from Grenville he was given the right to declare convicts whose term had expired to be free men) and was given a grant of land as early as November 1789 together with tools with which to work it, and some seed and stock. He set to work, cleared his land of timber, dug the ground over thoroughly, twice, and by the end of 1790 was married and had an acre and a half under wheat, half an acre under maize and a kitchen garden which did well. There were not many like him, but those few offered the

Governor some hope for the future. Though the assurances of self-sufficiency which he made to London were hedged about with 'if's and 'but's, he knew perfectly well that support, in the way of a continual supply of food, clothing and artefacts, would be necessary for some time to come.

The food situation was further eased by the fact that, especially after the *Surprize* and *Justinian* had sailed on with supplies for Norfolk Island, Sydney now had a smaller population than it had for some time – 35 male and 150 female convicts had left on the *Surprize*. The harbour, too, was quiet; after the *Neptune* sailed on 24 August there was no shipping at all at anchor. The Governor put forward a plan for the convict women to make clothes out of material which had reached the colony with the First Fleet – each was given enough material to make two shirts. Unfortunately they were so unskilled that the resulting clothing was unwearable and the scheme was soon dropped. At Rose Hill things were busier than in Sydney – the Governor had set out a plan for the township which would grow up there, with a main street a mile long which Tench thought would be 'of such breadth as will make Pall-Mall and Portland-Place hang their diminished heads.' There were already in November 1790 32 two-roomed thatched houses of clay and wattle, with 10 convict men living in each, though some housed as many as 14. More were being built for unmarried convict women – nine – in a street which crossed the first.

Apart from these there were other houses for 'convict families of good character', and at the centre of the settlement was Government House, a bungalow of lath and plaster 44 feet long and 16 feet wide with out-houses nearby and a new brick-tiled store-house 100 feet long by 24 feet wide, with a house nearby for the store-keeper. The foundation stone of a barracks had been laid within 150 yards of the river wharf where the boats from Sydney unloaded. There were also a barn, a blacksmith's shop, a stock-yard and a hospital (though this, Tench said, was 'most wretched [and] totally destitute of every conveniency'). Most gardens were in a poor state, due to a prolonged drought, but Tench was as impressed as the Governor by Ruse. Others, he was convinced, would follow the Cornishman's good example, and meanwhile he was convinced that Rose Hill was in a fair way to rival Sydney as an example of what could be done by good planning. The Reverend Johnson was not so impressed: 'While the Governor has one grand mansion at Sydney and another at Rose Hill [Johnson was] forced to live in a miserable hut, and that built at [his] own cost; and as for any place of worship, that is the last thing being thought of.'[153] On the other hand he now had an assistant – Thomas Barnsley, formerly a professional musician turned to crime – who became the clergyman's clerk (his wife Elizabeth became the colony's first professional midwife).

Back in Sydney there was now a little settlement up at South Head, where midshipman Southwell was in charge. He and 11 other men lived in a group of whitewashed cottages below the headland near the beach, where there was a stream of fresh water. The situation was really not unpleasant except that Southwell in particular felt cut off and ignored, and thought himself badly neglected by the Governor; indeed he grumbled about Phillip in his letters home, telling his family that 'many here, my friends, scruple not to speak of his conduct in terms of the highest disgust, and they do, it must be confess'd, bring much in support of the assertion.'[154] He does not elaborate – apart from occasional accusations that Phillip hoarded food, and that he kept official communications and orders too much to himself, none of those who complained about him ever elaborated. We may perhaps dismiss Southwell's words as the grumblings of a young man who thought himself unduly neglected, for only a short while later, having been invited to dinner by Phillip, he is remarking that the Governor 'treats us with more affability and is all at once so polite as to beg of my only companion, Mr Harris, and self, whenever we come to camp, to let him have our company, and I am tomorrow (having been so long a stranger) to wait upon him by particular invitation, several times repeated . . .'[155]

The invitation to dine came on 7 September, when Phillip was at South Head supervising the building of a column to help guide shipping into harbour. While he was there he heard that Bennelong, who had kept out of sight since his escape, had been seen at Manly with some of his tribe. The huge whale which had been responsible for the drowning of young Ferguson had been stranded there and killed by the Aborigines, who were feasting on it. When some marines had spoken to Bennelong, the latter had sent the Governor his greetings and a present of whale blubber. Phillip decided to go to see his Aboriginal friend, taking Collins and Lieutenant Henry Waterhouse with him.

According to Tench, Bennelong hung back and would not allow Phillip near him for some time, but then gradually became more friendly, produced Colbee, and the two began asking animatedly about their friends in Sydney – Bennelong asked particularly about one woman he had much admired and, on being told she was well, kissed Lieutenant Waterhouse with instructions to pass the message on. After they had been talking in a friendly manner for some time, a middle-aged, sturdy Aboriginal approached, and stood a little way off looking at Phillip. The Governor held out his hand and walked towards him, with Collins close behind. The nearer he came, the more apprehensive the Aboriginal became. Phillip, thinking to reassure him, took a knife from his belt and threw it to the ground. As if frightened at the rattle of the dirk, the man immediately raised his spear. Phillip called out '*Weé-ree, Weé-ree!*' – believed to mean 'Wrong! Wrong!' – but the man immediately threw the spear, which struck the Governor's right shoulder just above the collar-bone, the point emerging at his back. The assailant ran off into the woods, followed instantly by Bennelong and Colbee.

Lieutenant Waterhouse thought the Governor had been killed, and turned to run for the boats, but saw that Phillip was still standing – indeed trying to run, holding the ten-foot spear with both hands to keep the end off the ground, 'but owing to the length the end took the ground and stopped him short . . . He then begged me for God's sake to haul the spear out, which I immediately stopped to do and was in the act of doing it, when I recollected I should only haul the barb into his flesh again . . . I then determined on breaking it off and bent it down for that purpose, but owing to its length could not effect it. I then bent it upwards, but could not break it owing to the toughness of the wood.'

One might think that by this time if the Aboriginal had not killed the Governor, Lieutenant Waterhouse was in a good way of doing so. But Phillip managed to pull his pistol out of his pocket and fire it; this frightened the Aborigines, who had been throwing spears in the general direction of the party without hitting anyone else. They all immediately fled. With the help of a seaman, Waterhouse got the fainting Governor into the boat, and they pushed off, with Collins following in the second boat.

It was usually a five hour row from Manly to Sydney. The boat's crew did it in three, Waterhouse supporting the Governor in his arms the whole way, expecting any moment to hear his last breath. There was a surgeon among the party, but he was afraid to extract the spear without having proper instruments with him, besides which Phillip might bleed to death. It was a wise decision; when the boat had arrived at Sydney another surgeon, Balmain, attended the injured man properly. Phillip immediately asked how many hours he had to live, in order that he might put his affairs in order – but when Balmain had safely and speedily extracted the spear and examined the wound, he was confident of Phillip's recovery. Indeed the patient was up and about within 10 days.

The general view of the party, with which the Governor concurred, was that fear rather than animosity had been the cause of the incident – the Aboriginal had clearly been afraid that the Governor was going to kidnap him, as he had kidnapped Bennelong and Colbee. Orders were given that there were to be no reprisals, and no attempt to discover the assailant, though it was learned that his name was Wileemarin. The fact that Phillip made no attempt to punish him resulted in an easing of relationships between the Aborigines and the English, and indeed on 15 September there was a sort of international picnic on the north shore, when a party accompanied by Nanbaree and Abaroo was rowed across from Sydney to meet with Bennelong and a number of his friends, including some children who were particularly friendly. Bennelong was delighted when wine was produced, and this he drank freely with the bread and beef also provided. He persuaded one or two friends to taste the beef, though nobody would touch the bread. He then demanded to be shaved (which he had learned while living in Sydney), and this was done to the general astonishment and amusement of his friends, none of whom would allow the razor near them, though they allowed their hair to be trimmed.

Bennelong sent Abaroo for a woman who was seen half-hiding nearby, explaining that she was his wife, Barangaroo. He persuaded her to have her hair cut and combed, and the Englishmen were much impressed by her. Tench indeed wrote that Abaroo had put a petticoat on her, but she hated it, and much preferred to be naked – he thought 'she behaved so well, and assumed the character of gentleness and timidity to such advantage that had our acquaintance ended here, a very moderate share of the spirit of travelling would have sufficed to record that amidst a horde of roaming savages in the desert wastes of New South Wales, might be found as much feminine innocence, softness and modesty (allowing for inevitable difference of education) as the most finished system could bestow or the most polished circle produce!'[156]

Bennelong enquired about the Governor's health, and Tench said he should come to Sydney and see for himself. Bennelong however argued that Phillip should visit him first – and on 17 September he was well enough to be rowed across the harbour to which Bennelong and his wife were living. He told the Governor that he had beaten the man who had wounded him, and when he was asked to visit Government House happily agreed and appeared the following day with three companions. There was great excitement as they marched up to Government House, where Bennelong ran from room to room, showing the house to his friends, demonstrating how candle-snuffers worked, and making himself quite at home. When they showed signs of wanting to leave, Phillip made no attempt to detain them, in order to keep their trust. Before they went, Bennelong asked the Governor if he would build him a hut only slightly apart from the settlement, on the eastern point of the cove, and Phillip, delighted at his friendliness, promised to do so. The land on which it was built is today known as Bennelong Point.

# TWELVE

Though for a time amicable, by the winter of 1790-91, relations between the settlers and the Aborigines took a distinct turn for the worse. On a level closest to the Governor, Bennelong seemed to revert from a more or less friendly attitude to the white men, and Phillip in particular, to something more questionable. Phillip had hoped that he would continue to set a good example to his fellows, but the opposite was the case. In the closing months of 1789 he seemed to reject any idea of civilised behaviour.

On Saturday 13 November about 16 Aborigines turned up at Government House, and Phillip welcomed them courteously, as he always did if they showed signs of wishing to be sociable. Bennelong was among the group, together with the young woman he regarded as his wife; she had a fresh wound on her head, which he said was the result of a blow he had given her and which she had deserved – she had broken one of his best throwing-sticks.

Phillip remonstrated with him, but he would not listen – she had been 'bad', so he had beaten her. Another young woman in the group had been injured so badly that her broken scalp was visible. The Governor persuaded them all to go to the hospital, where the women's wounds were dressed, then they returned to Government House and sat down in the yard. Philip retired to his study to write some documents, and Bennelong went and sat at his side, carrying an axe with which he said he was going to beat his wife again. He was clearly in a very bad temper, and the Governor attempted to placate him, inviting him to dinner, but he got up and said he was going off to beat his woman. Phillip got up too, and said he was going with him and would see that he beat no one. He took the precaution of calling an orderly-sergeant to accompany him, and Collins also attached himself to the party.

When they reached Bennelong's hut they found several Aborigines, men and woman, lying about, and a girl of about 16 who when she saw Bennelong was clearly terrified and got up to leave. At this Bennelong rushed forward, seized some sort of sharp weapon, and before the white men could rescue her had wounded her twice, once on the head and once on the shoulder.

Neither the Governor nor any other white man could discover what offence the girl had committed, but Bennelong went on raving and promising to beat and kill her. Phillip attempted to reason with him, then ordered the sergeant to point his musket at him, but – as Tench relates – 'he seemed dead to every passion but revenge; forgot his affection to his old friends; and, instead of complying with the request they made, brandished his sword at the Governor and called aloud for his hatchet . . .'

The group of Aboriginals seemed to grow restive, and Phillip called for a party of armed men from the *Supply*, which was moored nearby. Their presence did not deter Bennelong in the least, who continued to swear he would sacrifice the girl and cut her head off. He told some rambling story about her assisting her father, his enemy, in battle. Phillip ordered the girl to be taken to the hospital, where a surgeon attended to her wounds; a quiet and gentle young man who appeared to be a relative, but had clearly been too wary of Bennelong to step forward previously, appeared and promised to take care of her. On Phillip's orders the couple were taken to Government House and given a room, but she was desperate to return to Bennelong's hut, though she must have known what reception would await her. She eventually did so – with what result we are not told. Phillip and everyone else found the whole incident incomprehensible – as Tench wrote, with reference to the general behaviour of the Aborigines as it appeared to the white men, 'Inexplicable contradictions arose to bewilder our researches, which no ingenuity could unravel and no credulity reconcile.'[157]

The incident again illustrates the emphasis Phillip laid on attempting to build a good relationship with the Aborigines. Apart from the fact that he had been ordered to do so, he was naturally disposed to be interested in them and to do his best to mitigate any ill-feeling between them and the intruders. He was conscious that the stealing of their land was a great offence, but one about which he could do nothing. He was, however, meticulous in punishing thieves who stole their goods, and when possible the white man would be punished in the presence of the Aboriginal from whom he had stolen. He was sympathetic when there were complaints that any white man had ill-treated an Aboriginal, and when assaults on convicts or marines were reported he was careful to enquire fully into the cases, and more often than not concluded that the Aboriginal had been provoked.

Certainly, as a man of his time it never for a moment occurred to Phillip to think that anything but good could come from 'civilising the natives'. 'When I shall have time to mix more with them,' he wrote, 'every means shall be used to reconcile them to live amongst us, and to teach them the advantages they will reap from cultivating land.'[158] On a personal level he always approached the original owners of the land in the most friendly way, joking with them when common ground for humour could be found (basic knockabout comedy appealed to them and, it seems, to him). He would display a gap in his front teeth as a sign that he was in some way one of them, and often seems to have been accepted as though in some way there was indeed an instinctive, almost psychic link between them.

His officers were not so assiduous – they did not find it easy to ignore the fact that compared to them the Aborigines were dirty, smelly and ignorant. Even Tench found it difficult to *like* them – Bennelong, whom they got to know better than any other, never became much more to most of the officers than a figure of fun; they were not in the least interested in finding out anything about his way of life. As to Aboriginal society, it was in their view basic and simple: 'theirs is strictly a system of Equality, attended with only one inconvenience, the strong triumphs over the weak.'[159]

As for the convicts, though on the face of it, compared to themselves the Aborigines showed a natural disposition towards honest behaviour and were violent towards the white men and women only when provoked, the convicts felt no warmth or kindness towards those they had dispossessed, and were always ready to think the worst of them.

However, at the end of 1790 an incident occurred which was to force even the Governor to uncharacteristic violence in his dealings with the Aborigines. On 9 December a marine sergeant with three convicts went out shooting with John M'Entire, a convict described as Phillip's gamekeeper. By all accounts he was not a pleasant man, and was generally disliked except by the Governor. The common view of him was that he was violently prejudiced against the Aborigines, and took every opportunity he could to steal from and ill-treat them.

The shooting party went out towards Botany Bay, where they had decided to spend the night in a hut set up there for just such parties, in which they could sleep during much of the day, and hunt for game (particularly kangaroos) at night or in the early morning. At one o'clock the sergeant was awakened by a noise and, thinking it was a kangaroo, roused his companions. But when they emerged from the hut they saw two armed Aboriginal men creeping towards the hut, followed by three more.

'Don't be afraid, I know them,' said M'Entire, and went towards them. They retreated and he followed them, speaking to them in their own language. One young man jumped onto the trunk of a fallen tree and hurled his spear at M'Entire, hitting him in the left side. The wounded man staggered back towards his party, calling out 'I am a dead man!' One of his companions broke off the spear and M'Entire, a strong and robust man, though severely wounded and bleeding heavily, lived long enough for the party to stagger back to Sydney. Before he died, as a Catholic he sent for Mr Johnson, to whom (Collins writes) 'he confessed that he had been a bad man and desired his prayers', accusing himself of having a thoroughly bad character and of having stolen from the Aborigines and been violent towards them, though he had only killed one when he himself had been attacked.

While he was still alive Colbee and several other Aborigines were brought to the hospital. They had heard of the attack and seemed genuinely sorry for it, naming the attacker as Pim-el-wi. The surgeon attending M'Entire was about to remove the spear, but the Aborigines gestured to him to leave it – if it were removed, they said, death would be immediate. It was left in the wound for two days before being removed; the patient lingered on, but no one really hoped for a recovery, and in fact he died during the first month of the New Year.

The Governor had been on a visit to Rose Hill when the attack took place. On returning he was unusually angry – it seems that for some reason he was the only man in the colony to respect and like M'Entire. He immediately issued an official order:

Several tribes of the natives still continuing to throw spears at any man they meet unarmed, by which several have been killed or dangerously wounded, the Governor, in order to deter the natives from such practices in future, has ordered out a party to search for the man who wounded the convict in so dangerous a manner on Friday last, although no offence was offered on his part, and to make a severe example of that tribe.

How severe that example was to be was made clear to Tench, who was summoned to Government House and told that he had been chosen to lead the retaliatory party, which would consist of two captains, two subalterns and 40 privates. They were to be ready to march at sun-up on the following day. Tench was to find the tribe to which the murderer belonged and kill 10 of them, cutting off their heads. Hatchets would be provided for that purpose and bags in which the heads were to be carried back to Sydney by two more men of the tribe, who were to be taken alive.

Tench, a thorough admirer of Phillip's humanitarian attitude to the Aborigines, was amazed and appalled. When he questioned the order, Phillip told him that since the settlers had arrived 17 white people had been killed or wounded by the natives. The tribe living near Botany Bay, known as the Bideegals, had been the chief aggressors, and he was determined to 'infuse them with a universal terror which might operate to prevent further mischief.' No women or children were to be harmed, however, and no property destroyed.

Tench, rather courageously, argued against his orders, and the Governor listened patiently. He had not so far attempted to take revenge for attacks on convicts, he said, because he had believed that these were the result of provocation or at least misunderstanding. 'To the latter of these causes,' he said, 'I attribute my own wound; but in this business of M'Entire, I am fully persuaded that they were unprovoked, and the barbarity of their conduct admits of no extenuation: for I have separately examined the sergeant, of whose veracity I have the highest opinion, and the two convicts; and their story is short, simple and alike.

'I have in vain tried to stimulate Bennelong, Colbee and the other natives who live among us, to bring in the aggressor: yesterday, indeed, they promised me to do it, and actually went away as if bent on such a design; but Bennelong, instead of directing his steps to Botany Bay, crossed the harbour in his canoe in order to draw the foreteeth of some of the young men; and Colbee, in the room of fulfilling his engagement is loitering about the look-out house . . . So that we have our efforts only to depend upon; and I am resolved to execute the prisoners who may be brought in, in the most public and exemplary manner, in the presence of as many of their countrymen as can be collected, after having explained the cause of such a punishment; and my fixed determination to repeat it when any further breach of good conduct on their side shall render it necessary.'

Perhaps seeing that Tench was still disturbed by his order, the Governor asked him if he himself had any suggestion to put to him, and the lieutenant immediately proposed that rather than slaughtering 10 men and exhibiting their heads (he did not add, in a barbarous manner, but the implication was clear), it would be better to take six captives alive, to punish three – presumably by execution – and to set the others free to communicate the message to the rest of the tribe.

The Governor's immediate furious reaction had perhaps by this time cooled, for he immediately agreed to Tench's suggestion – if six captives could not be taken, he said, he would hang two and give the impression that he had hanged them all by sending the other four to Norfolk, 'which will cause their countrymen to believe that we have dispatched them secretly.' He altered his orders accordingly: they now read:

> A party consisting of 2 captains, 2 subalterns, and 40
> privates (with a proper number of non-commissioned
> officers ) from the garrison, with three days' provisions,
> &c., to be ready to go out to-morrow morning at
> daylight, in order to bring in six of those natives who
> reside near the head of Botany Bay, or if that should be
> found impracticable, to put that number to death.

Tench set out with the substantial punitive party on 14
December: there was a captain of the New South Wales Corps,
lieutenants John Poulden and William Dawes, two surgeons,
Worgan and Lowes, three sergeants, three corporals and 40
privates. Dawes had been even more reluctant to obey orders
than Tench. Sometime later, his reluctance was described by
Phillip in a dispatch to Grenville:

> Lieut Dawes was to go out with the party, refused that
> duty by letter to the senior officer of the detachment
> (Capt. Campbell), who, finding it impossible to persuade
> Lieut Dawes to obey the order, brought the letter to the
> Governor, who likewise took great pains to point out
> the consequence of his (Lieut. Dawes) being put under
> an arrest. Late in the evening Lieut. Dawes informed
> Capt. Campbell that the Revd. Mr. Johnson thought
> he might obey the order, and that he was ready to go out
> with the party, which he did.'[160]

The punitive party faced considerable difficulty in achieving
their task: as Tench remarked, a party of Europeans encumbered
with thick cumbersome uniforms and burdened with provisions
and arms were no match for naked and unencumbered natives
when it came to pursuit and capture. They learned from Colbee,
who had suddenly appeared from the undergrowth, that the

tribesmen they sought had fled to the south, and that they would have no chance of catching them before their provisions ran out. They had no alternative but to return to Sydney.

Not pleased, Phillip immediately ordered a second expedition. This time the party found itself in countryside crossed and recrossed by rivers, which they had to ford up to their chests in water. Then the entire party got stuck in mud, and Tench and two others were actually unable to move until small branches had been cut and thrown to them to help them pull themselves free. A sergeant who had sunk to his chest was almost lost. Several knapsacks had been jettisoned and a number of rifles were so thickly coated with mud that they were unusable.

The Aboriginal tribesmen were still elusive, and a number of men were now so exhausted they could scarcely walk. The party dragged itself back to Sydney, and Phillip was reluctantly forced to give up his idea of exemplary punishment for the murder of M'Entire.[161] Perhaps the most unfortunate result of the failed expeditions was the souring of the previously good relationship between the Governor and young Lieutenant Dawes, who on his return unwisely told Phillip that 'he was sorry he had been persuaded to comply with the order', and made it very clear that he would not obey a similar order in future. He spoke out in the presence of two other officers, and the Governor told Grenville in a later dispatch that 'his expressions . . . were such as would have subjected him to a courtmartial had he been amenable to one.'

By the time of this unfortunate incident, there was a distinct feeling abroad that Sydney was settling down and beginning to recognise itself as a distinctive township with some sort of a society. One of the reasons for this was that, unlike the marines of the First Fleet, the officers of the New South Wales Corps had been allowed to bring their wives with them. The population had increased, and the Governor felt at last that he was presiding over a settlement which had some shape, some recognisable character. As he wrote to Grenville, 'The settlement is now so fully established that the great labour may said to be passed', though he could not forbear to add: 'It has, sir, been attained under every possible disadvantage though it is not in that situation in which I should wish to have it for it is not independent for the necessaries of life.'[162]

The 'starvation years' of which some books about the early history of New South Wales have spoken were in fact months rather than years – the period during which there was serious danger of the population of Sydney actually perishing was relatively brief, and by the end of 1790, though this was by no means a land of plenty, the situation had greatly eased. On 18 October the *Supply* had returned from Batavia with provisions. In mid-December a hired transport, the *Waaksamheyd*, anchored at Port Jackson with 171 barrels of beef, 172 of pork, 39 of flour, 1,000 pounds of sugar and 70,000 of rice. To the irritation of her master, Phillip ordered that all the provisions should be weighed as they came ashore; there turned out to be less rice than had been paid for, and Phillip accepted a quantity of butter in lieu.

The flour from Batavia, which should have been of real value, turned out 'though purchased at an excessive price' to be at least one-sixth bran, Phillip told Grenville, and the rice was bad. He really feared that there would be serious disaffection when this became known: 'despondency and discontent', once roused, spread quickly and were difficult to resolve. This was a severe psychological blow for the Governor, too – not given to despondency, he nevertheless felt obliged to relieve his feelings to his superior in London: 'A pain from which in more than two years, I have been seldom free has impaired my health, and at times puts it out of my power to attend to the charge with which his Majesty has been pleased to honour me in the manner I wish and the state of the colony requires.'[163]

The replies Phillip received from Grenville to his requests for leave were implacable – whether he asked to be allowed to attend to urgent business or complained about his health, the tone of the replied was the same:

> You have expressed a desire to be permitted to return to England. I am much concerned that this situation of your private affairs should have been such as to render this application necessary at a time when your services in New South Wales are so extremely important to the public. I cannot, therefore, refrain from expressing my earnest hope that you may have it in your power so to arrange your private concerns that you may be able, without material inconvenience, to continue in your Government for a short time longer. From the zeal which you have at all times manifested for the public service, I am inclined to believe that you will readily accede to this proposal, and I shall therefore only add, that as soon as your presence in the Colony can be dispensed with, you may be assured that everything on my part will be done to contribute to your accommodation. I am &c., GRENVILLE.

As the year ended Lieutenant Tench, that inveterate chronicler of the early history of Sydney, wrote in his journal his view of 'the state of the colony.'[164] It was on the whole more optimistic than he would have thought possible 12 months previously, and perhaps more optimistic than the Governor would have credited. The major problem was still the difficulty of cultivating crops in a country in which drought was beginning to seem a normal state of things. In November, he doubted whether all the brief showers of the past four months would amount to 24 hours of real rain. The gardens and farms were in a wretched condition. On the other hand, 'the convicts continue to behave pretty well; three only have been hanged since the arrival of the last fleet, in the latter end of June, all of whom were new comers', and as for the Aborigines, the settlers were now 'hand in glove' with them – the only problem being that they assumed that the food available to the colony should also be available to them, a species of communism being their creed.

As far as food production was concerned, the Governor had properly decided that the main efforts should be concentrated on slightly better land at Rose Hill (which Phillip decided, on 2 June 1791, should henceforth be known as Parramatta). At Sydney, relatively few convicts remained, and the main work that went on there was building: Samuel Wheeler, in charge of brick-making, continued to produce 40,000 bricks and tiles a month which he thought were good enough to fetch 24 shillings a thousand at Kingston-on-Thames, which had been his home before he was transported.

Up at Rose Hill there were now 450 male and 50 female convicts, 326 of them simply labourers, but with one master brick-maker and 52 labouring brick-makers, 28 bricklayers, 24 carpenters and five blacksmiths. The man in charge was Henry Edward Dodd, who had come out as Phillip's personal servant and had been put in charge of the government farms from the beginning. He showed Tench around, admitting that the best farmer in the country was probably the Reverend Mr Johnson, who certainly seemed to be more successful at growing vegetable marrows than at improving the morals of his flock. (He was however in bad odour with the convicts because he had become a Justice of the Peace, and had taken to ordering their provisions to be reduced if they did not attend divine service.) In general, James Ruse remained the best farmer in the colony, who had worked out his own system for improving the soil by burning the tree stumps and digging the ashes in, and taking care that the ground was properly tilled rather than simply being scratched over with a hoe, the lazier habit of the other convicts. He also manured his land with any refuse he could find, rather than letting it rot and go to waste. He was greatly helped by a good wife – Elizabeth Perry, who had arrived on the *Lady Juliana* and married him in September 1790.

Dodd had been able to report to Phillip that 200 acres of land had been cleared and cultivated – this figure was slightly faulty, for in many cases the stumps of trees had been left, and Tench calculated that a tenth of every acre could not be cultivated for that reason. However, 55 acres were in wheat, barley and oats, 30 in maize, and the remainder had been set aside for buildings, streets and private gardens. The latter were in a poor state – the drought, again – but at least there were reasonable crops of potatoes. There was also a number of tobacco plants; the planting of tobacco was not encouraged, but many men were desperate for it, as it fetched as much as 15 shillings a pound, and convicts would trade their whole week's ration for a small amount of the weed (shortly after this, Phillip was to make an order forbidding the cultivation of tobacco altogether).

There were four stockades of 20 acres each for the cattle expected to arrive in the colony, all supplied with water, and a conscious effort seemed to have been made to landscape the township, for the finest trees had been left, giving 'a park-like and beautiful appearance . . . the beautiful diversity of the ground (gentle hill and dale) would certainly be reckoned pretty in any country.' It is difficult not to see Phillip's hand in this; he and Dodd after all had worked together in the more amenable landscape of the New Forest (and for generations to come settlers were to go out of their way to counterfeit, where they could, a European landscape in the dry brown countryside of New South Wales). Meanwhile the town itself was growing steadily, with its broad main street and growing clutch of houses, the bungalow Government House, the beginnings of barracks, a small prison and a bakery where the flour distributed to the convicts could for a small fee be turned into bread.

Tench went back to Sydney fully conscious of the difficulties faced at Rose Hill, but equally convinced – as was the Governor – that circumstances there were improving slowly but steadily, and that all that was wanted to turn it into a thriving centre of cultivation was time, perseverance and of course supplies – particularly of stock – from England. As to Sydney, he reflected, as he found the town sweltering in a temperature of 42°C that more difficult months and years probably lay ahead.

# THIRTEEN

On 26 January 1791 the colony celebrated for the first time what much later became known as Australia Day. Collins noted it briefly: 'Our colours were hoisted in the redoubt, in commemoration of the day on which formal possession was taken of this cove three years before.'[165]

The year began with the death of one of Phillip's oldest allies in the colony, and perhaps the nearest person he could have called a friend, his former servant Henry Edward Dodd, the superintendent at Rose Hill. He had been failing for some time, but his death seems to have been brought about more or less by accident – he had heard some kind of disturbance during the night, had rushed out in his night-shirt, spent too long hunting for suspected thieves, and caught a chill. Phillip made no official note of the loss, but he must have been devastated – he had known Dodd since his first days farming in the New Forest. He was not the only man to respect and admire the dead man – Collins noted that 'The services rendered to the public by this person were visible in the cultivation and improvements which appeared at the settlement where he had the direction. He had acquired an ascendancy over the convicts which he preserved without being hated by them; he knew how to proportion their labour to their ability, and, by an attentive and quiet demeanour, had gained the approbation and countenance of the different officers who had been on duty at Rose Hill.' He was buried in a corner of a stock yard, at a funeral attended by every member of the Rose Hill community.

The funeral took place in dusty, dry heat, with a wind 'like the blast of a heated oven', as Collins put it. There was a January and February heat-wave – on the 10th and 11th February the temperature in Sydney reached 40°. 'Dogs, pigs and fowls lay panting in the shade or rushed to whatever water they could find.' Only man seemed capable of moving about, and even that – let alone work – was exhausting. The bodies of dead birds, flying-foxes and bats fouled the streams at Rose Hill and there was real fear that the Tank Stream would dry up, leaving Sydney without a regular water supply.[166] The Governor ordered a ditch to be dug on each side of the stream and a fence to be set up to prevent animals – or indeed humans – from approaching and further fouling it.

Despite the conditions, that most efficient of farmers James Ruse was able to report that in future he would not need provisions from the commissary, as he was now entirely able to support himself by the produce of his farm. Phillip, who had always trusted and admired the Cornishman, sent his congratulations and an agreement to give him 30 more acres of land to cultivate.

The *Supply* sailed into harbour on 26 February from Norfolk Island, Captain Hunter and his crew extremely anxious to return to England after having, they reported, almost starved to death – indeed many of them were so emaciated that they had to spend time in hospital. After a great deal of haggling, Phillip managed to hire the *Waaksamheyd* to carry them home. Tench reported that her master was wildly extravagant in his attempted charges, and though the Governor managed to beat him down his ship was 'perhaps the dearest vessel ever hired on a similar service, being totally destitute of every accommodation, and every good quality, which could promise to render so long a voyage either comfortable or expeditious.'[167] (It certainly was to be a long voyage: the *Waaksamheyd* took over a year to reach England.)

She left Sydney on 27 April with the crew of the *Sirius* on board. The Governor gave her an official send-off, standing at the salute with the marines and the New South Wales Corps and giving three cheers as the transport passed out of the cove. The marine officers were rowed alongside her as far as the Heads, and as she left Port Jackson she saluted the colony with nine guns. One of the marines, John Easty, recorded in his journal what many of the men must have been thinking: that 'there was two parties of men separated which had spent four years together in the greatest love and friendship as ever men did in such a distant part of the globe, both officers and men.'[168] On board, among others, were Lieutenant Southwell, Surgeon Worgan and Captain Hunter.

On the day that she sailed one of the most extraordinary adventures of the first years of the colony began. Governor Phillip was not especially involved, but the story cannot be ignored. It concerned William Bryant, a Cornish fisherman who had been transported for seven years and came out to New South Wales on the *Charlotte*, on which he met another West Country convict, Mary Broad, who had just given birth to a daughter. The two were among the first group to be married on 10 February 1788, and had a son together. Bryant impressed the Governor with his character and his seagoing expertise, and was the chief fisherman of the colony.

It is clear in retrospect that Bryant and his wife had an escape in mind for months, if not years. They found three other like-minded convicts, and with them stole the Governor's six-oared cutter and just before midnight set off with their children on a wildly ambitious voyage to freedom. Bryant could handle a boat and one of the other convicts, a man named Morton, had a sketchy knowledge of navigation and had managed to buy a compass and a quadrant from the captain of the *Waaksamheyd*.

They had a good start before their absence was discovered,

and their escape would have gone unnoticed for longer had not one of the convicts, James Cox, left a letter for his mistress hoping that she would continue to live a life free from the vices of her fellows. She talked, and the news of the escape thus reached the Governor, who immediately ordered a boat out to attempt to find the escapees. The attempt failed, and in what was a journey only equalled by Captain Bligh's more celebrated voyage after being thrown off the *Bounty*, the tiny boat sailed up the New South Wales coast, through the Straits of Endeavour, and 3,000 miles later reached Timor on 6 June.

If ever success was deserved, those five men and two children surely deserved it. They managed to persuade the authorities in Timor that they were the survivors of a shipwreck, until one of the men got drunk and talked too much. They were then arrested and sent to a prison in Batavia, where Bryant and his son died. The survivors were put on board the *Pandora* for Cape Town, where they transferred to the *Gorgan, en route* for England and trial. Tench happened to be on board, on his way back to England, and saw them. 'I confess I never looked art these people,' he wrote, 'without pity and astonishment. They had miscarried in a heroic struggle for liberty; after having combated every hardship and conquered every difficulty.'[169]

At their trial the judges were clearly impressed by the survivors' achievement and hardships and, rather than sentencing them to death (which might have been expected), ordered that they serve out the remainder of their original sentences. In a fascinating twist Mary's story was heard by James Boswell, Dr Johnson's biographer, who rescued her from prison and saw that she was returned to her home at Fowey in Cornwall with a small pension.

Unfortunately none of the escapees was literate enough to write an account of the voyage, and though several attempts have been made to describe it, these are largely fictional.[170] We do not know Phillip's emotional response to the story, but any anger he may have felt at the impertinent escape must have been moderated by respect for the convicts' astonishing feat of navigation. He certainly tightened up security as far as the small boats in the harbour were concerned, ordering that an officer's guard should be permanently placed on them and permission sought to remove any one of them – and that was to be granted only if the name of the person requesting it was on a Governor's list. Only for extraordinary reasons could a boat be taken out after dark, and in future the size of any boat built in the colony could not exceed 14 feet (about 4.5 metres).

Making one's way through the various memoirs, to say nothing of the reams of official documents of the period, it is easy to get the impression that Phillip was a workaholic with little time and perhaps small patience for anything but the running of the colony. His life had at least been quieter since the departure of Major Ross to Norfolk Island – Collins too rejoiced that since the Major's departure 'tranquillity has been our guest', adding the uncharitable wish that the wreck of the *Sirius* had disposed of Ross for good. The Governor was still hoping for permission to return to England, believing that the long voyage home might help him to recover from whatever medical problem was causing him such pain in his side – he thought perhaps inflammation of the kidneys. The fact that he was seriously unwell was clear to those around him, while new arrivals from England were shocked by his appearance: 'His health is very bad, he fatigues himself so much. He fairly knocks himself up and won't rest till he is not able to walk.'[171]

There are occasional signs that Phillip's interest in the Aborigines took on the complexion of a hobby, and certainly he also showed interest in the natural life of New South Wales, making notes on the birds and animals he saw around him. He successfully domesticated a dingo and kept four kangaroos (more probably wallabies) which slept in front of the fire in the kitchen of Government House. He sent two as presents to Sir Joseph Banks, with a note that they 'should sleep very warm and have a room to go to in which a good fire should be kept during the cold weather.' He also arranged for 60 tubs of 221 typical New South Wales plants to be sent to Banks at the most convenient sailing, together with plants for the King's gardens. A poor artist himself, he arranged for careful drawings to be made of all the plants and for these to accompany them. He had also hoped to send Banks the head of an Aboriginal, perhaps culled from a victim of smallpox, but the opportunity had not arisen.

These glimpses of Phillip's private life, such they are, are to an extent more puzzling than illuminating – the idea of his coldly acquiring a couple of Aborigine heads for a friend, presumably to be despatched along with the kangaroos, does not teach us to love him. On the other hand he was a man of his time, and the severed heads of natives of various continents were regularly arriving at London termini on their way to museums and private collections. Then there are brief glimpses of him which hint at a warmth of personality which is not shown elsewhere: an off-hand reference by an officer's wife, for instance, to the fact that he was often sending her and other ladies 'little presents'. What could they have been? Something more attractive, surely, than a cake made in the Government House kitchens from weevily flour?

As to his social life, although occasionally Phillip entertained his officers to luncheon or dinner, those do not seem to have been particularly festive occasions – though he often seems to have arranged that music should be played while people were lunching or dining. However, he himself was not extraordinarily interested in it – unlike Surgeon Worgan, who in March was preparing to sail for England and had given his piano to a friend, Mrs Elizabeth

Macarthur, sparing some time from his packing to begin to teach her to play it (before he left she could manage 'God Save the King' and something called 'Foot's Minuet'). Mrs Macarthur, the wife of an officer of the Corps, was an example of the gradually improving social life of Sydney – a lady who had no occupation other than being a lady. She made a point of cultivating Captain Tench – whom she visited almost every day – and Lieutenant. Dawes, to whose observatory she would walk, commissioning him to make orrereys for her and teach her basic astronomy. Unlike the officers' wives of only a year or so previously, she could tell her correspondents in England that she 'never was more sincerely happy.' Despite all the restrictions, Sydney was beginning to be a place where happiness was possible.

Of course it depended on one's character. As usual, the Reverend Johnson was determinedly looking on the black side, telling his correspondents that life had never been so entirely dreadful: 'In almost every respect things are truly wretched and uncomfortable. And when it will be better with us God only knows.' In fact, it was a little better already – he and his wife had moved recently into a house which he described to another correspondent as being 'as comfortable and convenient as I could wish.' He was in fact beginning to be in the minority – a considerable number of convicts whose sentences had been completed were now choosing to stay in the colony.10 seamen and two marines of the *Sirius* also decided to stay, some of them no doubt because they had taken mistresses and were reluctant to leave them for an uncertain future in England, choosing instead an only slightly less uncertain future in New South Wales. Phillip allowed them 18 months' provisions and 60 acres of land, with a house, two breeding sows, six hens and a cock, and a fair quantity of clothes, bedding and blankets.

At the same time the Governor made an order that no convict who had served his sentence should be allowed to return to England leaving behind dependants – wives or mistresses with children – to be cared for by the State; they should either take them to England or leave sufficient funds to care for them (the latter not ever likely to be possible). Collins drily commented that the order was 'designed as a check upon the erroneous opinion which was formed of the efficacy of Mr Johnson's nuptial benediction.'

April began with the now familiar decision from Government House that rations were again to be reduced. Phillip must have been conscious of the hardship this imposed – not only because less food was being provided, but because of its poor quality: unpalatable meat and rice full of weevils. Perhaps to take his mind off the grumbles and complaints of the marines, settlers and convicts, he set out on 11 April on another expedition, steering by compass through the wilderness, with Dawes working out at the end of each day their precise position and the course they had taken. The explorers, including the Governor, thoroughly exhausted themselves but alas found, as Tench put it, not a single area of land 'which could encourage hope, or stimulate industry, to attempt its culture.' The expedition was abandoned after five days.

At last, at the end of May, the drought broke, and Phillip noted that 'more rain fell in three days than had done in many months past, so that the low grounds were thoroughly soaked.' As a result 116 bushels of wheat were sown Rose Hill, where for the first time Phillip decided to celebrate the King's Birthday, marking the occasion with a ceremony at which he re-named the place Parramatta and relieved some convicts condemned for stealing vegetables of the iron collars they had been forced to wear. These had not in any event had much deterrent effect, for six men celebrated the royal birthday on their own account by breaking into the garden of Government House and assaulting the watchman (three of them were later caught and punished, and the watchman was given permission to carry arms). Rose Hill, now Parramatta, continued to thrive. There were 13 settlers at the Ponds and six at the Northern Boundary Farms, northeast of the town; 12 more had settled at Prospect Hill, four miles to the west, and three more south of the river.

In the now usual cycle, ships began to arrive from England – the first, the *Mary Ann*, came in on 9 July with 140 female convicts, six children and one free woman, all in surprisingly excellent health. She also brought quantities of clothing and some food supplies – more worm-eaten rice and putrefied pork and beef. Nevertheless on 27 August full rations were restored. To the disappointment of everyone, however, there were no letters and no newspapers or magazines. As Tench understandably complained, no one on the ship or at home had understood that anyone in Sydney could want to hear of events in the outside world. He asked if a new parliament had been summoned and everyone on the *Mary Ann* simply looked at him blankly – why should anyone wish to know such a thing? What had happened in revolutionary France? – 'Can't say.' For goodness sake, Tench said testily, why didn't someone pick up a couple of newspapers from a coffee house? Well, nobody had thought of it. Sorry.

No doubt the Governor shared Tench's disappointment, but he had other things to think about – for instance, the *Mary Ann* was the first ship of the Third Fleet, and was to be followed by nine more transports, carrying in all 2050 convicts. The *Matilda* arrived on 1 August with 205. She had had a less satisfactory voyage than the *Mary Ann*; 25 convicts and one soldier had died, and more were sick. The stores she brought, however – sufficient for nine months – were in better condition. On the 20th the *Atlantic* arrived, on the 21st the *Salamander* with 160 very healthy convicts, and on 28th the *William and Ann* with 181 more and a sergeant and 12 privates of the New South Wales Corps.

Phillip sent the convicts from the *Salamander* on to Norfolk Island with nine months' provisions and, keeping some of the most useful convicts from the *Matilda* in Sydney, sent the rest and 100 more up to Parramatta. Despite the fact that many of the new batch of convicts seemed healthy, the situation was not quite as satisfactory as Phillip had at first supposed. On 1 September he recorded that though there was little actual illness, a great number of men and women were weak from so many weeks' inaction during the voyage, while some had proved to have fever which had been passed on to the soldiers, so that 285 men were in hospital.

The considerable increase in the population of Sydney led for the first time to regular outbreaks of rowdy behaviour, and the Governor took steps to deal with it. Collins noted that 'the town beginning to fill with strangers (officers and seamen from the transports) and spirituous liquors finding their way among the convicts, it was ordered that none should be landed until a permit had been granted by the judge-advocate [himself]; and the provost-marshal, his assistant, and two principals of the watch, were deputed to seize all spirituous liquors which might be landed without.'[172]

There was a little light relief at the end of the month, when Bennelong announced that his wife, who was about to give birth, had decided she would do the Governor the honour of having the child at Government House. It was with some difficulty that Phillip persuaded her that a confinement at the hospital would be a much better idea. However, pleasure at the idea was soon shattered: despite medical attention, Barangaroo died. Bennelong decided on a ceremonial cremation; Collins supervised the building of a pyre, and the Governor attended the cremation. Sadly, the child also died, and was buried in the garden of Government House.

Good news came on 21 September with the arrival of the

*Gorgon*, a 44-gun warship which carried six months' provisions for 900 people, more stores for the marines, 200 fruit trees and a supply of seeds and – most welcome of all – three bulls, 23 cows, a bull calf, 68 sheep, and 11 hogs. She also brought Philip Gidley King, now officially pronounced Commander and Lieutenant-Governor, and brought with him Phillip's official seal – an impressive silver artefact bearing the motto *Sic fortis Etruria crevit*: 'Thus Etruria grew strong'. It bore the King's arms, and on the reverse a seated figure representing Industry, with a bale of wool, a beehive, a pickaxe and a shovel at her feet, three men and a plough, and in the foreground a ship and what purported to be the town of Sydney. With it came a new commission entitling him to the right to remit the sentence of any worthy convict.

Phillip showed off the new seal at a dinner-party at Government House. It was a valuable symbol, and he must have felt in some way that his mandate was renewed, the seal regularising not only his own position but that of the colony; it had always been subject to the King, the property of England, but the seal symbolised his authority under the crown, which previously had had little outward mark. Certainly it came on the cusp between bad and better times in New South Wales.

More transports arrived: the *Active* with 154 male convicts and the *Queen* with 126 male and 23 female convicts from Ireland. The Irish were in almost as bad a state as the passengers on the *Neptune* or the *Scarborough* had been, and several of them as they came ashore complained that the captain had withheld their provisions. The Governor ordered that he should go before an enquiry, and the magistrates found that 'great abuses had been practised'; they had no authority to deal with the matter in Sydney, but they sent a scathing report to the Secretary of State at home in England. Conditions on the *Atlantic* had been almost as bad – so bad that some convicts and a few of the crew had conspired to mutiny. The master, George Bowen, had shot the ring-leader just as he was about to kill the man at the wheel and two convicts had been hanged at the yard-arm.

The masters had also privately brought out with them a large quantity of things which they believed they could sell at a profit – 'articles of comfort', as Collins called them. The problem was paying for them – the colony had no currency, so deals were generally done in Spanish dollars, which were valued at anything between four and five shillings. Phillip, against his will, was forced to intervene and fix an 'official' exchange rate of 5s per dollar, while complaining to Nepean at the inconvenience of 'not having any money in the colony.' The rate of exchange was largely immaterial, for few people could afford what the masters were selling.

Made suspicious by the behaviour of the master of the *Queen*, Phillip began to look into the transports more carefully and found that on board her, and on the *Albemarle*, the *Britannia* and the *Admiral Barrington*, which arrived during October, there were other irregularities – some of them were carrying private cargoes for the Portuguese – cargoes of material like copper and iron which would have been extremely useful to the colony. He complained to Grenville that:

> the *Admiral Barrington, Albermarle*, and *Queen*, transports, had on board a very considerable quantity of copper, lead, iron, and cordage, the masters of those ships were sent for, and they acknowledged having received on board the quantities of *copper*, &c., specified in a list which the master of the Albermarle delivered . . . They say that most of those articles were received on board after they had taken in what stores and provisions Government had to send, that they never declared their ships full, and that it was known they had those articles

on board, which were received publickly and intended for a Portuguese settlement in India. They could not, I should suppose, have been put on board unknown to the agent employed by the Navy Board . . . Your Lordship will readily conceive of how much consequence it would have been to the settlement had two or three hundred tons of limestone been sent out, and which might have been done, if those ships found it necessary to bring so much shingle ballast; for the limestone might with little trouble have been changed for the stone of this country. The inconvenience which would attend unloading the ships will be seen, and without which it is impossible to say what they really have on board; but there is every reason to suppose that the account given in of copper and lead makes but a small part of what they have brought out. Of the cordage no account can be got; the quantity is supposed to be very considerable.[173]

This indifference on the part of the Admiralty to even his most urgent requests dogged Phillip like some perpetual nagging psychological illness. Though he was equally plagued by the indolence and misbehaviour of the convicts in his charge and continually grumbled about them, he had always expected that problem. He had not anticipated continual negligence on the part of his masters in London (though perhaps he should have done).

The convict population was now much increased – in addition to the men on the *Active* and the Irish on the *Queen*, 129 more men had arrived on the *Britannia* and 264 on the *Admiral Barrington*. In all, the Third Fleet had carried out 1,695 male and 168 women convicts, as well as eight women and nine children[174] – the families of convicts already at Sydney, who had sent for them, and whose passage seems to have been assisted by the Government, conscious of the great disproportion between

231

the male and female population of New South Wales.

The harbour was bustling with craft, but the fleet was soon to be dispersed – five of them to fish for whales off the coast of Brazil, the other five bound for Bombay to load with cotton. While the latter were in port, Phillip could hire them if he wished – and he was pleased to do so. Since the loss of the *Sirius* he had had no ship for general use – the *Supply* was in so poor a state that she could only be repaired in a British shipyard. He decided to send her to England for that purpose and to hire the *Atlantic* and the *Queen*, sending the former to Norfolk Island with King, who was to take up his position there as Governor, and to recall Major Ross and his marines. Johnson was also going forth to pay some attention to the spiritual well-being of the convicts on the Island, which he felt (not without reason) might have been neglected while they had been under the care of Major Ross. Ross was to return to England on the *Gorgon*. Collins had been considering the same voyage, but on hearing that Ross was to be on board speedily changed his mind: 'with him I would not sail were wealth and honours to attend me when I landed,' he told his father in a letter.

The Governor's dispatches to London were, as usual, full of politely phrased, discreet but unmistakably impatient grumbles. Though the colony was no longer starving, the supplies which had come out recently still provided less food than had been hoped for – only five months' supply of flour, 10 months of beef and pork, 23 days of oatmeal and 12 days of peas. It was more than merely inconvenient that he had no ships except those he could hire. 'The colony should never be without two ships,' he told Grenville, 'and I feel it my duty to say that I think no ships can with safety be employed on this station unless they are King's ships, that is, ships having commission, warrant, and petty officers on board them; and I think that more than one commissioned officer should be on board such ship[s].'[175]

Collins' return to England would leave him short of a Judge-Advocate, and he would be short of several officers; moreover it was extremely important that the population of convicts should be leavened by 'a few honest, intelligent settlers.'

His reasons for arguing for a supply of free settlers were sensible and based on experience: 'The vicious and the idle are not easily reformed while they are incorporated in one body. Precept has little effect, but example will do much, and although I can still say with great truth and equal satisfaction that the convicts in general behave better than ever could be expected, and that their crimes, with very few exceptions, have been confined to the procuring for themselves the common necessaries of life, crimes which it may be presumed will not be committed when a more plentiful ration renders those little robberies unnecessary; still we shall want some good characters to whom these people might look up. Having them will be attended with every advantage, and it is to be remembered that the business of cultivation is at present in the hands of few who ever turned their thoughts that way before they came to this country, and very few indeed have more than a very superficial knowledge in agriculture.'[176]

Another aspect of the problem of expanding good farming land was that so few men wanted to stay in New South Wales if there was the faintest chance of their returning to England. Expirees – those convicts who had served their terms – could chose either to take up land grants, work for others for a wage or return to England. A few chose to take the gamble of working the land, a few more worked for wages, but the great majority chose to return to England. This was as true of the marines as it was of the convicts.

Then there remained, as always, the practical matter of the shortage of equipment – the colony needed cross-cut saws, axes, combs, iron pots and 'two or three hundred frying pans'

– at present spades were being used to fry food, which speedily destroyed them as useful implements. Phillip would need, he told Grenville, to set up a windmill shortly, and iron mills and querns for grinding corn were in the meantime extremely necessary. There were now 2,570 male and 608 female convicts and 161 children to be clothed, and the Government had not sent a single length of cloth for shirts or shifts. With more and more official business to be done he also needed paper ('stationery', he told Grenville with a touch of irony, 'is not to be procured in this place.') Finally, could he please have some wax – he could not use his seal without it (one can hear him muttering, 'The fools might have thought of *that!*').

There was another problem. For some reason many of the new arrivals were convinced that China was 150 miles north of Sydney, and 15 or 20 of them had left to walk there, taking some stolen provisions with them. They had been traced as far as Lane Cove before all trace of them had been lost. Most had presumably perished, for they had never been found; a few had been brought back, naked, starving and dehydrated. Since most of the latest batch of convicts went out every day to work in the bush it was impossible to watch out for all of them and, though he hated to criticise a race of people among which he had many friends, Phillip had reluctantly to record that most of the foolish offenders were Irish.

Once again there was a heat-wave in the early summer; one convict died of heat-stroke and the general view was that the heat contributed to the deaths of the 50 people who also died during November. Water was once more short, and the Governor ordered that ships should water on the north shore rather than from the diminishing Tank Stream. He was also forced to reduce rations once again. Himself suffering from the heat, exhaustion and the pain in his side, and frustrated by the lethargy and lack of consideration of his masters, he sat down at

B

his desk in Government House on Sunday 21 November, and
wrote again to Grenville:

> My Lord,
> I am honoured with your Lordship['s] letter of the 19th
> of February in answer to mine to Lord Sydney, and beg
> leave to assure your Lordship that I should not hesitate
> a moment in giving up my private affairs to the public
> service; but from a complaint which so very frequently
> puts it out of my power to use that exercise which my
> situation requires, and the present state of this colony,
> in which I believe every doubt respecting its future
> independency as to the necessaries of life is fully done
> away, I am induced to request permission to resign the
> Government that I may return to England in hopes of
> finding that relief which this country does not afford.
> I have, &c.,
>
> A. PHILLIP.

How much he must have wished that he could have sailed home
on the *Supply*, which left Port Jackson on the 26th, carrying that
letter. Tench watched her on her way, 'the little ship which
had so often agitated our hopes and fears, which from long
acquaintance we had learned to regard as part of ourselves,
whose doors of hospitality had been ever thrown open to
relieve our accumulated wants and chase our solitary gloom.'
If he wished himself on board, at least he knew that the date
of his own departure was not far ahead – he 'would not say
that we contemplated its approach with mingled sensations: we
hailed it with rapture and exultation.'

# FOURTEEN

One can understand the reason why Phillip finally wrote out his letter of resignation – or rather his letter requesting permission to resign.  Given his physical condition, it is surprising that his decision did not come sooner.  Any other man plagued by physical pain and the frustrations of his office might well have taken the action much earlier; only Phillip's sense of duty had kept him in place until now.  All the same, had his health been better he might have delayed the final step, for in many ways he could have supposed that the next five years would see great advances in the colony which it would have been a pleasure to witness and supervise.

Mary Ann Parker, the wife of the captain of the *Gorgon*, left the fullest description by any disinterested person of the state of things in New South Wales four years after the first landing. It presents a much more positive view than that of anyone else whose records we have.  She was also delighted by the physical beauty of the landscape – something which understandably had not particularly commended itself to those who had had to cope with the stern business of actually scraping a living from it.  Governor Phillip and Judge-Advocate Collins came on board the *Gorgon* soon after she had dropped anchor on 21 September, dined with Captain Parker and then took him and his wife ashore to show them around.

When we went on shore we were all admiration at the natural beauties raised by the hand of Providence without expense or toil; I mean the various flowering shrubs, natives of this country, that grew apparently from the rock itself. The gentle ascents, the winding valleys and the abundance of flowering shrubs render the face of the country very delightful. The shrub which most attracted my attention was one which bears a white flower very much resembling our English hawthorn; the smell of it is both sweet and fragrant and perfumes the air around for a considerable distance. There is also plenty of grass which grows with the greatest vigour and luxuriance but which however, as Captain Tench justly observes, is not of the finest quality, and is found to agree better with horses and cows than with sheep.

Our amusements here, although neither numerous nor expensive, were to me perfectly novel and agreeable: the fatherly attention of the good Governor upon all occasions with the friendly politeness of the officers rendered our *séjour* perfectly happy and comfortable . . . [Government House] always provided a home for me: under this hospitable roof I have often ate part of a kangaroo with as much glee as if I had been a partaker of some of the greatest delicacy of the metropolis, altho' latterly I was cloyed with them and find them very disagreeable . . . Our parties generally consisted of Mrs King, Mrs Johnson[177] and the Ladies who reside at the colony.

We made several excursions up the cove to the settlement called Parramatta. I upon first arrival at Parramatta was surprised to find that so great a progress had been made in this new settlement which contains above a thousand convicts besides the military. There is a good level road of great breadth that runs nearly as mile in a straight direction from the landing place to the

Governor's house which is a small convenient building placed upon a gentle ascent and surrounded by about a couple of acres of garden ground.[178]

Mrs Parker was not blind, however, to the less admirable aspects of the colony. She was taken to the hospital in Sydney, where her tranquillity was seriously disturbed: 'In every bed and on every side lay the dying and the dead. Horrid spectacle, it makes me shudder when I reflect that it will not be the last exhibition of this kind of human misery that will take place in this country whilst the present method of transporting these miserable wretches is pursued.'

Governor Phillip's own tranquillity was somewhat disturbed by the arrival on the *Queen* on 5 December of Major Ross, who reported to Government House that he had brought with him all the marines who had decided to remain on Norfolk Island. Why he had done this, except possibly to annoy, remains a mystery – he said it was 'to sign their accounts.' At any rate Phillip had to pay to have them all returned to the island. His only comfort was that at least Ross would soon be permanently out of his life – virtually the last glimpse he had of the Major was as he stormed out of his tent to fight a duel with a Captain Hill on 13 December (for what reason we do not know; nor do we know the result, except that no one was injured even after each had taken two shots at the other).

Phillip's relationship with Ross had not in any way sweetened during the latter's time on Norfolk Island, and there is no doubt that Ross had some reason to criticise the Governor. Phillip's original commission had instructed him to occupy the island and colonise it to prevent its occupation by any foreign power, and also to look into the possibility of there being large quantities of flax there. The idea of cultivating flax had failed, but the island had been useful in other ways, in particular as a dormitory for unwanted prisoners from Sydney, for though at first cultivation had been almost as difficult there as in New South Wales it had seemed capable from the first of supporting a considerable population. After the failure of the harvest in New South Wales in 1789 and with supplies from England failing to arrive at Sydney Phillip was convinced he should begin to transfer people to the island when the opportunity arose. In May of that year he sent over 21 male convicts, six women and three children; they would have a greater chance of survival on the island. In February of 1790, when Sydney was still seriously in want of food and the *Supply* arrived from Norfolk Island with reports of a plethora of fish and birds there, he decided to send her back with the *Sirius* carrying both convicts and marines – 116 male and 67 female convicts, 27 more children and two companies of marines.

If from Phillip's point of view this seemed not unreasonable, the Lieutenant-Governor of the Island, Gidley King, loyal to Phillip as he was, cannot have been entirely delighted, for it speedily became clear that the Governor was using Norfolk Island as a dumping-ground for undesirables – convicts and indeed marines who had proved difficult to control. These included men like marine Henry Wright, who had been found guilty of raping a child, and the black convict Caesar, who had a knack of escaping from any prison or set of chains by which he was confined.

Especially after he had relieved King of his duties and sent Major Ross to the island as Lieutenant-Governor (together with his almost equally splenetic second-in-command, Captain James Campbell), there was a degree to which Phillip set Norfolk Island aside in his mind; unsurprisingly those on the island felt this, especially when he was quick to send them convicts and the dregs of the marine corps but slow to forward on to them a share of what supplies reached him in Sydney.

Their anger reached a peak in August of 1790, when the people on the island heard of the arrival of supplies at Sydney two months earlier, which had still not reached them. Lieutenant Bradley told his journal that 'the reason for their having been so long delayed seems only to be known to our very *humane Governor* who, no doubt, must have *felt much* for the distressed situation of the five hundred Inhabitants on Norfolk Island. If we even allow him to possess only those feelings which a reasonable being would have for a fellow creature, it is unaccountable what could have kept him from retrieving us.'[179]

However, when Phillip left the antipodes, he could count Norfolk Island as a success. Of a population of 1,115, 812 were self-supporting. There were 123 settlers made up of emancipated convicts, seamen and marines, who between them had 179 wives and children. The marine officers and free people, with their wives and children, numbered 121. King thought that within a year it could be entirely self-supporting, yet within two years he was suggesting that it should be abandoned as being too remote and difficult for shipping and too costly to maintain. Slowly, the settlers were wrenched from the land they had worked so hard to cultivate and by 1808 only 200 people remained on the Island; by 1813, a year before Phillip's death, it was deserted. 11 years later the British Government instructed the then Governor of New South Wales to use the island as a place to which to send 'the worst description of convicts' and it became notorious for the cruelty and degradation inflicted on its unfortunate prisoners.

When the *Gorgon* sailed on 18 December she carried Ross, Tench and the marines who had come out with the First Fleet. Another passenger who may have sailed on her was Lieutenant Ralph Clark, who had come in on the *Queen*, sea-sick all the way and unable to see to the comfort of Mary Branham, who was below decks nursing their five month old daughter Alicia.[180] Also on board the *Gorgon* was Lieutenant William Dawes.

His decision to leave the colony caused the Governor some difficulty. Dawes actually very much wanted to stay, but had become embroiled in an implacable quarrel with Phillip. The trouble had started when he had questioned the Governor's orders to join the punitive expedition in 1790, after the murder of M'Entire. Phillip had never been able to forgive this. Then he had had to reprimand Dawes for leaving his observatory without sufficient cause, when he had been supposed to be on duty there. On that occasion, the Governor claimed, the young man spoke to him in language which in other circumstances – for instance, if Phillip could have afforded to lose a useful young officer – would have merited a court martial. (In the somewhat peculiar circumstances of the settlement Phillip had often, he told Grenville, found it necessary 'to pass over improprieties which could not otherwise have passed unnoticed'.) Finally, he accused Dawes of buying extra rations from a convict, when that activity was strictly forbidden.

As he told Grenville, Phillip would have been pleased to have kept Dawes in Sydney, 'had he seen his error', but the officer must acknowledge his faults.

Dawes replied with all a young man's assurance that he had thought it was perfectly in order for him to buy flour from the convict baker to the garrison, which the man had had left over from his normal batch. As to the language he had used to the Governor when charged with leaving his post at the observatory, he had not meant this to be improper or disrespectful, but thought he should do himself the justice to 'deny such charge in terms sufficiently clear and expressive to leave no possibility of misconception.'

Phillip was equally forthright:

REPEATED orders had been given to prevent the convicts from selling any part of their ration, but which they continued to do, and carried on that trade with those who from their situation were not likely to be suspected, consequently detection was not very practicable. Robberies were too frequently the consequence, and it was not possible that it should be otherwise, for every man could eat his ration, and with which very few of those people were satisfied; at the same time they made a practice of joining together a part of their ration of flour, and giving ten pounds of flour for a bottle of rum, and thirty pounds of flour for a pound of tobacco. This was at a time when the ration was only four pounds of flour for a man for seven days. A convict being detected, who, it appeared on his examination before the magistrates, had made a practice of receiving flour and other species of provision from the convicts and exchanging them for spirits and other articles, he declared that Lieut. Dawes was one with whom he had made such exchanges, having given forty pounds of flour for twenty pounds of sugar to that officer. It does not appear that Lieut. Dawes could [not] know to whom the flour belonged, as the man of whom the purchase was made (a blacksmith ) carried on that trade for a variety of people; nor can the Governor admit that Lieut. Dawes never purchased any other species of provisions, as his Major-Commandant had been some time before desired to point out to him the impropriety of his purchasing pease from convicts.

Dawes was certainly being a little less honest than was strictly necessary, and certainly Phillip's point of view can be appreciated, but the fact that he demanded a full and unconditional apology, and also insisted that if Dawes remained in Sydney he must transfer to the New South Wales Corps and lose seniority, made it impossible for the young man to climb down. So he sailed on the *Gorgon* – perhaps leaving behind an Aboriginal mistress, Patyegarang; he had forged a close relationship with her while compiling a dictionary of Aboriginal languages, and in the notebook used for the purpose there is a note describing her 'standing by the fire naked',[181] which suggests that discussion of the vowel sounds of the Cameragal dialect did not occupy all their time.

Tench, before he joined the ship, attended church service for the last time in Sydney – now, he reflected, merely a depot for stores. The future of the colony seemed to be concentrated on Parramatta. There, there was some optimism and reason for it. Here in Sydney he looked around him at the congregation and was depressed: 'Several hundred convicts were present, the majority of whom I thought looked the most miserable beings in the shape of humanity I ever beheld: they appeared to be born down with fatigue.'[182]

The marines lined the decks of the *Gorgon* as she sailed out on 18 December, few of them sorry to take their last look at the harbour of Port Jackson. Collins quite rightly paid them tribute: they were 'as valuable a corps as any in his Majesty's service. They had struggled here with greatly more than the common hardships of service and were now quitting a country in which they had opened and smoothed the way for their successors and from which, whatever benefit might hereafter be derived must be derived by those who had the easy task of treading in paths previously and painfully formed by them.' [183]

Christmas was celebrated in Sydney by the robbery of 22 gallons of spirits from the main store, and perhaps partly fired up by this a crowd of convicts went to Government House to demand that their rations, lately been distributed daily, should again be given out once a week on Saturdays, as had previously been the case. Phillip came out to them and told them he was in no mood to grant their demand, and when they started to mumble and grumble told them that he knew perfectly well the names of the men who had organised the protest, and would not hesitate to make examples of them if there was any more trouble. Collins reported that 'This was the first instance of any tumultuous assembly among these people, and was now to be ascribed to the spirit of resistance and villainy lately imported by the newcomers from England and Ireland.' What it was, in fact, was the first instance on the continent of political action, but of course it failed, and 'before they were dismissed [the protesters] promised greater propriety of conduct and implicit obedience to the orders of their superiors and declared their readiness to receive their provisions as had been directed.'[184]

Irritated by the incident the Governor issued his first proclamation of 1792, ordering that in the case of any future riot anyone found outside his or her hut at the time of the disturbance would be deemed to have taken part in it, and would be dealt with accordingly. What this meant was underlined at the court at Parramatta on the same day, when Collins and the Reverend Jackson awarded 15 convicts a total of 1,950 lashes for various offences including 'going to Sydney without leave' and stealing potatoes. The convict who had made an unwarranted expedition to Sydney was deterred from a similar excursion during the next six months by having heavy irons attached to one of his legs.

If the floggings seem overly severe, one should remember that the store of food supplies available in the colony was still varying wildly between relative plenty (after harvest-time) and real want, and that even at the best of times the instinct to get hold of as much food as possible, whenever possible, was strong — one result being that one-sixth of the harvest each year was lost through thieving. Phillip no doubt felt obliged to do something about this, despite not really having the power to do a great deal. The increased population of the colony had brought a proportionate increase in crime and there was strong fellow-feeling among the convicts responsible (most of them comparatively recent arrivals, particularly the Irish). Consequently, though generous rewards were on offer to anyone 'peaching' on his fellows, this had no result. It was also difficult to punish the offenders adequately. Collins reports that most of them were so weak from hunger and so emaciated (the reasons for their thieving in the first place) that flogging would probably kill them, and putting them in irons carried a danger of permanent injury. The Governor did not want to be seen as a man who murdered starving men for stealing food. Even those of the military who grumbled against him acknowledged his difficulties — Richard Atkins, a free settler who had disgraced himself in England by his addiction to alcohol and had come to redeem himself in New South Wales, commented that people might exclaim against the Governor, but he doubted whether any other man could do as well.[185]

The *Pitt*, arriving at Port Jackson on 14 February, carried the replacement for Major Ross — the new Lieutenant-Governor, Major Francis Grose, Commandant of the New South Wales Corps, who arrived in the company of 319 male and 49 female convicts, five children and seven free women, with some provisions (though only enough to serve the colony for 40 days). Grose was an experienced soldier who had served during the American War of Independence and was often described as jovial and amiable, neither of which quality he was to display in his relationship with Phillip — partly no doubt because he was impatient at being merely a second-in-command with little real power. He was as undistinguished in manner as in his military career; Captain William Bligh, a future Governor of New South Wales who met him at Cape Town on his way out, described him as 'a man not blessed with any great share of knowledge.' He had raised three companies of the Corps — over

300 men – and sold captaincies and lieutenancies to a number of them, building the foundation of what became a substantial fortune. The fourth company of the Corps had been raised by the Governor himself and consisted of men of the First Fleet Marine Corps who had decided to stay on in the colony. Grose's commission was publicly read at six in the morning of 17 March when he reviewed the Corps, whose colours were raised for the first time in New South Wales. The Governor attended and received the salute of the Corps and a 15-gun salvo from a ship in harbour. He was no doubt hoping that his relationship with his new lieutenant would be less confrontational than that of his predecessor.

The Reverend Johnson was meanwhile nagging Phillip, once again, about the moral state of the colonists – in particular the fact that there was no centre of worship and he still had to hold services in any old barn that happened to be available on any particular Sunday. He did not wish, he said, 'or mean to interfere with anything that does not concern myself, but as the clergyman of the colony and intrusted with the spiritual charge of these unhappy people around us, I submit it to your Excellency's own consideration whether, before the approaching winter, some place could not be thought of and built both here and at the new settlement for the purpose of carrying on public worship.'[186]

Johnson seems to have got nowhere with that request, but Phillip did respond to another of the clergyman's suggestions, acceding to the setting up of the first schools in the colony – one in Sydney and one at Parramatta, with a schoolmistress in each who taught the convicts' children religion, morality, reading, writing and arithmetic for free, and those of the military for a small fee.

The colony now not only had schools, but shops, or at least a market. The masters of visiting ships had for some time been given permission to set up stalls to sell goods they had brought for the purpose – the latest was one established by the master of the *Pitt*, whose goods were as usual too expensive for most people to afford. Now, the free settlers began to trade among themselves, with the Governor's encouragement: they could sell grain to each other, and to the commissary, at a fixed market price. Phillip set up a market at Parramatta for grain, fish, clothing and anything else anyone wished to sell. There, laying hens sold at between seven and 10 shillings each, eggs at threepence each, fresh pork at a shilling a pound, potatoes at threepence a pound, cabbages at a penny each and coffee, a great luxury, at two shillings and sixpence a pound. Convicts were allowed to trade, though great care was taken to attempt to ensure that there was no traffic in stolen goods (this had become much more prevalent since the road between Sydney and Parramatta had been improved and stolen property could be carried from one to the other and disposed of before the thieves could be identified).

Phillip was concerned that trade should be encouraged, but was equally concerned that it should not be at the expense of the settlers and to the profit of private *entrepreneurs* like the masters of visiting vessels. In any case, what possible value to the colony was there in pieces of millinery for the ladies or fancy waistcoat buttons for the military when the colony was desperately short of basic clothing for the convicts and such necessities as cooking pots and spades? Certainly some clothing had arrived, but it was of material so thin and so badly stitched that 'most of the people are naked a few weeks after they have been clothed.' Phillip pointed out to Henry Dundas, Grenville's successor in London[187], that 'The Commissary being obliged to purchase various articles out of the *Pitt*, where the private property sold in this settlement importations amounted to upwards of 4,000 pounds, may serve in some measure to point out what might be brought by a ship loaded wholly on the account of Government.

Many of the most necessary articles which had been put on board that ship were afterwards landed, and yet the stowage of those articles would not have taken up one-quarter of the stowage which the private trade took up. It is not, sir, to reflect on the person who commanded the *Pitt* that I make this observation, but from feeling the obligation of pointing out a circumstance which may prevent a similar evil, the effects of which are at this moment severely felt in the colony.'[188]

Once again, as had been the case every year since his arrival, the Governor was worried about supplies. In early April there were storms at Parramatta which beat down the unharvested corn and spoiled it, while down in Sydney most of the houses had leaking roofs and some had collapsed; plants and seeds were sluiced out of the gardens and the bridge over the Tank Stream was washed away. Cold weather began, and the convicts huddled in their damp hovels in their thin clothing, now once more on short rations. The Irish who had come out on the *Queen* suffered most — of the 126 men who had landed from her, only 50 remained alive by May. Phillip had ordered that the weakest of them should be excused from hard labour, but as Collins remarked 'it was not hard labour that destroyed them, it was an entire want of strength in the constitution to receive nourishment, to throw off the debility that pervaded their whole system, or to perform any sort of labour whatever.'[189]

The sick and semi-starving were not greatly comforted by the fact that the Governor himself laid the first stone of the foundations of a Town Hall at Parramatta, but he was pursuing a vision of the town as a real and thriving centre of food production. He took Atkins up to the area to show him around Prospect Hill, where 13 convict settlers had set up a community, and despite their primary occupations — there was a weaver, two carpenters and a butcher among them — were working hard to establish wheat on the poor land of their allotments.

Then there was the Ponds, with 14 more settlers, one or two of whom were doing well – particularly an ex-seaman John Ramsay and his wife, who had a good plot of corn and a small, well laid-out garden. Phillip Schaffer, who had been sent out on the *Guardian* to supervise the convicts (difficult, for he then spoke no English), had established a really sound farm with 140 acres, 14 of which were in maize and corn, vines and tobacco. Schaffer was busy clearing the rest, and was living in a sound brick house.

There were other settlers with individual farms – Mr Arndell, an assistant surgeon, held six acres, Christopher Magee, an emancipated convict, had eight acres well-cultivated, and of course James Ruse, the most ambitious and successful of all. Atkins settled at Parramatta as magistrate with admiration for the settlers and the (somewhat remarkable) conviction that 'they are in every particular much better situated than they could possibly be in England.' He was also filled with admiration for the Governor, who could not be praised too highly for 'the paternal care he gives to all and each of [the settlers] who deserve it.'[190]

No-one had a great deal of energy or enthusiasm with which to celebrate the King's Birthday on 4 June, but as usual Phillip gave his officers dinner at Government House – kangaroo was served, hunters having recently had some success in killing a number (they now hunted with greyhounds, some of which had arrived from England), and there were fresh vegetables from his garden. The customary salvo was raised, bonfires were lit and rum was distributed to the soldiers from the store at the hospital to which the Governor had sent all the rum that remained from the *Sirius* and *Supply*. He got together the convicts in Sydney and gave them the usual loyal address, releasing from their leg irons all those convicts condemned to wear them, except for the most criminal. He also apologised for having had yet again to reduce the food ration, told them that he expected supply ships within days rather than weeks, and that provided they remained patient, orderly and cheerful (the latter rather a big ask), they would then reap their reward.

In fact, yet again, ships were slow in arriving, and the return of the *Atlantic* from India, where she had been sent to buy food, did not relieve matters, for she was loaded only with rice – though Lieutenant Bowen, who commanded her, had also bought two bulls and a cow, 20 sheep and 20 goats. She was unloaded – with great difficulty, as the men of the colony were once more so weak that really hard work could not be expected of them – and sent on to Norfolk Island. Six days later however, on 26 July, the *Britannia* arrived with four months' supply of flour and eight months' of beef and pork. It also brought the news that the reason why more supplies had not already reached Sydney was that the Government had believed that Phillip was going to acquire all future stores from India. How his clear messages could have been misunderstood is another tribute to the opaque understanding of the British civil service. In a sense that was beside the point: the Governor could again increase rations, as he had promised – a change, Collins remarked, that 'gave universal satisfaction.'

Phillip was as positive as possible in his October 1792 dispatch to Dundas, but was also entirely realistic in his estimate of the colony's future:

Of the present state of this settlement, I have the satisfaction of assuring you that the soil and its produce more than answer the expectations which I have formerly given. Our last year's crop of maize, notwithstanding the long drought, was 48,442 bushels, of which 26,492 bushels have been issued as bread for the colony, 695 bushels reserved for seed and other purposes, and not less than 1,500 bushels were stolen from the grounds, notwithstanding every possible precaution was taken to prevent it. From the time the corn began to ripen to the time it was housed, the convicts were pressed by hunger, and great quantities were stolen and concealed in the woods; several convicts died from feeding on it in its crude state, when carrying the grain to the public granary. But in speaking of these people, it is but just to observe that I can recollect very few crimes during the last three years but what have been committed to procure the necessaries of life.

One thousand acres of ground are in cultivation on the public account, of which 800 are in maize, the rest in wheat and barley, agriculture, at Parramatta and a new settlement formed about three miles to the westward of Parramatta, and to which I have given the name of Toon-gab-be, a name by which the natives distinguish the spot. The soil is good, and in the neighbourhood of this place there are several thousand acres of exceeding good ground. The quantity of ground in cultivation by the settlers is 416 acres, and they have 97 acres more ground cleared of timber . . . And I flatter myself that the time now approaches in which this country will be able to supply its inhabitants with grain; but no dependance must be placed on a crop while it is in the ground, consequently regular supplies of flour, &c., from Europe will be necessary until there is a sufficient quantity in store to serve the colony for one year at least. . . . The crop may fail from a dry season, or be lost from fire or other accidents, and to which it may naturally be supposed the crops in this country are more exposed than in Europe.

My letters by the *Supply, Gorgon,* and *Pitt* will have

shewn that I look to England for the necessary supplies, of which we still stand in great need, and which I doubt not are now on their passage; but the great length of time in which this colony has remained in its present state takes away hope from many, and the consequences must be obvious. It has, sir, been my fate to point out wants from year to year; it has been a duty the severest I have ever experienced. Did those wants only respect myself or a few individuals I should be silent; but here are numbers who bear them badly; nor has the colony suffered more from wanting what we have not received than from the supplies we have received not arriving in time.

He had no sooner laid down his pen after writing his dispatch than he had more domestic trouble to sort out – stirred by none other than the Lieutenant-Governor. As far as his talent to annoy was concerned, Major Grose was to prove a worthy successor to Major Ross.

# FIFTEEN

On 4 October Governor Phillip was amazed to receive a completely unexpected letter from Major Grose, the Commandant of the New South Wales Corps:

> Sir, The situation of the soldiers under my command, who at this time have scarcely shoes to their feet, and who have no other comforts than the reduced and unwholesome rations served out from the stores, has induced me to assemble the captains of my corps for the purpose of consulting what could be done for their relief and accommodation. Amongst us we have raised a sufficient sum to take up the *Britannia*, and as all money matters are already settled with the master, who is also an owner, I have now to request you will interest yourself in our favour, that you will, by representing the necessities of my soldiers, protect this ship from interruption as much as you can, and that you will assist us to escape the miseries of that precarious existence we have hitherto been so constantly exposed to. With every respect, &c., FRANS. GROSE,[191]

Phillip thought this an abominably impertinent letter. Grose had absolutely no authority to hire the *Brittania* and send her off to the Cape in what amounted to a private trading mission. Who knew whether the goods brought back would be genuine necessities or supplies to be re-sold within the colony? The proposal seemed to open up the probability of future illicit trade with the Cape and more personally it raised the old *canard* which had dogged Phillip ever since his arrival; that he maintained a better table for himself and his favourites at Government House than others in the colony could enjoy. He fired off an immediate response to the Major: the master of the *Britannia*, if he hired his ship to the Major and his officers, would be acting outside his licence from the East India Company and he, the Governor, could have no responsibility to protect it. Moreover:

> I am sensible that the garrison suffers many inconveniences from the necessary supplies not arriving, and which I should gladly do away by any means in my power, yet I cannot acquiesce with you in thinking that the ration served from the public stores is unwholesome; I see it daily at my own table; I am sorry to see that it is neither so good nor in that quantity as I would wish it . . . As to the nature of the ration, it is, I believe, nearly as good as what is issued to the army and navy in India, and I think that there can be little doubt but that an ample supply of provisions from Europe will arrive before the *Britannia* can return to this port; and there is every reason to expect that a very few months will remove the inconvenience the colony labours under . . . When the *Atlantic* was sent to Calcutta, every officer was permitted to send for such articles as he wanted, and which will always be allowed, and everything else done for the accommodation of the officers and men under your command which the public service admits. I am sorry that I cannot, with propriety, take any official step in this business. I am, &c., A. PHILLIP.[192]

Grose immediately went up to Government House where we can assume there was a more or less heated discussion, but that in the end tempers cooled. An accommodation was reached, at all events, and the *Brittania* sailed for the Cape. Phillip's reluctant permission was, as he had suspected, a mistake – the voyage was the first of an increasing number which comprised an illicit trading operation.

The dispatch Phillip was completing when Grose's letter interrupted him bears a strong resemblance to every other dispatch he sent from New South Wales during his tenure of office there. He repeated once more his pleas for material assistance: he had asked again and again for iron pots – perhaps no one in London quite realised how necessary these were, or surely they would have been sent? There was less excuse for the neglect to send cross-cut saws, axes and other tools necessary for farming and building – certainly, through sheer necessity, they had found ways of making some of them in the colony, but the demand was greater than the supply – these things wore out so quickly. The working clothes which had been sent had been thin and delicate, and often packed so badly that they were affected by damp and had fallen to pieces the first or second time they were washed.

It was the old, old story, and with the old, old result – promises, promises. A letter from Dundas brought out on the *Royal Admiral* together with 289 male and 47 female convicts (10 had died from fever) at least seemed to acknowledge Phillip's letter of resignation: 'I cannot conclude this letter without assuring you how much I lament that the ill state of your health deprives his Majesty of your future services in the Government of N. S. Wales and I have only to hope that on quitting the settlement you will have the satisfaction of leaving it in a thriving and prosperous situation.'[193]

Did this mean his resignation had been accepted? Phillip wrote back to Dundas asking for a clearer explanation of what was expected of him. Was it the case that the King had given permission for him to return to England? Or was it, as he feared, that he was expected to remain there, perhaps for some years? Meanwhile he also wrote to Nepean complaining that the state of his health really made it necessary for him to leave New South Wales, but he did not want to take passage home and arrive to find that he was not expected. In the event he had no option but to make his own plan and follow it, since Dundas simply ignored his request for elucidation of his ambiguous replies.

The *Royal Admiral*, besides the convicts and a batch of letters, had brought various 'private goods' for sale to the settlers, and they were clearly more realistically priced than had usually been the case, for the master was able to sell £3,600 worth of them before sailing and left the remainder (valued at £750) for later sale.

Meanwhile an illicit trade in rum had started, which was later to run completely out of control. For once, Phillip miscalculated his attempts to govern it; he issued licences to sell porter, under certain restrictions, but these were used to sell rum, and since people were also getting their hands on the wine he had been sent from Britain with instructions to sell it only to officers and men of the New South Wales Corps, the streets were full of rolling drunkards who, in the way of rolling drunkards, not only fought and injured each other and beat their wives but stole and damaged property.

Materially, however, by August and September the colony was in much better shape. More supplies had arrived, with welcome new clothes – each convict was issued with two 'frocks' of coarse cloth, two pairs of trousers of the same material, a hat, a pair of yarn stockings and a pair of shoes and a comb; the women got a petticoat each and a coarse shift, with stockings and shoes, soap, needles and thread, a thimble and a pair of scissors.

At the end of October, Phillip let it be known in the colony that he would be standing down and sailing home on the *Atlantic* in mid-December. It was a good decision, for had he waited until the arrival of the next store-ship he would have found that the dispatches she carried made absolutely no reference to his desire for leave. His relatively sudden decision is out of line with his usual behaviour, and one can only put it down to an increase in physical discomfort and mental strain (particularly in his dealings with Major Grose).

There was general consternation at the news of his resignation – not only on the part of the Governor's admirers, but even those who constantly criticised him: better the Devil you know. To those closest to him the news was no real surprise; though he had done his best to conceal it, his failing health and the increased pain he suffered had been obvious.

His last weeks at the colony were filled with just the mixture of positive and negative events he had always experienced. There had been few unalloyed positive aspects to any day in his life as Governor. He was happy to be able to buy 569 barrels of American beef and 27 of pitch and tar from the brigantine *Philadelphia*, which docked from America. She was the first American ship to enter the harbour – the world was beginning to discover that New South Wales was a place with which trade was possible: within months trading vessels began to call regularly from England, Ireland, Calcutta, Batavia, America and Chinese ports. Phillip was unhappy to hear that after the *Philadelphia* had sailed her quartermaster and six sailors were discovered to have deserted her and remained in Sydney – why the master did not discover this, or was content to sail without them, is a mystery. The quartermaster, who had served on the *Sirius*, declared that nothing would induce him to return to England; he was imprisoned until he changed his mind. With his ironic humour, Phillip simply put the sailors in a longboat and made them row to and fro to the North Shore until they could be deported.

The *Royal Admiral* sailed on 13 November, and five days later the *Kitty* dropped anchor at Port Jackson. The Governor had been much looking forward to her arrival, for on board there should be 50 families of Quakers who, he had been told, wished to make a new life for themselves in the colony. Clearly, they would be just the sort of free settlers that were needed. Alas, they had decided at the last moment that they had made a rash decision, and decided to remain in England. Phillip sighed, but remembered that on the same vessel there should be 10 artisan convicts – more carpenters, bricklayers and joiners. Of these, all had escaped from the ship during the voyage, presumably at some interim port, except one brick-maker and a joiner.

Moreover, the batch of iron pots which were so badly needed turned out to have been seriously damaged during the *Kitty's* rough voyage, and all but a few were broken. The one welcome piece of cargo on board consisted of two chests packed with 3,870 ounces of silver dollars with which the colony could establish a proper currency (about £90,000 in modern currency). Philip was able to distribute much of this in back pay for his civil servants. He was also able at this time to increase rations.

To the last, his Lieutenant Governor remained a thorn in his side. Grose had been storming up to Government House on a regular basis with the old complaint that Ross had so often made – that the Governor, when reducing the convicts' rations, also reduced everyone else's – including those of the soldiers of his Corps. Moreover, the officers had to suffer the same proportionate reduction as the private soldiers, so (he complained in an official letter to the Under-Secretary for War in London) 'the captain of a company and the convict transported for life divide in share and share alike whatever is served out . . . and what makes our situation the more unpleasant is that the Governor does not feel himself authorised to indulge with grants such as would wish either for comfort or amusement to cultivate a small quantity of ground.'[194] Phillip had told him that he had frequently written to London on the subject but had received no reply; still Major Grose hoped for the Under-Secretary's 'interference'. Happily by the time the question was taken any further, Phillip's interest in it had become theoretical.

He was by the end of November starting to pack what belongings he wanted to take back to England – including a large collection of insects he had gathered over the years, the packing of which he entrusted to Richard Atkins, who in the brief time he had been in the colony had begun to count himself the Governor's friend. Others, too, were packing their few pieces of clothing and a souvenir or two – among them the few remaining marines who had come out with the First Fleet and who had remained in Sydney after the bulk had returned to England (47 decided to stay in the colony). As he prepared to embark on the *Atlantic* John Easty recorded in his journal the fact that he had been, like the Governor himself, four years, 10 months and eight days in New South Wales, 'when we have been three parts of our time on short allowance and hardships. Very much has been undergone, as must be expected by settling a new colony.'[195]

One of Phillip's last acts was to add a pound of flour to the weekly ration; when he left, convicts, marines and settlers were receiving a basic three pounds of flour, five of rice, four of pork or seven of beef and six of oil. The prospects for the harvest were good, the ears of wheat long and full and the straw excellent. Apart from his attention to the rations, the Governor's last official order was to require fire-breaks to be burned around the cultivated areas of land at Parramatta, where a bush fire on 5 December had destroyed one house and several gardens. Two days earlier the Governor had been at Parramatta to open the new hospital, a sturdy brick building near the river, well away from houses and surrounded by a protected area in which the patients could walk and relax.

He left New South Wales with a population of 3,108, including 16 free men and 24 free women, 52 ex-convict settlers and eight emancipated convicts. The total number of convicts amounted to 1,948 men, 414 women and 127 children. In addition there were 1,115 people living on Norfolk Island.

On 10 December, Easty noted that 'This day Arthur Phillip, Governor and Commander in chief and Captain-General in and over his Majesty's territories in New South Wales, embarked on board the *Atlantic* for England, when the New South Wales Corps was under arms and paid him all the marks of honour.' At six in the morning he left Government House to join Lieutenant John Poulden and the last of the marine detachment which had come out with him in 1788. He may have smiled ironically as Major Grose saluted him – now acting Governor, he could deal with the problems Phillip's solutions to which had so irritated him.

The *Atlantic* weighed anchor and sailed out of Port Jackson, and most of the principal officers rowed alongside her until she reached the Heads at eight o'clock, when they gave three cheers to send her on her way. She sighted Falmouth on May 19 and next morning Arthur Phillip stepped ashore in the old country.

# SIXTEEN

*The London Packet* of 29/31 May announced that 'Governor Phillip has brought home with him two natives of New Holland, a man and a boy, and brought them to town'. On board the *Atlantic* with Phillip together with a selection of kangaroos, dingoes and other animals and birds were two Aboriginal men – Bennelong and Yemmerrawannie. The latter was first known to the Governor as a suitor for the hand of Abaroo – Tench described him as 'a slender fine looking youth . . . about sixteen years old.' He had become a favourite of Phillip's and for some time lived at Government House, where he was persuaded to wear clothes and taught to wait at table; he much impressed Mrs Macarthur when she was given lunch there during her visit. Clearly Phillip thought him as nearly 'civilised' as Bennelong, and likely to impress the British public.

While Phillip busied himself with reporting to the Home Office and the Admiralty, the two native Australians were equipped for their expected appearance at the Royal Court. Phillip ordered new clothes for them – they were to appear dressed identically in green coats, blue and buff striped waistcoats, slate-coloured knee-breeches and silk stockings. They were also given extra quilted waistcoats and cotton 'under-waistcoats', another pair of breeches each and later another 12 shirts and eight cravats, with hats, stockings, shoes and shaving equipment. This cost Phillip £30 (today about £2,400), which he presumably met out of his own pocket.

Having got the visit to St James's Palace and the audience

with King George III over, the two Australians were moved into fashionable Mount Street, off Grosvenor Square, attended by a servant, their clothes mended and washed, a small library of books sent in and a master hired to teach them to read and write, as Phillip had always intended. He believed that when and if they could acquire a thorough understanding of the English language, they would be able to pass on an enormous amount of useful information about the Aboriginal way of life.

Apart from all this, they were thoroughly entertained – or at least entertainment was offered them. No doubt they enjoyed riding about London in a private coach to St Paul's, the Tower and elsewhere, but whether they enjoyed bathing in the chilly waters of the Serpentine is more doubtful. On 15 August, carrying gloves and a walking stick each, they were taken to Sadler's Wells Theatre to see a show, with acrobats, tableaux illustrating *The Honours of War; or, The Siege of Valenciennes . . . the late Operations of the Allied Armies Commanded by His Royal Highness the Duke of York*, and finally a sort of pantomime entitled *Pandora's Box; or The Plagues of Mankind*. What can they have thought of it all?

Possibly because of inclement weather, by mid-October Yemmerrawannie was not at all well, a doctor was engaged and both men were sent to Eltham, seven miles or so outside London, to the house of some friends of Phillip, who cared for them. Their house was quite near that of Lord Sydney, now retired from politics, who was very hospitable to the two men. Yemmerrawannie seems to have recovered somewhat, for in November the couple was back in Mount Street, where they found a new wardrobe provided by Phillip, with warmer winter clothes including two pairs of heavy breeches, two pairs of 'fine flannel Drawers, four flannel underwears to wear next the skin' and two waistcoats each; later he gave them greatcoats and night-caps.

But the cold winter weather got its claws into the failing Yemmerrawannie. The doctor bled him and he stayed in bed while Phillip took Bennelong to Covent Garden Theatre to see *The Suspicious Husband* and *Harlequin and Faustus, or, The Devil Will Have His Own*, with 14 scene changes – the sort of display more likely to have interested the Australian than his visit to the trial of Warren Hastings, of which he would surely have made little. Yemmerrawannie was too sick for such outings and was probably looking forward to the day when he and Bennelong would set out on the return voyage to Port Jackson. This seems to have been in train by the new year, when Phillip spent yet more money on clothing for them – two suits, two blue coats, two waistcoats and two pairs of nankeen breeches.

It was about this time – on 8 May 1794 – that Phillip married a second wife – a Miss Isabella Whitehead, about 40 years old, the daughter of a former Sheriff of Lancaster. His estranged wife had died (leaving him £100, or about £8,000 at today's value); the new Mrs Phillip's father died four months after their wedding, and through his wife's estate Phillip became once more a man of considerable means, able to move in society with a freedom which would not have been possible for him, even as ex-Governor of a British colony, on his naval pay. Given the lack of personal documents, we can only guess at the success or otherwise of the second marriage (though recently some letters have been discovered which suggest that the second Mrs Phillip was not a particularly amiable or well-balanced person). She does however seem to have cared for Yemmerrawannie in what proved a terminal illness, for he died, at only 19 years old, on 18 May 1794, and was buried in the graveyard of St John the Baptist church at Eltham. Bennelong said goodbye to Phillip for the last time, visited Yemmerrawannie's grave and sailed for home from Plymouth early in February 1795.

In August of the following year, he wrote to Lord Sydney's steward, Mr Phillips:

Sir, I am very well. I hope you are very well. I live at the Governor's. I have every day dinner there. I have not my wife; another black man took her away; we have had muzzy [bad] doings: he speared me in the back, but I better now . . . all my friends alive and well. Not me go to England no more. I am at home now. I hope Sir you send me anything you please Sir. hope all is well in England. I hope Mrs. Phillips very well. You nurse me Madam when I sick, you very good Madam: thank you Madam, & hope you remember me Madam, not forget. I know you very well Madam. Madam, send me two Pair stockings. You very good Madam. Thank you Madam. Sir, you give my duty to Ld Sydney. Thank you very good my Lord. very good: hope very well all family, very well. Sir, send me you please Some Handkerchiefs for Pocket. you please Sir send me some shoes: two pair you please Sir.[196]

Back in England Phillip, at 53, felt old and ill; he realised that another period in Australia would probably kill him, asked permission to resign the Governorship and almost immediately left London for Bath, where he hoped the waters would alleviate the pain in his left kidney, which had been troubling him for at least two years. He took rooms in South Parade, where Sir Walter Scott had lived as a child, and gave himself over to a doctor who in one way or another seems to have given his patient good advice, for Phillip's health gradually improved – so much indeed that in October of 1793 he informed the Admiralty that he was ready for active service, and returned to London. He naturally continued to take an interest in the affairs of New South Wales, pressing the Home Office to ensure that the colony was properly supplied and most concerned at the growing reliance on rum, which was becoming more and more used as currency, with certain men making small fortunes at the expense of the Crown. He also did his best to respond to requests from officers at New South Wales who appealed to him for his influence on their behalf, and was particularly active on behalf of his friend Philip Gidley King. He failed in his attempt to have King appointed his successor as Governor, but he did manage to have his friend's salary as administrator of Norfolk Island increased.

While at first he seemed to be enjoying married life and to some extent the social whirl which it entailed, his mind was on other things – and on things which would offer him more opportunities than a life in retirement with occasional calls for advice from the Home Office about the colony he had left behind him. The war with the French was not going well in Europe, but Britain still ruled the waves, and Philip returned to active service in 1796 as captain of the ship on which he had served in 1778 – the *Alexander*. Back then he had been first lieutenant; now he was commander.

He joined her in Plymouth. She did a little escort duty – some patrolling, some lying inactive in harbour – then he left her for the *Swiftsure*, which again patrolled the Channel without seeing any action – except the unwelcome action of winter storms. Meanwhile Spain joined France at war and the British were forced to evacuate Corsica and Elba and withdraw from the Mediterranean. There was a welcome victory at Cape St Vincent under Sir John Jervis and Admiral Nelson, and the *Swiftsure* was one of the warships escorting store-ships to Gibraltar. During 1797 Phillip had some difficulty on board with drunkenness and theft – the mutiny at Spithead sent echoes throughout the entire fleet, but Phillip knew how to maintain discipline, and when Nelson came on board to inspect the ship in June he reported her in excellent order and fit for service. That service took in patrol in the Atlantic in April and May, then until September supported Nelson's blockade of Cádiz. Phillip was then sent from the *Swiftsure* to the *Blenheim*, which he found in every way unsure – the crew on the very edge of mutiny, and the ship herself almost unseaworthy.

Moreover, the *Blenheim's* former captain, Admiral Charles Thompson, had been removed from command as the result of a vicious row between himself and his superior officer, Lord St Vincent (as Jervis had now become). St Vincent had executed two sailors for mutiny on a Sunday, and Thompson accused his chief of profaning the Sabbath. St Vincent told the Admiralty that either Thompson must go, or he would. Thompson went, but he had been a popular captain of the *Blenheim*, and his departure did not make things easy for his successor.

St Vincent, however, approved of him, and sent him to Lisbon under the excuse that the *Blenheim* needed repairs, but with the ulterior notion that he might eventually take virtual command of the Portuguese navy. The Portuguese had shown signs recently of weakening in the battle against Spain and France; their backbone clearly needed strengthening, and Phillip should offer their navy 'every assistance' – with any luck as Commodore of an Anglo-Portuguese squadron.

Unfortunately for Phillip, to whom this move offered a great opportunity for advancement, the Spanish and French declined to invade Portugal. Then Rear-Admiral Frederick arrived at Lisbon and insisted on flying his own flag from the masts of the *Blenheim*. Furious but helpless, forsaken by St Vincent (who could do nothing against the will of a Rear-Admiral), Phillip must have felt entirely frustrated, as indeed he was. He had no recourse but to return to England, 'under the most mortifying circumstances' as he told Nepean.[197]

Shore bound, he found himself placed in charge of the Hampshire Sea Fencibles – a sort of Home Guard of volunteers given a rough training in the use of pikes and cannon – and meant to arm the Martello forts along the coast. He may have been frustrated, but taking a house in Lymington he went about his new duties with his usual determination, recruiting over 300 men and attending to their training. This done, and with rumours of a negotiated peace in the air, he was sent to inspect the accommodation of French prisoners-of-war in ships and hospitals at Portsmouth, Porchester and Forton. Just has he had done in New South Wales, Phillip demonstrated his care for cleanliness, efficiency and sound medical attention.

As Rear-Admiral of the Blue (from January 1799) he again offered himself for active service, but the signing of a peace treaty in March 1802 reduced the need for active officers, and though he expressed enthusiasm, St Vincent – now First Lord at the Admiralty – did nothing for him, at least in that respect. He was instead asked to inspect the Impress Service. He had had experience of press gangs at almost every stage of his naval career and disapproved of them in every way, but as far as the Admiralty was concerned they were a necessity and the concern was not so much at the methods employed by the gangs as by the fact that a sufficiently large number of pressed men was not forthcoming, considering the large amount of money spent on organising the gangs.

Phillip, with a secretary, travelled to Scotland and then down the east coast to Suffolk and along the south coast to Falmouth, producing a report which showed up a number of ways in which local authorities took advantage of the Impress Service – for instance by reporting all the local lay-abouts and drunkards as deserters, so that they would be impressed, relieve the parishes of the problem of looking after them and provide the navy with totally useless men. He also found that some officers given the duty of running press gangs had the habit of attending local assizes and picking up more inadequate men there.

Phillip continued to make himself useful in other ways – for instance by loaning the Admiralty his own charts of some of the harbours in which he had dropped anchor, including Rio, and other South American ports. He also asked the Admiralty to appoint him Admiral in the Leeward Islands. Though his request seems to have been sympathetically received it was never granted, and when instead he was offered the command of British warships based in Ireland he turned it down.

In the spring of 1803 he began once more inspecting the Sea Fencibles – England was by now seriously concerned that Napoleon might invade her coast – and by the end of the year was, with a secretary, inspecting the whole force; he spent the whole of 1804 on the task, travelling north as far as Scotland, and covering parts of the west coast and Wales as well as the south.

Prime Minister Pitt praised and talked up the Fencibles in much the same way as Prime Minister Churchill did the Home Guard during the days when another invasion was feared almost a century and a half later. Phillip agreed that they would be of use, but was not quite so confident that they would be of enormous service should an invasion come – indeed he suggested that some of the Fencibles might more profitably be used as conventional members of the navy.

Though he did all this work with the efficiency and thoroughness confidently expected of him, he may well have longed for a more active occupation – or rather for one which would at least take him to sea once more. He was now a Rear-Admiral of the White, and it must have been galling to realise that he was probably never again to have command. Then, in December 1804, his appointment as inspector of the Fencibles was ended. With what sounds very like desperation he suggested to the Admiralty that in the case of an invasion he should be placed in command of all vessels capable of defending the coast. Even his friend Nepean was unpleasantly surprised at what was very like impertinence, and was forced to tell his old friend that he should refrain from making any requests unconnected with his official duties. Phillip ended his last report on the Fencibles with the words: 'I will not take up their Lordships time with any further observations and remarks.'[198]

The words marked a rather sad end to his naval career.

Mrs Phillip had, during the past 10 years or so, lived at Bathampton, a village about two kilometres east of Bath. Now, Phillip bought, for £2,200, a substantial house in Bath itself – at 19, Bennett Street. Bath was a fashionable centre, and Phillip will have known several of the naval officers who also lived there, and welcomed old friends such as Philip Gidley King, who sought him out. He will have had few financial problems, for he had a pension of £500 a year and an admiral's half-pay of £750 a year – a total which today would equal about £100,000. At his death he was able to leave his wife an estate valued at around £20,000 (today, about one and a half million pounds), together with an annuity of over £650,000. Where quite such large sums came from is something of a mystery – perhaps his time abroad had not been spent simply in gathering information for his Government.

Life seems to have been as pleasant as it could be for a formerly active man who may not have felt that he was entirely spent. Unfortunately, he was, especially as far as his health was concerned, although he was happy to entertain old friends, particularly those who could bring him news of the prospering colony of which he had laid the foundations, what seemed half a lifetime ago. It is interesting that, on a holiday at Clifton, near Bristol, he met in 1811 a young architect called Francis Greenway. The following year, Greenway was found guilty of forging a document and sentenced to death, but instead was transported for 14 years, arriving in Sydney in February 1814 and subsequently designed St Matthew's Church, Windsor, St Luke's, Liverpool, and St James's, Sydney.

Phillip died on 31 August 1814. His poor health, indifferent all his life and failing for the past 10 years, suggests a natural death, and the rumours that he committed suicide seem entirely unfounded – not only because they only originated in the twentieth century, but also because he was certainly given church burial at Bathampton, and the church would have been strictly against consecrated burial for a suicide.

Isabella Phillip lived for another nine years and puzzlingly died leaving a mere £5,000. How she managed to spend all her husband's money during the final years of her life remains a mystery; they had no children and so no one to support except herself. She also left the house in Bennett Street completely empty of any documents relating to her husband's life and career – the one known portrait of him, by Francis Wheatley, survived and is now in the National Portrait Gallery in London. In March 1823 she joined Phillip in St Nicholas's Church, Bathampton – almost certainly the only church in England with kangaroos in the stained-glass windows, which show the coats of arms of Australia and its six states. Phillip's grave, marked by a plaque in the floor of the church, attracted little notice for over 80 years, until 1897, when the Premier of New South Wales, Sir Henry Parker, had it and the nearby memorial restored.

The church itself has strong physical Australian associations: the floor is of Wombeyan marble, and all the furniture of black bean. In Bath itself, there is a memorial in the Abbey, which bears the inscription 'To his Indomitable Courage, Prophetic Vision, Forbearance, Faith, Inspiration and Wisdom was due the Success of the First Settlement in Australia at Sydney.'

# WHAT HAPPENED AFTERWARDS

Bennelong, having returned to Sydney with Captain Hunter on the *Reliance*, became somewhat distant and bettermost in his relationship with other Aboriginals, took great care of his western dress and disapproved his relatives' continued preference for nudity. He found his wife, Goroobarrooboolo, living with another man, but seduced her into returning to him with the help of some petticoats and other clothing he had brought back from London. However, she remained faithful for only a few days, returning to her lover and a state of undress. Bennelong would indeed occasionally himself remove his clothing, folding it carefully before leaving Government House for an excursion into his tribe's country and resuming coat and trousers on his return. He clearly also resumed his attentions to the ladies and on one occasion was badly beaten by his friend Colbee for seducing the latter's wife. He had ambitions to become a sort of ambassador to Government House, improving relationships between his people and the white settlers, but does not appear to have done more than assert this intention. He became seriously addicted to alcohol and often so violent he could not be controlled. His health quickly deteriorated and he died at Kissing Point on 3 January 1813, the year before Phillip's own death. The obituary note in the *Sydney Gazette* was not especially positive: 'Of this veteran champion of the native tribe little favourable can be said. His voyage to and benevolent treatment in Great Britain produced no change whatever in his manners and inclinations, which were naturally barbarous and ferocious.' His grave is unmarked, and there is no memorial.

William Bradley, on Phillip's recommendation, was promoted master and commander in 1792. He took part in the battle of the Glorious First of June in 1794, and was automatically promoted captain. In September 1812 he was further promoted Rear-Admiral of the Blue. In 1814 he was tried for defrauding the postal authorities and sentenced to death, but reprieved on condition that he was transported for life. He died in exile in France in1833.

Arthur Bowes Smyth, more generally referred to as simply Bowes, left Sydney in May 1788. He died some months after his return to England and was buried on 31 March 1790 in Tolleshunt D'Arcy, Essex.

Ralph Clark seems to have died in about 1794, killed while fighting the French in Haiti. Unknown to him his wife had died giving birth to a still-born child. Their other son died of yellow fever while on the same ship as his father. Nothing is known of the fate of his convict mistress Mary Branham and their daughter.

Colbee lived until about 1830 and was granted land both at Windsor and Bathurst. To an extent he became part of the settlement, which may account for the number of disputes he had with his fellow Aboriginals, who remained at a distance. In 1797 he killed a man called Yeranibe during a fight; as a result he had to engage in combat with the dead man's tribe, and would have been killed but for the intervention of some soldiers. He is said to have been buried in the same grave as Bennelong.

David Collins remained in the colony until 1796; he had requested to return to England some years earlier, but could not be spared from his work as Judge-Advocate. He had two children by a convict Nancy Yeats, though back at home was pleased to be reunited with his wife Maria, who had remained in England. Unjustly refused reinstatement in the Marine Corps on a technicality, he made a considerable sum on the publication of his book *An Account of the English Colony in New South Wales* (1898), and he produced a second volume two years later. He returned to Sydney in 1803 as Lieutenant-Governor of Port Philip (later renamed Melbourne), but moved to Tasmania to establish the settlement at Hobart in 1804. There he had two children by Margaret Eddington, the daughter and wife of a convict. He died in 1810, leaving a widow – the novelist Maria Collins – who had never left England.

William Dawes went to Sierra Leone in 1792 as advisor to the Governor, and he himself took over that post later the same year. In 1793 he was promoted to First Lieutenant and placed on half-pay; he became mathematics master at Christ's Hospital and helped to train missionaries for the Church Missionary Society. In 1813 he went to Antigua as a correspondent of the Church Missionary Society, established schools for the children of slaves and travelled to Dominica and St Vincent. He died in Antigua in 1836. One of his sons, William Rutter, became an eminent astronomer.

John Hunter returned to England after the loss of the *Sirius,* published *An Historical Journal of the Transactions at Port Jackson and Norfolk Island* and served on the *Queen Charlotte* before in 1795 becoming Governor of New South Wales. His time as Governor was racked with problems resulting from an inefficient bureaucracy in Sydney and a slow and complex system of advice from London. Problems had also arisen during an almost three-year gap between Phillip leaving Sydney and Hunter returning to the colony. Though almost self-sufficient in grain, the settlers had to rely heavily on supplies from Europe, and these were often uncertain. There was tension between

Hunter and the military, and he was uncertain of his authority to cope with them. The settlers' complaints of profiteering by officers of the Corps, which had reduced some of them to near bankruptcy, angered Hunter, but he failed to deal with them, relying on complaining to London while remaining inactive himself. Recalled to London in 1799, he lived for a time on half-pay before somewhat rescuing his reputation in his book *Governor Hunter's Remarks on the Causes of the Colonial Expense of the Establishment of New South Wales [with] Hints for the Reduction of Such Expense and for Reforming the Prevailing Abuses.* He was granted a pension for his services and served in command of the 74-gun warship *Venerable*, which in his hands was totally wrecked with a heavy loss of life. He was exonerated and continued to serve, dying in 1821 as Vice-Admiral.

The Reverend Richard Johnson and his wife had two children, a son and a daughter. They continued as gardeners, becoming regular farmers and making money from their crops: by 1799 they had a farm of 350 acres. He also continued his pastoral work. He and his family returned to England in1800, two years later giving up the idea of returning to New South Wales and resigning his position as chaplain. He continued to work in the church, and died in 1827.

Philip Gidley King left Norfolk Island for England in 1796, returning to New South Wales in 1800 as Governor. After an uneasy term of office due to various disturbances in the colony he retired in 1807 and died in England the following year. In 1832 his wife Anna returned to live with her daughter near Parramatta and when she died in 1844 left 26 grandchildren in New South Wales. While on Norfolk Island, King had two sons, Norfolk and Sydney, by Ann Inett, a convict from Worcestershire. They both became lieutenants in the navy. His only legitimate son, P. P. King, married Harriet Lethbridge of Cornwall.

Nanbaree, adopted by Surgeon White, was 'christened' by

him as Andrew Snape Hammond Douglas White, but resolutely refused to use the name. He acted as a sort of gamekeeper to White, and later became a seaman serving on HMS *Reliance* and with Flinders on the *Investigator*. He died in 1811.

Robert Ross returned to England in 1791 with the marines and continued his career with them, dying in 1794. His son John, who had accompanied him to Australia, served with distinction in France, but died at the age of 20.

James Ruse sold his land in 1793 and the following year started a farm at the junction of the Hawkesbury River and South Creek, but was wiped out by flooding and had to work as a seaman; his wife, Elizabeth (with whom he had seven children) remained to work the land, and in the end rescued him from bankruptcy. After 1828 he worked as an overseer for a landowner at Minto and died at Campbelltown on 5 September 1837. On his tombstone are carved the lines:

*My Mother Reread Me Tenderley*
*With me She Took Much Paines*
*And when I arrived in This Coelney*
*I sowd the Forst Grain and Now*
*With my Hevenly Father I hopr*
*For Ever To Remain.*

Watkin Tench returned to England in 1791, where he married Anna Maria Sargent, the daughter of a Plymouth surgeon. They had no children, but adopted four orphans, two of whom became captains in the navy, one a bank manager in Plymouth. Tench was promoted to Brevet Major, fought under Captain Bligh, was captured by the French and spent six months as a prisoner-of-war. Liberated, he served in the Channel fleet and then on shore until retiring on half-pay as major-general in 1816. Three years later he returned to active duty as commandant of the Plymouth Division, retiring in 1821 with the rank of Lieutenant-General. He died at Devonport in 1833. He wrote the two best books about the early years of the New South Wales settlement – *A Narrative of the Expedition to Botany Bay: With an Account of New South Wales, its Productions, Inhabitants &c* (London, 1789 – it went into three editions, and was published in Dublin and New York and translated into French, German and Dutch) and *A Complete Account of the Settlement at Port Jackson, in New South Wales, Including an Accurate Description of the Situation of the Colony; and of its Natural Productions; Taken on the Spot* (London, 1793; German and Swedish translations). He also published a third book, conceived during his imprisonment in France – *Letters Written in France, to a Friend in London, Between the Month of November 1794 and the Month of May 1795* (London, 1796).

John White remained in Sydney until December 1794, when he returned to England. He was put on half-pay in 1820 and died in 1832, leaving a fortune which today would amount to about £100,000. He had a son, Andrew Douglas, by a convict, Rachel Turner, transported for stealing clothes from her mistress. Andrew followed his father to England in 1800, joined the Royal Engineers, fought at Waterloo and returned to Australia in 1823.

# ACKNOWLEDGEMENTS

I am grateful to the following institutions, and often to individuals within them:

The State Library of New South Wales, in particular the Mitchell Collection; the library of the University of Sydney; the National Library of Australia, Canberra; the Library of the University of Canberra; the British Museum Library; the London Library; the Bath Central Library; the Library of the National Maritime Museum, Greenwich; the UK National Archives at the Public Records Office; Sydney Museum; Mosman public library. The publication of Volume One of the Historical Records of Australia on CD is a wonderful resource which has been of the most invaluable assistance

I am also grateful to Geoffrey Robertson and Rick Pool, and in particular to Professor Alan Frost, whose excellent *Arthur Phillip: his voyaging* (a book which, published in 1987, should never have been allowed to go out of print) was an invaluable guide.

Finally I have as always to thank my wife, Julia Parker, whose reading of the manuscript has revealed more typographical errors than any reasonable person would have thought possible, and whose advice and criticism has once again been invaluable.

# BIBLIOGRAPHY

Anon. *The History of Botany Bay in New Holland* (London 1790)

Anon. *The Voyage of Governor Phillip to Botany Bay; with an Account of the Establishment of the Colonies of Port Jackson and Norfolk Island* (London, 1790)

Atkins, Richard, *Journal 1791-1810*, MSS In National Library of Australia.

Barrington, G., *An Account of a Voyage to New South Wales* (London, 1810)

Barton, G. B. an Britten, A., *A History of New South Wales from the Records* (Sydney, 1888-94)

Becke, G. L. and Jeffrey, W., *Admiral Phillip: the Founding of New South Wales* (London, T. Fisher Unwin, 1899)

Bowes Smyth, Journal of a Voyage from Portsmouth to New South Wales and China in the *Lady Penrhyn*, 1787-1789. (Sydney, 1979)

Clark, Manning, *A History of Australia* (Vol.I., Melbourne University Press, 1962)

Clark, Ralph, *The Journals and Letters of Lt Ralph Clark, 1787-1792* (ed. Fidlom, Paul G. and Ryan, R. J. (eds) (Australian Documents Library in association with the Library of Australian History Pty Ltd, Sydney, l981)

Collins, David, *Account of the English Colony in New South* (London, 1798, 1802), and available at
http://www.gutenberg.org/files/12565/12565-8.txt

Easty, John. Memorandum of the Transactions of a Voyage from England to Botany Bay, 1787-1793 (Angus & Robvertson, 1965)

Egan, Jack: *Buried Alive* (Allen & Unwin, Crow's Nest, 1999)

Eldershaw, M. Barnard, *Phillip of Australia* (Harrap, London, 1938)

Fowell, Newton, *The Sirius Letters,* (ed Irvine, Nance, Fairfax Library, 1988). Also available at http://setis.library.usyd.edu.au/ pubotbin/toccer-new?id=fowjour.sgml&images=&data=/usr/ot &tag=explorers&part=10&division=div1

Frost, Alan, *Arthur Phillip: his voyaging* (OUP, Melbourne, 1987)

Haslam, J., *Convict Ships. A Narrative of a Voyage to New South Wales in the year 1816* (London, 1819)

Hughes, Robert: *TheFatal Shore* (Knopf, New York, 1986)

Hunter, John, *An Historical Journal of the Transactions at Port Jackson and Norfolk Island, &c* (London 1793; reproduced by the Libraries Board of South Australia, 1968.)

Nagle, Jacob, *The Nagle Journal: a diary of the life of Jacob Nagle, Sailor, from the year 1775 to 1841.* (Weidenfeld & Nicolson, 1988)

O'Brien, E., *The Foundation of Australia* (Sydney, 1950)

Phillip, Arthur, *Voyage to Botany Bay*

Rawson, G., *The Strange Case of Mary Bryant* (London, 1938)

Tench, Watkin: *Narrative of the Expedition to Botany Bay; Complete Account of the Settlement at Port Jackson.* Published as *Sydney's First Four Years* by Angus & Robertson in association with the Royal Australian Historical Society, Sydney, 1961. Also available on-line at http://setis.library.usyd.edu.au/ozlit/pdf/p00044.pdf

White, John, *Journal of a Voyage to New South Wales* (London, 1790), also available at
http://gutenberg.net.au/ebooks03/0301531h.html

Worgan, G. B., *Journal of a Fleet* Surgeon, http://setis. library.usyd.edu.au/pubotbin/toccer-new?id=worjour. sgml&images=&data=/usr/ot&tag=explorers&part=2&divisio n=div1

*Historical Records of Australia,* Series 1, Vol. 1
*Historical Records of New South Wales,* Vol. 1 pt 2

## 1   NOTES
HRNSW = *Historical Records of New South Wales*
HRA – *Historical Records of Australia*

### Notes to Chapter One
1   Why was New South Wales named New South Wales? Captain Cook didn't use the name until he was writing his diaries on the voyage home from New South Wales.  Unfortunately he didn't go into any details about his reasons and we can only assume he thought it looked like South Wales.
2   *see* Frost, Alan, *Arthur Phillip: his voyaging* (OUP Melbourne, 1987)
3   Public Record Office, Admiralty Papers, 73/390
4   Arthur to Rebecca Phillip, 21 June 1756, Public Record Office 30/8/52
5   A midshipman was an apprentice officer.  The word derives from the area of the ship, *amidships*, where they were berthed.   The midshipman usually served seven years on the lower deck, and was roughly equivalent to a present day petty officer in rank and position.6   There is no suggestion that he ever did so.
7   See Frost, Alan, *Arthur Phillip: his voyaging* (OUP, Melbourne, 1987) p.32
8   Pocock to Cleveland, 9 October 1762, quoted by Frost op. cit.  p.42
9   The pound in 1760 is calculated to be worth about £80/90 in today's currency
10   Op cit

### Notes to Chapter Two
11    Becke, Louis, and Jeffery, Walter, *Admiral Phillip: the Founding of New South Wales* (London, T. Fisher Unwin, 1899) pp.286-9
12    Quoted Becke and Jeffery, op cit, p.319-20

### Notes to Chapter Three
13    Evan Nepean (1752-1822) entered the navy as a clerk and served as a purser in ships on the American coast during the rebellion of the American colonies.  In 1782 he was appointed secretary to Lord Shuldham, Port-Admiral at Plymouth, and later that year became under-secretary of state in the Home Department.  It is in this post that he was concerned in the arrangements for the dispatch of the

First Fleet and the administration of the newly established penal colony in New South Wales during its early years.

14    Admiralty Papers, 1/2306, Phillip to Sandwich, 19 July 1790
15    Sandwich F/28/49 quoted in Frost p.99

**Notes to Chapter Four**

16    Histoire des Navigations aux Terres Australes (Paris 1756)
17    Journal of the House of Commons, 1778-80, vol. 37, col. 311
18    Eden, William, *Discourse on Banishment* (1787)
19    Thomas Townshend, Baron Sydney of Chiselhurst (1733-1800) became one of the lords commissioners of the treasury in 1765; in 1782 he was appointed secretary at war.
20    Quoted Clark, M, A History of New South Wales Vol 1, p.71
21    HRNSW Series I, Vol. i, p.22
22    HRNSW Vol I, Pt II, pp.1-2
23    Vessels under charter to the Navy (whether to carry troops, convicts, or provisions) were classed as 'naval transports'; those which carried provisions were called 'provision ships' or 'victuallers'.
24    Ibid. p.14
25    Ibid pp.9-15
26    The term 'natives' was in common use at the time, and I have also used it when in context. No disrespect is of course intended to the indigenous original inhabitants of Australia.
27    Ibid pp.9-15
28    HRNSW Vol 1 Part II pp51
29    HRNSW p.52
30    Ibid
31    Ibid
32    HRNSW p.51
33    Teer to Navy Board 7 December 1786 ADM 106/243
34    Ibid. Vol 1 Part II pp58-9
35    HRNSW p.58
36    Quoted Hughes p.63
37    King, Philip Gidley, *Journal*, 1786-1790, MS at Mitchell Library, Sydney.
38    White to Nepean, 27 February 1781 (C.O. 201/2)
39    *The Gentleman's Magazine*, November 1786

## Notes to Chapter Five

40 Naval Chronicle Vol VI (1801)
41 Tench, Watkin, Sydney's First Four Years (Sydney, 1961) p.11
42 The Journals and Letters of Lt Ralph Clark, New South Wales Documents Library in association with the Library of New South Wales History Pty Ltd, Sydney, l981, pp241-3
43 Quoted Frost, op. cit., p.37
44 Tench, Ibid, p.13
45 Ibid. pp.13-14
46 Clark, Journal, May 15, 1781

## Notes to Chapter Six

47 Tench, Watkin, A Narrative of the Expedition to Botany Bay (London, 1788) p.14
48 Nagle, Jacob, *The Nagle Journal: a diary of the life of Jacob Nagle, Sailor, from the year 1775 6o 1841.* (London,1988)
49 Clark, ibid., p.12
50 White, John, *Journal of a Voyage to New South Wales* (London 1790) pp.18-19
51 White, ibid., pp.20-21
52 Johnson to Mr Tucker, Tenerife, 30 May 1787; original in library of St Paul's Cathertal, Melbourne, quoted Clark, Vol I, p.83
53 RNSW Vol II p.520
54 White, op. cit., pp.34-38
55 Oil of tar is obtained by the distillation of wood tar; it is sometimes used as an inhalation with hot water, and externally, it is used as an antiseptic and stimulant in eczema and other skin diseases.
56 White, op. cit., p.29-30
57 Ibid. p.31
58 Clark, op. cit., 5 July 1787
59 'Mother Bank' – i,e., on the Thames
60 Clark, op. cit., 5 July 1787
61 White, op. cit., p.24
62 Tench op. cit., p.24
63 White., op. cit., p.45
64 Ibid., p.68
65 Tench, op. cit., p.22
66 White., ibid.

67    Collins, D., *An Account of the English Colony in New South Wales* (London, 1798-1802) p.37
68    Tench op. cit., p.24
69    There is some doubt what Phillip meant by this: traditionally casada is a dish consisting of rice and beans, meat, cabbage salad and fried plantains. Perhaps by casada he meant plantains.
70    Hunter, op. cit., p.22

**Notes to Chapter Seven**
71    7 September 1787
72    Clark op. cit. 11 October 1787
73    He was generally known simply by the surname Bowes, which is how he will be referred to henceforth.
74    Bowes Smyth, Journal of a Voyage from Portsmouth to New South Wales and China in the *Lady Penrhyn*, 1787-1789; no pagination.
75    Tench, *op. cit.*, p.27
76    White, John, *Journal of a Voyage to New South Wales* (London, 1790) p.93
77    Ibid 95-6
      Hunter p.31
78    Tench, *op. cit.*, p.28
79    HRNSW p.60
80    White, op cit p.102
81    HRNSW Vol II p533
82    Bowes, op. cit.
83    Collins op. cit. xxxvi
84    Clark, 1 January, 1788
85    Tench, op. cit., p.35
86    Ibid. p.32
87    Quoted Eldershaw M. Barnard, *Phillip of Australia* (London, 1938), p.92; not found in Tench.
88    Collins, op. cit.

**Notes to Chapter Eight**
89    Completely naked – not even a fig-leaf
90    Collins, p.v
91    Nagle, Jacob, *The Nagle Journal: a diary of the life of Jacob Nagle, Sailor, from the year 1775 to 1841.* (London, 1988) p.34

92   White, op. cit., p.118
93   HRNSW vol II p.666-7
94   Collins op. cit., p.6
95   Known later, and still, as the Tank Stream
96   HRA p.19
97   HRA p.35
98   Bowes, Journal, 23 Feb 1788 p.74
99   Campbell to Lord Duycie, quoted in Hughges, op cit, p.89
100   Clark op. cit., February 1 1788
101   Psalm 116, v,12
102   Tench op. cit., p.39
103   Collins, op. cit.,p.34
104   HRNSW p.23
105   Bowes op. cit., p.81
106   Flax was an important element in the preparation of rigging for England's ships
107   COMMISSION OF PHILIP GIDLEY KING.  By His Excellency Arthur Phillip, Esq., Governor-in-Chief and Captain-General in and over his Majesty's territory of New South Wales and its dependencies, &c., &c., &c.  HRA p.32

**Notes to Chapter Nine**
108   HRA p.21
109   Admiral Lord Howe was First Lord of the Admiralty
110   Tench op. cit., p.59
111   HRNSW p.36*ff*
112   HRA p.30
113   Worgan, George B., Journal,  24 May 1788
114   Clark, op cit 28 Feb  1790
115   A centuries-old drink, an ale made with highly dried malt, nearly burned, and naturally carbonated.
116   Many years later wild cattle were discovered which were fairly obviously the descendents of the missing bull and cows
117   HRNSW p.176
118   Captain James Campbell: a marine captain, and not the naval captain with whom Phillip had served in the Caribbean
119   Letter, quoted  in Frost, Alkan, op. cvit., p.121

## Notes to Chapter Ten

120  9 July 1788
121  HRNSW Vol. II p.694
122  HRA p.69
123  HRA p.46
124  Later, the Governor re-named Rose Hill as Parramatta
125  HRA p.49
126  John Easty, *Memorandum of the Transactions of a Voyage from England to Botany Bay, 1787-1793* (Melbourne, 1965) p.43
127  Tench p.150
128  HRA p.110
129  See Clark's journal for 6 Dec 1787
130  Collins, op. cit., p.47
131  Tench, op. cit., p.152
132  Hunter p.143
133  Tench, op. cit., p.154
134  HRNSW p.154
135  HRNSW II p.289
136  HRNSW II 302
137  Ibid.
138  Tench, op. cit. p. 159
139  Ibid.

## Notes to Chapter Eleven

140  Tench p.162-3
141  Now Jakarta
142  HRA p.171
143  HRNSW II p.330
144  Tench p.165
145  Can this punishment have taken places? Given the severity of the lashings, it would surely have killed Lane?
146  Tench, op. cit., p.169
147  HRNSW II p.332
148  Collins, op. cit., p.122
149  HRNSW II pp.386-9
150  HR HRA p.197
151  NSW II p.372
152  HRA p.197

153 The diaries and journals continually allude to 'church' services, but presumably when they wrote of 'going to church' they mean going to any hut where Mr Johnson might hold a service
154 HRNSW II p.816
155 Ibid.
156 Tench, op. cit., p.184

**Notes to Chapter Twelve**
157 Tench p.201
158 HRA I P.24
159 Tench, op. cit., p/205
160 HRA p.293-4
161 Tench's account of the incident is in Chapter XII of his second book; pp.205-16 of op. cit.
162 HRA II p.262
163 Ibid.
164 Tench pp.191-198

**Notes to Chapter Thirteen**
165 Collins p.148
166 During the 1790 drought three storage tanks had been constructed in the sandstone beside the stream which ran into Sydney Cove, and it is from these that the stream got its name
167 Tench, op. city., p.218
168 Easty, ibid.
169 Ibid. p.213
170 The most reliable is in Frederick A. *Pottle's Boswell and the girl from Botany Bay* (London, 1938)
171 William Neate Chapman, letter, quoted Egan, Jack (ed) *Buried Alive* (Sydney, 1999)
172 Collins, op. cit., p.105
173 HRA p.295
174 200 had died on the way out
175 HRA p.279
176 HRA p.272-3

**Notes to Chapter Fourteen**

177  The wife of the Reverend Johnson
178  Parker, Mary Ann, *A voyage round the world in the Gorgon man of war, Captain John Parker, performed by his widow* (London, 1795) pp.73-92
179  Bradley, *Journal*, pp.208-9
180  Whether they also sailed home on the *Gorgon* is unknown, as is the reception Ms Branham received from Mrs Clark, if indeed they were introduced.
181  Quoted *Buried Alive,* op cit., p.276
182  Tench, op. cit., p.273
183  Collins op. cit., p.127
184  Collins op. cit., p.128
185  Atkins became a respected magistrate
186  HRA p.216
187  Henry Dundas, First Viscount Melville, later First Lord of the Admiralty, impeached for misappropriation of public funds.
188  HRA  p.377
189  Ibid.
190  Atkins, Richard, *Journal 1791-1810*, MSS In National Library of Australia.

**Notes to Chapter Fifteen**

191  HRNSW p.381
192  Ibid.  381-2
193  Ibid.  p.355
194  HRA p.381
195  Easty op. cit.. 9 December

**Notes to Chapter Sixteen**

196  MS National Library Canberra.
197  Admiralty Papers 1/2317, quoted Frost p.238
198  ADM 1/581:83-4 quoted Frost p.247

# INDEX

eager for action, 23; praised by Lavradio, 24-5; does not command fireship, 27; as spy, 28-9; sails to India, 32*ff*; to France on 'private affairs', 34; reports on French fleet, 35; selected as Commander and Governor, 44; thoughts on his commission, 50*ff*; chooses officers, 65-6; final preparations, 57*ff*; transfers to Supply, 104; plans for arrival, 109; first sight of Port Jackson, 115; raises the flag, 119; Commission read, 126; addresses colony, 127-8; expeditions 140, 144, 171-2; quarrels with Maj. Ross, 142-4, 166-7; appeals to Sydney and Nepean, 150 ; plans Sydney, 153-4 ; pleads for provisions, 157, 158; kidnaps Aboriginals, 161-2, 179-80; rebukes Ross, 176; requests leave, 184-5, 214-5; and the Second Fleet, 193*ff*; wounded, 202 ; anger, uncharacteristic, 210; conflict with Dawes, 212-13, 242-4; leave denied 215; receives seal, 229; and indifference of government 231, 232; requires free settlers, 233; asks permission to resign, 234, 237; deals with 'riot', 244-5; encourages schooling, 247; future of colony, 251-3; trouble with Maj. Grose, 255-7; queried resignation, 257-8; announces departure, 258-9; returns to England, 262; introduces Aboriginals to London, 263*ff*; second marriage, 265; returns to active service, 267; the Sea Fencibles, 168-9, 270; Rear-Admiral, 269; and Impress Service, 169; retirement, 270; death, 272. PERSONALITY AND CHARACTERISTICS viii-xiv Aborigines, attitude to, ix-xi, 114, 158-60, 161-2, 179-80, 207-8, 209-10, 223; and capital punishment, 55, 138, 149, 210; convicts, attitude to, 78, 127, 163-4; convicts, concern for,

87, 91, 94, 114-15, 121, 203; convicts, criticism of, 123; discipline, attitude to, 78-9; fearlessness, 114; firmness, 100; health, xii-xiii, 16, 45, 148, 223, 234, 237, 258, 266; hospitality, 238; and ladies, 224; respected, 90; marines, criticism of, 123-4; marriage, attitude to 14; social life, 224-5; workaholic?, 223;
Phillip, Elizabeth (mother), 2
Phiullipo, Isabella (second wife), 265
Phillip, Jacob (father), 2
Phillip, Margaret Charlotte (first wife), 14*ff*
Phillip, Rebecca (sister), 2
piano, Australia's first, 168
*Pilar*, 21
Pinchgut, 130
*Pitt*, 246, 248
'police force', *see* watch
Port Jackson, 115; described, 118-9
Poulden, Lieut John, 142, 212, 262
*Prince of Wales*, HMS, 1, 56, 90, 106
*Princess Louise*, HMS, 8
prison system, 37-0

*Queen*, 229, 231, 239

*Ramilles*, HMS, 7-9
Readhead, William, 4-5
*Recruiting Officer, The*, 168-9
Rio de Janeiro, 33, 81, 90*ff*
Rocha, Francisco José de, 21
Rodney, Admiral George, 12
Rose Hill, see Parramatta
Rose, Mary, 190-1
Ross, Maj. Robert, 66-7, 81, 94, 101, 103, 126, 171, 239, 241, 277; quarrels with Governor 141-2, 165, 166-7, 177-8; opposes night-watch, 175; complains of Governor, 150-2, 178-9, 232, 239; rebuked, 167; to Norfolk Island, 184; fights duel, 239
*Royal Admiral*, 257, 259
rum, illicit trade in, 258
Ruse, Elizabeth, 198, 200

ALSO BY DEREK PARKER
and available from Woodslane

# BANJO PATERSON

## The Man who wrote Waltzing Matilda

A. B. `Banjo' Paterson was not simply the author of the words of
`Waltzing Matilda', Australia's unofficial national anthem, and many
other classic ballads such as `The man from Snowy River' and
`Clancy of the Overflow'. Though it is now almost forgotten, he
was a first-rate war correspondent for the Sydney Morning Herald.
His dispatches from the Boer War are as vivid and exciting to read
today as when they were frantically scribbled under the guns of Boer
sharp-shooters, and delivered on daring rides from the front to the
nearest telephone office. He was a friend of `Breaker' Morant, whose
notorious trial and execution was one of the sensations of that war.
He was also an expert horseman, a man who knew everything there
was to be known about horses and horse-racing, winning prizes at
polo matches and race meetings. Returning from South Africa, *The
Banjo* (as he always signed himself) worked for Sydney newspapers,
and travelled to China and England (where he stayed with his friend,
the poet Rudyard Kipling), and for a while led a relatively sedentary
life as editor of The Sydney Evening News. At the outbreak of World
War One, he failed to get accreditation as a war correspondent,
and served as an ambulance driver in France, and finally to Egypt
where he headed a team of rough-riders and trained horses. Major
Paterson came back to Sydney to edit The Sportsman and the earliest
collection of traditional bush songs, and to become a popular and
well-known broadcaster in the early days of radio. By the time he
died everyone in Australia knew the verses of `Waltzing Matilda' but
scarcely anyone could have told you they had been written by `Banjo'
Paterson as he had sold the copyright outright for five pounds!

Hardback  $34.95  ISBN: 9781921606076

# OUTBACK

## The Discovery of Australia's Interior

In 1800, while the coast of Australia had finally been charted, the vast interior of the continent, and routes across its deserts and mountains from north to south and east to west lay all undiscovered. By 1874, its lands had been all but won. Derek Parker's exciting book gathers together the stories of those intrepid explorers who, often against great odds, on journeys of months or even years, beat starvation, inadequate information and mapping, disease and loss, to forge a routes which would enable the country's development. From early explorers, who were generally escaped convicts, to the son of a Lincolnshire surgeon who coined the name 'Australia'; from explorers Major Mitchell, who slaughtered aborigines, to Sir George Grey, who learnt their language, recorded their culture and came to love and understand them; and from the greatest overland expedition in Australian history in 1844 to continued failed attempts to find a mythical 'inland sea', this is a fascinating read.

Paperback   $24.95   ISBN: 9781921203923